Europe's Indians

POLITICS, HISTORY, AND CULTURE
A series from the International Institute at the University of Michigan

SERIES EDITORS   George Steinmetz and Julia Adams

SERIES EDITORIAL ADVISORY BOARD

Sponsored by the International Institute at the University of Michigan and published by Duke University Press, this series is centered around cultural and historical studies of power, politics and the state—a field that cuts across the disciplines of history, sociology, anthropology, political science, and cultural studies. The focus on the relationship between state and culture refers both to a methodological approach—the study of politics and the state using culturalist methods—and a substantive one that treats signifying practices as an essential dimension of politics. The dialectic of politics, culture, and history figures prominently in all the books selected for the series.

# Europe's Indians

## PRODUCING RACIAL DIFFERENCE, 1500–1900

## *Vanita Seth*

DUKE UNIVERSITY PRESS

Durham & London 2010

Library of Congress Cataloging-in-Publication Data appear
on the last printed page of this book.

Dedicated to my father, Sushil,
and in loving memory of my mother, Vimal

CONTENTS

## ACKNOWLEDGMENTS

ONE OF THE HEROIC mythical figures of the modern age is that of the Author, a solitary individual who, through research, contemplation, and angst, produces works of originality. Thankfully, the genre known as the "acknowledgments" puts any such self-delusions to rest. This work is the product of institutional support, the generosity of colleagues and friends, and the patience and love of family.

From its birth as a dissertation to its metamorphosis as a book, this project has benefited from the support of a number of institutions. The Political Science Department at the University of Melbourne housed me as a graduate student, and it was there that I returned as an honorary visiting scholar in the summer of 2002. The Government Department at the University of Sydney offered a similar invitation in 2003. I am grateful to both institutions for their generous sharing of resources and the collegiality of both faculty and staff. At the University of California, Santa Cruz (UCSC), where the thesis slowly morphed into a manuscript, I thank the Committee on Research for funding my overseas research in 2003 and 2004. The staff at the Nehru Memorial Museum and Library and the India Office Library, London, made such research as painless as possible. A special thank you also to Patricia Sanders and Marianna Santana for their editorial and formatting assistance. The colloquium series and conferences organized by Cultural Studies, under the directorship of Gail Hershatter and Christopher Connery, offered a source of intellectual support and interdisciplinary conversation. Thanks also to the Duke series editors, George Steinmetz and Julia Adams, for their unfailing support of this project. An earlier version and briefer version of chapter 4 previously appeared in *When World's Collide*, edited by Peter Euben and Karen Bassi (Lanham, Md.: Rowman and Littlefield, 2010), and I am grateful to Rowman and Littlefield for permission to republish here. Finally, I pay homage to one institution that is rarely mentioned in such pages: the café. It is in coffee shops around Sydney, Melbourne, and Santa Cruz that much of this work was written—a heartfelt thanks to them all.

Then there are friends. Thanks to Terry Shakinovsky for her humor, retail therapy, and hospitality, and Robin Archer for our talk-fests in Oxford, as well as a hug and thanks to Lisa, Nicki, and the gang in Kentish Town for making London a home away from home. Wendy Jemmi, the matriarch of the Kentish Town household and my surrogate mother in London, never quite understood why, in my late twenties, I was still at "school." I would like to think if Wendy were alive today she would be persuaded that it was a good idea. Leela Gandhi, Elaine Jefferies, Deborah Kessler, Amanda Macdonald, Pauline Nestor, Fiona Nicol, Kate Price, Haripriya Rangan, and the editorial team of *Postcolonial Studies* all offered support through the early years of this project—most notably, by offering much needed distractions from it.

Alongside old friends I am fortunate enough to be thanking new ones. Radhika Mongia and Daniel Vukovich offered not only friendship, intellectual conversation, and wonderful food, but for someone far away from home, they provided the closest thing to family. To them both I extend my love and thanks. Dinner parties, cafés, and pubs were where I argued, gossiped, exchanged references and writing, shared my enthusiasms with, and inflicted my frustrations on Mark Anderson, Dean Mathiowetz, and Megan Thomas—my work and my life would be poorer without them. The transition from city to small-town life was less lonely and more enjoyable thanks to the friendship, conversations, and intellectual generosity of Noriko Aso, Alan Christy, Annette Clear, James Clifford, Christopher Connery, Tony Crowley, Carla Freccero, Gail Hershatter, Ronnie Lipschutz, Lourdes Matinez-Echazabal, Robert Meister, Helene Moglen, Sheila Namir,

Micah Perks, and Juan Pobleto. A warm thank you to John Hutnyk for his close readings of earlier drafts of this work and for the conversations and drinks we have shared in London and Manchester. A special thanks to Pal Ahluwalia for his unqualified support of this project. In his various roles as mentor, advocate, and adviser, Pal has supported this project in innumerable ways. Finally, Michael Dutton deserves special mention. His support of and critical engagement with my work as a dissertation supervisor has yet to be matched. Michael continues to be a mentor, but I am fortunate also to call him a friend.

Finally, family. From childhood games to pub crawls, Nishad Pandey basically grew up as this dissertation and then book was being written. He has always been willing to distract me from my work, for which I am eternally grateful. Rajyashree Pandey has been a confidant, friend, and intellectual companion—for the laughter, intellectual conversations, late-night gossip sessions, and pop-psychology sound bites, I am sincerely indebted. Sanjay and Suman Seth have provided me with sustenance in all aspects of my life. They have been ardent listeners, intelligent critics, wise advisers, intellectual mentors, patient editors, and merciless teasers. My own work has been profoundly influenced by Sanjay's writings and our long conversations on politics, history, and theory. *Europe's Indians* is a product of those conversations. Suman Seth has patiently (and at times not so patiently) forced me out of my intellectual comfort zone—it is thanks to him that this work has benefited from the scholarship of historians of science.

One confronts the limitations of language—indeed, the absurdity of attempting—to thank one's parents. My father, Sushil, has been a profound influence in my life. It is to him that I credit my intellectual curiosity and my political formation. I have come this far because he had faith in me when I had little in myself. My mother's anxiety over her wayward child was notably relieved when I returned to university, finished my undergraduate degree, and embarked on this project as a dissertation. It is with sadness that I arrive at the end of this journey without her loving, gentle presence. It is to my father and in loving memory of my mother, Vimal Seth, that I dedicate this work.

# Introduction

IN A PUBLIC PARK in Potsdam (the palatial summer residence of many a Prussian king) there stands a peculiar monument that dates its history back to 1757. The structure is a replica of a Chinese teahouse, around the circumference of which is built a verandah. On the verandah are a series of figures—Chinese men and women pouring tea, playing musical instruments, gazing in the distance, grouped together in conversation. The surreality of stumbling upon this structure in the middle of a park in Germany is heightened on a closer look at the statues themselves. Their "foreignness" is depicted in the clothing the male figures wear (pointed hats with large rims) but absent—indeed, strikingly absent—from the perspective of the modern observer is any racial representation. No "slanted" eyes, "yellow" complexion, or long, thin pigtails adorn these Chinese replicas. Indeed, many of the female figures are garbed in the flowing gowns of the German nobility—they are more Fräulein than foreign. What was to define European (and North American) representations of the Chinese in the nineteenth century does not appear to have obstructed the vision of the eighteenth-century sculptors.[1]

In 1894, E. R. Henry, in his capacity as inspector-general of police in colonial Bengal, submitted a report to be distributed to all district police superintendents. The published document, *Criminal Identification by Means of Anthropometry*, contained detailed instructions on the use of anthropometrical instruments and the significance of the data that they provided:

> Upon the assumption that these anthropometric data remain constant throughout life—and experience may be held to have demonstrated this—it is certain that if these immutable measurements . . . can at any time be obtained for any particular criminal, his identity is fixed in a manner which will render nugatory any efforts he may make to confuse it by change of name or residence or by personal disguise.[2]

The use of calipers, sliding bars, and measuring standards and gauges (diagrams of which are generously scattered through the report) were to be provided to all police stations to measure (in strict order) the length of the left middle finger, the left forearm, the left foot, and, finally, the culprit's height. The administrative recording of this information required the maintenance of cards (one card per individual) detailing the anthropometrical data of each convict. On a single card could be found two hundred and forty three principle headings, which in turn were subdivided "according to height, span, length, and breath of the ear, height of the bust, and eye color, this latter providing seven divisions."[3] The imperative, Henry was to argue (in a revised report dated 1900), "of being able to fix human personality, of being able to give to each human being an individuality differentiating him from all others . . . cannot be overestimated."[4]

In the later report, Henry was in fact to recommend the superiority of fingerprinting over that of anthropometry as a means of identifying criminals. British India was to be one of the first places to introduce this new science. And yet, if policing methods were soon to change, the site of differentiation was not. The body had come into being.

From the spectacle to science, from clothing to calipers—much had changed from the mid-eighteenth century to the late nineteenth century. Representing difference, it would appear, has a history of its own.

It is this history that the present work seeks to narrate. *Europe's Indians: Producing Racial Difference, 1500–1900*, traces European representations of difference from the time that Columbus inadvertently, and unknowingly, stumbled upon the American continent through to the time when racial theorists, quite self-consciously, were subjecting culture to the measuring instruments and evolutionary gradations of racial science.

Clearly, covering a history that spans some four hundred years in a single book would be too ambitious a task if my intention were to offer a detailed history of events and thinkers. This however, has not been my objective. Rather, this work seeks to account for the historical particularity of European representations of the New World and India by studying Renaissance, Classical Age (seventeenth-century and eighteenth-), and nineteenth-century discourses on the non-West within what I describe as epistemic traditions. The central premise underwriting this work is that to speak of European knowledge is not to evoke a singular history (humanity's journey from superstition to science) but to identify historically bounded and historically contingent traditions of knowing. It is these traditions, I suggest, that mediated the ways in which Europeans saw, ordered, conceptualized, and lived in the world—traditions that provided the rules and logic of their reasoning and thus the grounds on which to recognize "truth" and distinguish it from the "irrational," "false," or "superstitious." It was these same traditions of reasoning through which European commentators identified, translated, and conceived of difference—difference as it was encountered in the wake of colonial expansion and conquest. It was not the singularity of Reason but historically particular forms of reasoning that framed European efforts to identify, contextualize, and translate the culturally unfamiliar.

Thus, the objective of this work is not limited to detailing the content of Renaissance, Classical, or nineteenth-century representations of the non-West. It aims to excavate the epistemic conditions that enabled the thinking of difference at different historical junctures. In so doing, a number of unquestioned assumptions underwriting the histories of European interaction with the colonial non-West come to be challenged.

The prevailing and pervasive presumption that European representations of difference have always already been mediated through the oppositional category of self–other is one such truism that can no longer be sustained. As I elaborate in the next chapter, contemporary scholarship has tended to presume that while European representations have changed historically they are nevertheless always filtered through the mutually exclusive categories of self and other. In other words, self and other exist as two trans-historical containers the contents of which may alter over time, but the form of their articulation remains constant: The Greek/barbarian is simply displaced by the Christian/pagan. While chapter 1 challenges this thesis directly, chapters 1 and 2 also offer alternative readings of European representations of the New World in the sixteenth century and in the Classical Age, respectively. Thus, in chapter 1 I argue that it was not otherness but similitude that underwrote Renaissance epistemology. It was not radical difference but commensurability mediated through the familiar that rendered the New World knowable. In the Classical Age, we can recognize a noticeable shift from the preceding centuries and yet again, otherness is not the medium through which the Americas are translated. Instead, the indigenous Americans are posited, in contradictory fashion, as both the model of universal reason, freedom, equality, and property-accumulating individuality and a deviation from these same universal norms. It is only in the nineteenth century (the historical backdrop of chapters 3 and 4) that the oppositional logic of self–other becomes a privileged medium through which difference is tabulated and classified.

Situating European representations of difference within the epistemic possibilities and constraints that produced them also reveals a very different interpretation of the historicity of race than traditional historical narratives currently permit. References to forms of "proto-racism" in antiquity, or the medieval preoccupation with "gens" (lineage), as well as the biblical tale of Ham (the exiled son of Noah who settled Africa), can be, and have been, read as reflective of racial thinking in the pre-modern period. To do so, however, risks imposing a particularly modern form of reasoning to bear on pre-modern and early modern traditions of thought.

Recent scholarship that has sought to defend the modernity of racial thought has been no less problematic. In identifying the emergence of racial discourse with evolutionary science, transatlantic slavery, New World conquest, nationalism, or colonialism, this literature has tended to obscure a more fundamental question: How did race become available to thought? Was it simply an outgrowth of colonialism, slavery, science, or colonialism, or is racial thinking itself reflective of and contingent on historically specific forms of reasoning? It is the latter thesis that I defend in chapter 4, arguing that to classify human difference in racial terms is only intelligible through, and necessarily reliant on, certain pre-existing epistemological conditions— namely, the elevation of man as the sole bearer of knowledge and agency and the transformation of the body into a transparent and immutable object available for human representation. It is only within an epistemic con text that permits the confluence of these two premises—man as subject in a world of objects rendered meaningful through representation—that race can find expression. A meteoric tour from late-medieval through nineteenth-century representations of the body provides the groundwork for arguing, in chapter 4, that it is only in the context of modern (nineteenth-century) reasoning that race can and was appealed to as an organizing principle for cataloguing human difference.

But if, as I have suggested thus far, European representations of difference during the Renaissance, Classical Age, and nineteenth century were born of and contingent on particular traditions of reasoning, it is equally necessary to recognize that these very traditions were themselves informed by Europe's interaction with the colonial non-West. It is significant, as I argue in chapter 3, that the European fascination with history in the nineteenth century—including the vexed question of what precisely constituted the "historical"—was fashioned within a colonial context wherein History came to be identified with European genius. The denial of historical subjectivity, as a number of scholars on the New World have argued, was a feature of early European writings on the indigenous Americans.[5] In contrast, however, India in the early years of its colonization was presumed to have a past stretching back to the ancient Greeks. By the middle of the nineteenth century, celebrations of India's antiquity had all but ceased. Against European history we confront Indian tradition; against progress through and in time, we encounter native lethargy and unreflective custom. Thus, while the historical etymology of both history and tradition long prefigured the modern, their usage and meaning were thoroughly reconfigured through the colonial prism.

It was this very appeal to historical progress posited against "tradition" that enabled nineteenth-century European philosophers and historians to privilege Europe as the birthplace of a new, superior form of selfhood: the autonomous, individuated, and individualized subject. The European individual stood in sharp contrast to the collective identities that characterized the non-West, beholden as the natives were to tribal, religious, caste, and familial affiliations. And yet, as I argue in chapter 2, it is a little observed fact that the exalted free, equal, rational individual so celebrated in liberal thought and so central to early contractarian philosophy was located in a New World state of nature wherein the indigenous American could be encountered in his alternating and conflicting role as both the archetype of and contrastive foil against the self-interested, self-regulating, rational individual.

The dual concern with situating European representations of difference within the multiplicity and historicity of colonially configured traditions of reasoning positions this work at the nexus of two bodies of literature that can broadly (though not always precisely) be identified as postmodern and postcolonial histories.

The first of this literature includes an eclectic body of work that nevertheless shares a methodological affinity: the writing of histories that do not presume historical continuity. The influence of Michel Foucault looms large in this project, but the works of Thomas Kuhn, Ian Hacking, and Arnold Davidson has equally influenced my thinking.[6] The value of this scholarship lies in its effort to produce histories of European thought and practice that recognize such histories to be fractured, nonlinear, and resistant to totalizing and monolithic narratives of progress. In different ways these scholars have sought to locate "thought" within the episteme (Foucault), paradigm (Kuhn), or style of reasoning (Hacking and Davidson) of a given period that made such thought possible. For this reason, such histories are less concerned with the works of individual thinkers or with narratives of cause and effect than they are with the question of possibilities: What conditions made it possible for particular sets of statements to be grouped together, to be rendered as knowledge, and to be constituted as truth in one historical moment—and not in another?

Underwriting such questions is the recognition on the part of these scholars that pre-modern knowledge did not consist of chaotic, incoherent, random, or arbitrary statements. Pre-modern knowledge, in other words, was not bereft of an internal logic for assessing truth and falseness. Rather, the Renaissance and the Classical period, no less than the nineteenth century, possessed a highly elaborate and cogent system of rules and norms that constituted the foundations of their knowledge production. Thus, Thomas Kuhn argued that the more carefully one studies "say Aristotelian dynamics, phlogistic chemistry, or caloric thermodynamics," the more evident it becomes "that those once current views of nature were, as a whole, neither less scientific nor more the product of human idiosyncrasy than those current today."[7]

In a similar vein, Foucault's use of the term "episteme" also works to privilege the historical contingency and historical specificity of knowledge production. Where Foucault's episteme differs from Kuhn's paradigm is in the expansiveness of the term: the fact that an episteme speaks beyond the confines of specific scientific traditions to encompass the entire edifice that produces and sustains truth claims in a given historical period. An episteme, Foucault has argued, is a means of organizing "in a coherent way an entire region of empirical knowledge."[8] The episteme of a given period may not necessarily be recognized or known by its contemporaries, but it finds expression through the repeated appeal of a shared set of rules across widely divergent disciplines or fields of study. Thus, in *The Order of Things*, Foucault traces the historical specificity of Renaissance, Classical, and nineteenth-century studies of language, life, and exchange by excavating the epistemic foundations that rendered these seemingly disparate areas of study commensurable and intelligible to the contemporaries of a given age. In other words, knowledge production, irrespective of the field of inquiry, was recognized as knowledge, was recognized as truth, within the possibilities and constraints of a specific epistemic tradition.

It is this same effort at excavating the rules and unconscious logic at work in the production of truth claims that informs Arnold Davidson's and Ian Hacking's concept of "style." Borrowed from art history, Davidson's and Hacking's respective appeal to "styles of reasoning" is a recognition that Reason, far from being singular and trans-historical, is multiple and historically contingent. Accordingly, Hacking relativizes truth by historicizing the logic by which we arrive at truth—or, to put it in his words, the "propositions to which we reason get their sense only from the method of reasoning employed." In other words, as Davidson elaborates, "Different styles of reasoning . . . determine what statements are possible candidates of truth-and-falsehood."[9] Thus, while Renaissance truth statements may appear to the modern reader as so many superstitions, a familiarity with Renaissance styles of reasoning would reveal a "systemacticity, structure and identity," "a well defined regularity" that corresponds to rules and norms from which Renaissance statements of truth-and-falsity derive their intelligibility.[10]

Adding to an already overcrowded lexicon of terms, Hacking's and Davidson's appeal to style as a methodological tool for tracing the histories of reasoning is nevertheless a valuable contribution to the existing literature. This is so because Hacking's and Davidson's work brings to the fore the necessity of studying concepts as a means for gauging larger epistemological shifts. The emphasis here is not on tracing the etymology of a word so much as in recognizing that the presence or absence of a concept—its disappearance from the lexicon, its sudden emergence into language, or its radically different renderings over different historical periods—is illuminating precisely because all these permutations offer a point of entry into particular styles of reasoning.

Ultimately, for all the differences that might distinguish their scholarship, there is a certain shared emphasis in the works of Kuhn, Foucault, Hacking, and Davidson that can be identified and summarized in two parts. First, the histories explored by these scholars—scientific traditions (Kuhn), knowledge formation (Foucault), statistics (Hacking), and psychiatry (Davidson)—lay stress on the fact that pre-modern knowledges, like modern knowledge regimes, contained an internal logic, an intelligibility born out of particular knowledge traditions that grounded thought within well-governed and regulated systems of reasoning. Out of this first thesis we recognize a second—namely, that if different historical periods were governed by different paradigms, episteme, or styles of reasoning that are often not intelligible to those outside its logic, then the history being written by contemporary historians influenced by Kuhn, Foucault, Hacking, and Davidson will not necessarily correspond to a traditional historiography, reliant as it is on presumptions of progress, incremental development, or individual agents. And indeed, the historical scholarship produced by Kuhn, Foucault, Hacking and Davidson has, at least in some instances, laid emphasis on the discontinuity of European history (the emergence of new styles of reasoning, epistemic frames, or paradigms), the grouping of old concepts or statements in radically different ways, the incommensurability between different bodies of knowledge—revealing in the process how meta-histories of "European thought" can simply not sustain the overarching unity the classification seems to promise.

The enormous value of this scholarship, however, should not obscure one of its chief weaknesses—namely, its failure to recognize and engage with the mutually constitutive relationship between European knowledges and colonial expansion. In so saying, I am not demanding that scholars of European history re-train, for example, as scholars of India, but that to write of European thought in the Renaissance, Classical Age, or nineteenth century without any recognition of the extent to which colonial expansion may have informed such thought detracts from, and simplifies, the history being written. Herein lies the significance of the other body of scholarship I alluded to earlier—what can loosely be identified as "postcolonial" theory.

A fundamental tension exists between these otherwise sympathetic bodies of scholarship. I say sympathetic because at one level postcolonialism has benefited from the debunking of European meta-histories that posit European history as an inevitable and natural outgrowth of historical development—a development that traditionally has been lauded as a tribute to European genius while simultaneously offered up as a universal promise available for emulation by others. Recognizing the particularity of European thought and thereby challenging its universalist pretensions has been a central theme of much postcolonial scholarship. But such scholarship has not simply been reactive. Rather, postcolonial scholarship has proved to be a necessary corrective to Europe-centered histories in two crucial ways.

First, it has alerted us to the extent to which European thought has been profoundly shaped by the fact of colonial interaction and colonial subjugation. Thus, Anne McClintock's work has helped to complicate feminist histories of patriarchy, gender, and domesticity by tightly interweaving European discourses of gender with imperial rule and racial representations.[11] In a similar vein, Ann Laura Stoler has offered a critical rethinking of Foucault's *The History of Sexuality* by detailing the extent to which European discourses on sexuality were configured and constituted through reference to colonized and racialized bodies.[12] Enrique Florescano has discussed the ways in which early Spanish colonists reconfigured their understanding of history with reference to the geography and peoples of the New World.[13] And yet other scholars have interrogated the colonially implicated history of an imperial discourse organized around seemingly benign concepts such as "culture" or "tradition," revealing a history thoroughly immersed within, and born out of, colonial relations.[14]

But if one intervention of postcolonial scholarship has been to detail the extent to which colonialism is implicated in European discourses and knowledge production, the second significant contribution lies in its recognition that non-Western knowledges may be resistant to, or incompatible with, Western categories of thought. In so arguing, postcolonial scholars are not engaging in a crude relativism—their concern is not to defend the "traditions" of other "cultures." Rather, the objective of at least some postcolonial scholarship has been to interrogate and dismantle the presumed universalism and neutrality of the categories through which Western knowledge has been constituted. The contention of many postcolonial scholars has been that using concepts such as "tradition," "culture," or "religion" necessarily distorts (because it reconfigures within Western categories) the multiplicity of ways in which the world has been lived, experienced, conceptualized, and articulated.

Thus, the works of Enrique Florescano and Serge Gruzinski offer detailed accounts of the complex cosmologies that framed the worlds of indigenous Americans at the time of conquest.[15] Their works trace the hybrid and entangled ways in which indigenous cultures were both incorporated within and transformative of colonial thought and settlement. In the context of India, Ashis Nandy and Dipesh Chakrabathy's critiques of historiography go beyond the more familiar criticism that the non-West has been traditionally constituted as a-historical.[16] Nandy's and Chakrabarthy's intervention is less a plea for historical inclusion than an argument for particularizing "history," for recognizing in "history" a particular relationship to time that was not and is not universally shared. In a similar vein, Sanjay Seth's book *Subject Lessons*, while ostensibly about education debates in colonial India,[17] is concerned less with the colonial content of such education or with the often disparaging British commentary regarding Britain's colonial subjects. Rather, the emphasis of the work is on how knowledge as it was rendered in nineteenth-century European thought necessarily presumed on particular types of subjects. In other words, it is the cultural and historical neutrality presumed in Western understandings of knowledge and subjectivity that are the objects of Seth's critique.

Postcolonial histories therefore should not be confused with liberal discourses of tolerance. Postcolonial history does not demand the recognition of difference so much as it challenges the knowledge structures through which difference traditionally has been accorded recognition. For this reason, an integral part of postcolonial scholarship has involved not only unpacking the particularity that underwrites European knowledge but also exploring the radically different cosmologies and knowledge systems that have enabled and framed radically different ways of being in the world. Detailing the multiplicity of ways in which people have lived, related to their gods, ordered their world, and rendered it meaningful is thus a crucial feature of much postcolonial literature.

Yet my own intellectual allegiance to this scholarly enterprise is somewhat qualified by the fact that, in their efforts to critique colonial discourse or to detail the particularity of non-Western knowledges, postcolonial scholars have at times been guilty of reproducing the meta-Europe that historians such as Foucault have sought to challenge—a Europe that is epistemologically uniform, historically linear, and conceptually monolithic. In other words, if the strength of postcolonial scholarship resides in its efforts to retrieve and foreground the rich, multifarious, and colonially subordinated forms of knowledge and types of reasoning produced by societies outside the West, the effort to produce such histories sometimes inadvertently presumed as its opposition the trans-historicity of Europe itself. What effectively gets erased is the critical work of scholars of European history who have done much to alert us to the particularity, contingency, and fractured nature of European knowledge. Edward Said's effort to trace the genealogy of Orientalism from the ancient Greeks to the twentieth-century North American academy is an exaggerated example of the intellectual pitfalls of such scholarship.

It is the tension between these two bodies of scholarship wherein my own work lies. This work first emerged out of a simple question: If, following Foucault, knowledge as it was constituted in the Renaissance, Classical Age, and nineteenth century relied for its coherence, intelligibility, and (following Hacking and Davidson) ability to discern truth and falsity within the restraints of historically located epistemic traditions, then what implication did this have for European representations of the non-West?

As is usually the case, this initial question quickly provoked another: To what extent was knowledge constituted within the epistemic particularity of European history born out of, and informed by, Europe's relationship with a world outside its borders?

It was out of these initial questions that *Europe's Indians* eventually took shape. My concern in this work is, thus, twofold. The first is to trace representations of difference from the late fifteenth century to the late nineteenth century while recognizing that such representations were beholden to specific historical contexts that belie our efforts to read continuity from one historical age to the next. In other words, my objective in this work is not simply to catalogue European representations of the non-West but also to map the conditions of possibility that enabled and constrained these representations. Colonialism, not surprisingly, emerged as a crucial "condition" in the history being narrated. Thus, a second, interrelated concern of this work has been to emphasize the extent to which European regimes of knowledge were not hermetically sealed from, or indifferent to, corresponding histories of colonial expansion and colonial interaction.

These dual themes, which offer a unifying structure to the book, are explored in each chapter through reference to very different literatures and via unconventional routes. Most notably, this work traces the historical shifts in European forms of reasoning and, thus, European representations of difference with reference to two specific colonial sites: the New World and India. Both the New World and India were malleable (albeit in different ways) to accentuating the historical faces of European representations of difference over the four hundred years that this work covers. Moreover, in tracing European representations of the Americas and India, it becomes possible to recognize the heterogeneity of European discourses of difference; that the "non-West" was not conceptualized by travelers, philosophers, or colonialists as a homogenous, monolithic site of uniform difference.

While the existence of Africa, like that of India, was known to Renaissance Europe, the very "newness" of the American continent permitted a rare insight into fifteenth-century and sixteenth-century forms of reasoning. More specifically, it dramatized the fact that confronting the "newness" of the New World did not shake the foundations of Renaissance epistemology. Rather, the Americas were simply woven into the lining of existing knowledge. The subsequent reinterpretation of the New World as a state of nature in the writing of Thomas Hobbes, John Locke, and Jean-Jacques Rousseau, as well as their respective efforts to read in the indigenous Americans the example par excellence of man in his natural state, offered similarly rich possibilities for exploring the epistemological terrain of Classical thought.

In a similar vein, but for very different reasons, India also possessed a specificity that was particularly revealing of European representations of difference. Most notably, the mythological status that India had long possessed (while true of China, Egypt, and Persia, as well) was exemplified by the privilege accorded to Sanskrit in the late eighteenth century and early nineteenth century. The discovery of a linguistic affinity between Sanskrit and ancient Greek and Latin heralded not only a "discovery" of ancient Sanskrit literature but facilitated the contentious debates concerning the definitional contours of history and tradition. Precisely because of the earlier colonial fascination with Sanskrit and philology, the shift away from textual studies of ancient scriptural sources to anthropological studies of contemporary communities is most dramatically played out in the context of nineteenth-century British India. If India was crucial to European formulations of history in the early and mid-nineteenth century, it was also central in late-nineteenth-century debates concerning race, criminality, and policing: Anthropology rather than philology became the privileged discipline aiding colonial knowledge production. India, in short, became the experimental laboratory for the emerging technologies of criminal identification. Indeed, it is in India that fingerprinting was first introduced.

If the coupling of the New World and India in a single work is unconventional, so, too, is the history this work seeks to narrate. For in insisting that European discourses on the non-West were produced within particular traditions of knowledge, it became necessary to resist the temptation to narrate European representations of difference within a developmental history. Thus, through exploring the multiple representations of difference produced out of the epistemic particularity of the Renaissance, the early modern period, and the nineteenth century, a space was opened up to pursue questions that a more traditional historical method might not be equipped to ask—for example, what permitted certain representations of difference to be articulated as truth claims at one point in history and not in another? Did different periods in history presume on different subjectivities? If so, what relevance, if any, did subjectivity have on the nature of the knowledge produced? When did the body become an object of knowledge? What does it mean for questions of diversity if God, demons, witches, angels, and monsters are accorded volition and agency? What does it mean for our understanding of Man if he is not privileged as the sole source of knowledge and agency? Why did some of the most respected scientists of the nineteenth century adhere to what we can only regard today as the "pseudo-science" of racial biology? What did it mean for Classical conceptions of the individual when the free, equal, rational individual was identified with the New World Indians? To what extent was nineteenth-century historicism shaped by nineteenth-century discourses on "native traditions"? How did historicism reconfigure the historically resilient concept of savagery? Was the conquest of the New World a precursor to racial discourse? What are the correlations between physiological fixity, policing technologies, and the introduction of fingerprinting in British India?

These questions, like the commentary thus far, provide a very general survey of the concerns that preoccupy this work. I now turn to a more detailed discussion of the individual chapters.

Chapter 1 questions the historical efficacy of evoking self–other as the defining matrix through which difference has been represented throughout European history. Engaging briefly with contemporary works on this subject, I go on to argue that interpreting early European contact with the New World in terms of self–other—where Europe marks the self and the indigenous American is the site of otherness—is problematic if for no other reason than it is difficult to discern either a European self-identity in the Renaissance or the production of a discourse about the "native."

This chapter argues that Renaissance knowledge formation was not articulated through oppositional narratives, but was governed by the logic of similitude. In so saying, I am appropriating and extending Foucault's study of Renaissance epistemology to better understand and contextualize early European representations of the New World.[18] I suggest that the New World was rendered into a very old world, because it was enveloped into a pre-existing world—one malleable to commensurability through reference to ancient texts, biblical Scriptures, and popular travel stories.

Chapter 2 is also concerned with European representations of the New World, but with the focus turned toward the seventeenth century and eighteenth century. Through the social-contractarian writings of Thomas Hobbes, John Locke, and Jean-Jacques Rousseau, it is possible to dramatize the disjuncture between Renaissance and seventeenth-century and eighteenth-century epistemologies. Having left a world where the hand of God is always present, where society is divinely ordained, circumscribed, and predetermined by His Will, we enter the Age of Man. In evoking the writings of Hobbes, Locke, and Rousseau, I am not suggesting that their works represent building blocks in the gradual cementing of liberal ideals. Rather, their writings provide, through the bounded world of the text, an insight into the larger epistemological terrain of the seventeenth century and eighteenth century. What we encounter in the works of Hobbes, Locke, and Rousseau is the gradual ascendance of Man as the architect of order, the author of meaning, and the agent of history. Man in this context is constituted as a free, equal, and rational individual who is first encountered in a state of nature significantly located on the distant shores of the New World. This individual is no less than the Indian himself.

In other words, the individual in the imagination of Hobbes, Locke, and Rousseau is personified through the figure of the indigenous American. This relationship between colonial contact and the emergence of discourses around individuality not only complicates existing literature on the history of the "individual" by insisting on the relevance of colonialism in the making of European individual subjectivity,[19] but it also works to elucidate one of the defining features of seventeenth-century and eighteenth-century epistemology. For I argue that through the organizing principle of the universal individual, difference comes to be constituted as the "exception." It is a deviation from a norm, a deviation that finds expression through irrationality in Locke or degeneracy in Rousseau. But what is notable in the work of all three contractarians is that, even though the New World is constituted as a state of nature, this fact does not transform the indigenous American into an object to be studied. He is an archetype of universality (the free, equal, rational individual) or exceptionality (the irrational, familial miscreant), but he is not a figure invested with any historical, cultural, or racial particularity.

This ceases to be true in the nineteenth century—the focus of chapter 3. This chapter traces the shift from, and differences between, the universal histories produced in the seventeenth century and eighteenth century and the emergence of history as a disciplinary science in the nineteenth century. Among the many characteristics that distinguish nineteenth-century thought is the emergence of and emphasis placed on historicism. The principle of universality that underwrote Classical thinking comes to be complicated with a newfound concern for identifying particularity—most notably, in the context of history and culture. Where I complicate this familiar narrative is in arguing that a history of historical thought within Europe cannot be narrated solely with reference to Europe. Exploring this argument through European representations of colonial India, it becomes possible to trace a gradual distinction emerging, over the course of the nineteenth century, between two "types" of subjects—historical actors and traditional peoples, where the former denotes agency and consciousness, and the latter denotes habitual, unreflective practices. Through tracing this distinction, mapped over Europe and its colonies, it becomes possible to discern the extent to which concepts such as "history," "tradition," the "past," and "culture" cannot be presumed to have an a priori intelligibility. Rather, they were categories of differentiation born out of the specificity of nineteenth-century colonialism. It is only once we recognize the historicity of these concepts that it becomes possible to account for the paradoxical representation of India as possessing a vast antiquity and yet being bereft of history.

But if history constituted one site on which discourses of difference came to be articulated in the nineteenth century, racial science was an equally potent source of explanation. I approach the subject matter of nineteenth-century racial discourse via a circuitous route, which in fact subordinates the history of racial representations to a history of the body and shifting conceptions of subjectivity. Accordingly, chapter 4 begins with Renaissance representations of the body as an entity that is malleable, volatile, and transgressive. The fluidity and permeability attributed to the body in Renaissance thought—explored through reference to the wild man, monsters, hermaphrodites, and medical treatises of the time—constrained the possibilities of recognizing the body in clearly demarcated and racialized terms. The body for the Renaissance did not lend itself to categorical precision. In the Classical Age, a changed epistemic foundation no longer recognized the world and knowledge as divinely ordained. In this new context, only man was recognized as a subject, and it is only with reference to man that meaning, knowledge, and order were deemed possible. Within the episteme of the Classical Age, the body ceases to have volition and agency, and while it retains its malleability, it does so only in reference to the actions of men. Through reference to seventeenth-century and eighteenth-century writings on the imagination, pedagogy, and wild children, I argue that the body in the Classical Age is represented as subordinate and subjected to human reason and that for this very reason the body is not accorded the deterministic significance it was to have in the nineteenth century. It is in the nineteenth century that the body emerges as an intransigent, impassive, and impermeable object. Through reference to nineteenth-century criminal-identification techniques—particularly in the context of colonial India—I suggest that the very impermeability, fixity, and thus measurability of the body accords it with the paradoxical authority to both mark difference (for example, between races) and establish individualized identity (as in the case of policing technology). This chapter, in short, seeks to demonstrate that any effort to write a history of race requires first and foremost that one trace the shifting contours of European conceptions of the body and subjectivity.

We arrive then at the end of the nineteenth century. There is no culminating endpoint to this history, for, as I argue in the epilogue, European encounters with and representations of cultural difference are no less fraught than they have been through the course of the history I narrate. What should be evident by the conclusion of this work is that contemporary representations and engagements with difference are not the fallout of some inevitable and self-evident historical logic but, rather, the product of a history that is indebted to human practices and human thought. The point of the epilogue—indeed, the utopian impulse of this book as a whole—is to suggest that this history can be unmade.

# 1  Self and Similitude

## Self and Other: Figures of Modernity

IT HAS BECOME an increasingly common feature in contemporary writings on European colonialism to articulate the relation between the colonizer and the colonized in terms of self and other, West and non-West. While the narrative I allude to is all too familiar, it is a narrative that, nevertheless requires unpacking.

Simply put, when we speak of the self in opposition to the non-European other, are we appealing to a metaphysical rendering of the West as an entity that, following Nietzsche, can be traced back to the ancient Greeks, or are we to understand the conceptual grid of self–other as a historically bounded reference to modernity—one that locates the West-as-self within the context of the post-Enlightenment?

If it is the former, if it is a metaphysical category to which we are appealing, implicit in our understanding is a recognition that the West–non-West binary has always already inhabited the conceptual geography of self–other—at least as far back as classical antiquity. In other words, the West has always already been a self-referential subject. Alternatively, if we seek to subject the self–other narrative to historical specificity, if we wish to situate it within the world of the modern, our premise by necessity has to presuppose that the oppositional apparatus of the West–non-West binary was indebted to a particular set of historical conditions, whether these be capitalist economic relations and Enlightenment universalism, the emergence of nation-states and a distinctively modern form of governmentality, or the ascendance of science and reason and the catch-cry of secularism.

It becomes apparent, therefore, that when we speak of self and other, we need to be alert to the fact that, from this point of reference, we can traverse two radically distinct theoretical terrains—one that is organized around the trans-historical sign of the West, and the other that subjects the West to historical specificity. As I will go on to argue, the distinction drawn is an important one, and yet in some of the contemporary literature engaging with the production of the Western self and non-Western other, there often appears an ambiguity, a "collapsing together" wherein metaphysics and history intermingle in a confused interchangeability.

Illustrative of my point is Edward Said's decidedly seminal text *Orientalism* (1978). Said's work provides a now canonical reading of European colonialism through the conceptual grid of self–other, the Occident–Orient. In so doing, he renders a more complex appreciation of power wherein power is identified not simply with bullets, governance, and wealth extraction but with the very production of knowledge.[1]

The fact that Said engages with nineteenth-century European literature and the twentieth-century North American academy is suggestive of the fact that he situates the oppositional binary Occident–Orient within the template of modernity. And yet while Said encloses his subject matter within a historical frame, this temporal imposition coexists with a temporal transcendence, a constant oscillation between the category of the West and the category of the modern. What is implicit throughout Said's thesis becomes explicit when he argues: "In classical Greece and Rome geographers, historians, public figures like Caesar, orators and poets added to the fund of taxonomic lore separating races, regions, nations and minds from each other; much of that was self-serving and existed to prove that the Romans and Greeks were superior to other kinds of people."[2]

What we witness in Said's text, dramatized in the quote, is the collapsing together of Julius Caesar's Rome and the reign of Queen Victoria. Yet what remains a largely ambiguous positioning of the Classical period in Said's work finds full expression in François Hartog's thesis that Herodotus's *Histories* represents one of the earliest expressions of the Greeks' efforts to understand their neighbors through radical opposition. *The Mirror of Herodotus: The Representation of the Other in the Writing of History*, as the title suggests, offers an in-depth textual reading of *Histories* from an interpretative position that construes Herodotus's references to the Persians, Scythians, Libyans, and other non-Greeks as emblematic examples of the representational production of self–other in classical antiquity.[3]

While Hartog's *Mirror of Herodotus* provides both an insightful and sophisticated reading of the *Histories*, the interpretation of the *Histories* as a text of otherness has a currency that goes beyond the jacket of his book. If Said oscillated from ancient Rome to nineteenth-century Europe, more contemporary works have found no hesitation in mapping Herodotus's *Histories* over Renaissance representations of the New World. Thus, in a work concerned with first contact between Spanish voyagers and indigenous Americans, Stephen Greenblatt's *Marvelous Possessions* retraces the roots of European constructions of the other back to Herodotus, whose ethnology, he argues, constitutes "the first great Western representation of Otherness."[4] In a similar vein, Michel de Certeau parallels the *Histories* with Michel de Montaigne's famous essay *On Cannibals*, suggesting that both function as texts that offer "a representation of the other."[5]

In works as different as that of Said, Hartog, Greenblatt, and Certeau—works that engage with radically distinct intellectual projects—a shared theoretical premise nevertheless exists: that it is possible to speak of the West as an entity that extends itself back to antiquity, an entity that is malleable to all historical conditions. Thus, implicit in this narrative is the contention that one can traverse centuries, from the dizzying peaks of Greek and Roman civilization to the glory of European imperialism, and encounter, throughout this breathless history, a self-defining identity of the West as conceived through the oppositional representation of the non-Western Other. It is precisely this proposition that this chapter seeks to question.

In light of the literature I have briefly reviewed, it becomes evident that in appealing to the classics for testimony of representations of otherness, we are investing the self–other distinction with no other significance than that of cataloguing—the registering of hierarchical difference. If this is the case, however, it is a practice that can hardly be preserved as the exclusive intellectual property of the West. After all, numerous civilizations throughout history have engaged in the intellectual and practical exercise of distinguishing themselves from their neighbors and have often predicated this distinction on a self-proclaimed superiority. Such an accusation could be directed at the Aztecs and Chinese no less than at the Greeks and the Romans. However, if our understanding of self and otherness is reduced to only recognizing this fact, its value is of a very limited scope. In attempting to explain everything, it fails to tell us anything. Indeed, in rendering self–other as ubiquitous, we are denied precisely that which makes such organizing categories significant—the possibility to distinguish over time and space, to acknowledge history and recognize power.

What is striking when reading a text such as Herodotus's *Histories* is that even if we allow for an interpretation that construes the *Histories* as ethnocentric (a fact that is itself questionable, given Herodotus's effusive praise of the Libyans), it is difficult to argue that power mediated the relations between the Greeks and the barbarians. Not only was the wealth and might of the Persians difficult to deny, but even the Scythians, for all their "barbarity" were regarded by Herodotus as simply indestructible—given their nomadic existence, "How . . . can they fail to be invincible and inaccessible for others?"[6]

In failing to recognize that the self–other binary was a grammatical feature of *colonial* representations, we risk losing sight of the fact that the ubiquitous power of modern colonialism lay not only in the unparalleled success of Europe's domination of much of the globe but also in the corresponding appropriation of the discourses of modernity by the colonized peoples[7]—a fact immediately apparent in the narratives of nationalism, modernization, and science, and in the universalization of the language of rights and the individual. What we also risk ignoring is precisely that which makes the self–other binary an integral feature of modern colonial relations—that in the context of nineteenth-century European colonialism, the self not only constituted, defined, and represented the other for its own consumption (a charge one might level at Herodotus), but that it translated that knowledge as "truth" both in the realm of discursive practices and in the production of material realities.[8]

Yet my objection to the temporal transmigration of the self–other binary to ancient times is not simply limited to its consequent rendering of power and history as obsolete. More significantly, once we subsume all intersocietal contact from antiquity to the present within a dialogue between self and other, we risk rendering ancient knowledge into a textual alibi in the very defense of modernity itself. It is not my intention to deny the fact that the Greeks sought to differentiate themselves from their neighbors or that their observations were mediated through categories that at times employed the language of negation to represent the antithetical non-Greeks—be she or he a Scythian nomad, an Amazon, or one of the panoply of monstrosities believed to populate India. Clearly, it is possible to interpret the *Histories* as a testimony to Greek constructions of self and otherness—numerous scholars, after all, have done so. And yet, I would argue that while such a reading is indeed possible, the very fact of that possibility, the very fact that the *Histories* can be rendered into a text of otherness, speaks less to Herodotus's Greece than to modernity more generally, and to nineteenth-century colonialism more specifically. In other words, it is from the vantage point of colonial history, a history that has in part been mediated through the grid of self–other, that we transpose our (modern) reading onto ancient texts.

Thus, while it is undoubtedly true that *Histories* is one in a pantheon of classical texts that has helped to shape the contours of a European self and its Oriental, African, Asian, and American other, it has become so through a process of translation wherein an ancient text has been rendered malleable to modern categories and then appealed to as confirmation of the antiquity of those self-same categories. Integral to the logic of this circular argument is the premise that from Herodotus's time to our own, the categories employed to conceptualize the other have remained unchanged; that the conceptual grids through which we order our world resonate in the texts of pre-Christian times; that the division between an East and West has always already existed; and that ancient texts are the oracles of our modern condition.

In the final analysis, to privilege the self–other binary in a reading of ancient texts is to assume that knowledge was ordered, structured, and imported through this very grid. It represents a failure to recognize even the possibility that such reading may require the visual aid of retrospective lenses. In ignoring this possibility, we risk rehearsing Said's intellectual position, whereby in extending his critique back to antiquity to historicize and debunk the truth claims of modern European colonialism, he is in fact forced to rearticulate its premises, ignore its implications, and confirm its self-made historical trajectory. Thus, in an act of imaginative migration, ancient Greece and modern Europe can speak to each other as familial brethren, sharing a language encoded with the same timeless categories of West and East, Self and Other.

The problem is: What constituted the West, and who precisely was the Self?

## Europe: An Idea

In A.D. 800, Charlemagne was dubbed *Pater Europa*, the father of Europe.[9] Pope Pius II, on hearing of the fall of Constantinople, feared that "now we have really been struck in Europe, that is, at home."[10] Erasmus of Rotterdam wrote in a letter dated 1530 of "the prosperity of Europe," while the cartographer Abraham Orelius could, in his *Geographical Encyclopedia* (1578), confidently instruct his readers, "For Christ see Europe."[11] Francis Bacon, in 1623, presupposed the comprehension of his readers when he spoke of "we Europeans," while 1689 saw Fontelle endeavoring to recognize a distinctive European "quality of mind or genius."[12] More than a hundred years later, Edmund Burke pronounced that "no European can be a complete exile in any part of Europe," while the conquered Napoleon conceded that his aim had been "to found a European system, a European code, a Supreme Court for all Europe; there would have been a single European people."[13]

All of these quotes have been extracted from a growing body of literature that has sought to trace the "idea of Europe." In an area fraught with disagreement on a number of fronts (including as to when Europe "really" emerged, when it distinguished itself from Christianity, and when it captured a collective imagination), what is nevertheless recognized in the very nature of this exercise to identify the "origins" and development of the idea of Europe is the premise that Europe was an "idea," that Europe and Europeans were never natural, self-evident, immutable, or historically neutral entities. Rather, as Gerard Delanty argues, Europe was a concept, a cultural construction. Consequently, "To speak of Europe as an 'invention' is to stress the ways it has been constructed in an historical process; it is to emphasize that Europe is less the subject of history than its product."[14]

While the origins of the word "Europe" can be traced back to ancient Greek mythology, made famous by Albrecht Dürer's painting *The Rape of Europe* (ca. 1495), it is generally recognized that Europe held little political, cultural, or economic meaning for the ancients. The Greeks were largely ignorant regarding the geography and inhabitants of Europe, while the Roman Empire, extending over three continents, displayed little apparent loyalty to Europe per se.

It is, rather, in the Middle Ages that an idea of Europe that expresses some significance, however vague, comes to emerge. The title bequeathed to Charlemagne as "Father of Europe" is a popularly cited early medieval example. So, too, is the late medieval reference by Pope Pius II to Europe as a home. Peter Burke also points to the increasing number of references to Europe in literary works such as that of Petrarch, where Europe is referred to with some regularity, and in Dante's Latin works, wherein Europe is cited on thirteen separate occasions.[15] Burke is quick to point out, however, that while "Europe" may appear with increasing regularity from the thirteenth century onward, one should be wary of exaggerating the significance of the idea of Europe in the Middle Ages. After all, if Dante mentions Europe three times in his *Divine Comedy*, this in itself is only of limited significance when compared with the far greater number of references to Italy (eleven), Christian or Christianity (fifteen), and Florence or Florentine (twenty-two).[16] Similarly, while Pius II is often cited in the corpus of early references on Europe, Denys Hay notes that in fact he uses *Respublica Christiana* far more frequently.[17]

This alerts us to a contentious issue regarding the history of the idea of Europe—namely, at what moment did "Europe" itself come to be invested with autonomous meaning, with cultural and political significance. As Hay points out, "If by Christendom [Pope Pius II] meant Europe, that was precisely the ambiguity which was to persist."[18] Until well into the seventeenth century, Hay suggests, Europe and Christendom were interchangeable terms.[19]

The ebb and flow of references to Europe throughout the Middle Ages often correlated with the successive invasions first by the Mongols and later (over a protracted period of time) by the Turks. The frequency of references to Europe became pronounced precisely at those moments when Christendom was increasingly giving ground to Turkish invasions, when its authority was being narrowly contained within Europe.

Given this fact, many historians have argued that, while in the fifteenth century and sixteenth century it would not be viable to speak of a distinctive European community or of an all-encompassing identity, the idea of Europe was nevertheless emerging under the rubric of Christianity. In other words, while cultural disparities and political rivalries made a secular European identity untenable, Europe as the geographical and spiritual center of Christianity nevertheless carried emotive claim. It is in this context that Ortieus's brief instruction "for Christianity see Europe" speaks volumes, leading many historians of the idea of Europe to argue, as Delanty does, that "Christianity gave to Europe its identity."[20]

While there is certainly some truth to this conclusion, I would suggest that the unifying role of Christianity has tended to be overstated. Two reasons lend themselves to explaining why we should be wary of defending the idea of Europe as an expression of Christianity and thus, by implication, elevating the significance of Europe itself.

First, while Hay suggests that Europe and Christianity were synonymous concepts throughout the Renaissance, there is much to suggest that Europe was a concept entirely overshadowed by, and secondary to, Christianity. Delanty himself makes this point when he argues that Europe was "subordinated to Christianity which was the dominant identity system in the West."[21] It is not surprising, therefore, that Dante and Pope Pius should evoke Christendom more than Europe or that Columbus should pronounce that his discovery should benefit "not only Spain but all of Christendom."[22] While the threat of Islam may have helped to shape the contours of Europe, that very same threat, as M. E. Yapp argues, imposed limitations on the possibilities of a European identity: In the face of Ottoman successes, it was less Europe than Christianity that found expression.[23]

The mapping of Christianity over Europe is further problematized by the fact that both the Crusades and Turkish incursions made the distinction between a Christian Europe and Islamic Asia a questionable division. Christian crusades were operative in the Levant by 1493, after the fall of Constantinople, when as much as one-quarter of European territory was under Muslim rule, and by 1530, the Ottomans had captured most of Greece, the Balkans, much of Albania, and all of Bosnia, Bucharest, Belgrade, and Budapest.[24] Again it is Yapp who makes the important and qualifying observation that "the pretensions of Christendom remained universal." Thus, the Crusades expressed not a European movement but, rather, an obstruction to "the elaboration of that concept."[25]

Hence, while Europe was an indeterminable figure residing in the shadows of Christianity, Christianity itself was far from being a monolithic and coherent entity. It is notable, as Stephen Greenblatt observes, that on the eve of his execution, Thomas More's appeal to the "holy saints in heaven" only heightened "the sense that to affirm in 1535 the essential singleness of the whole corps of Christendom was to affirm that which ordinary earthly vision could not see."[26]

Temporal vision had been blind to the divine unity of Christianity as early as 1054, when the linguistic and ecclesiastical differences between the Byzantine orthodoxy and the Latin church became firmly cemented. The already loosened threads of the Christian coil were unraveled altogether when papal authority was challenged with the events leading up to Henry VIII's divorce and the Protestant revolt. Along with the undermining of church authority was the gradual ebbing of its cultural hegemony, a fact most profoundly witnessed in the decline and eventual redundancy of spoken Latin.[27] Hence, the fundamental undermining of the language of *Republica Christendom* gradually released the idea of Europe from Christian to secular significance.

While the breakup of Christendom gestured toward the gradual secularization of the idea of Europe, it is in fact Columbus's discovery of America to which monumental significance is attributed.[28] As Burke argues, "If the first context in which people became aware of themselves as Europeans was that of being invaded by other cultures, the second was that of invading other cultures, in other words discovery and exploration."[29] Thus, the discovery of America permitted a shift in identity from that of Europe by default (a geographical and cultural recognition of Turkey's military success) to Europe as the confident heir of the spiritual *and* temporal throne. By 1572, the title page of the Ortelius atlas centered the majestic but stern female figure of Europe holding the specter of world domination, while the female personifications of Asia (richly clad), Africa (semi-nude), and America (nude and in possession of a human skull—the spoils of her cannibal feast) were all sitting subserviently at Europe's feet.[30]

Yet despite the fact that references to Europe figured more frequently in the art and in the literature of the Renaissance, it is to the eighteenth century to which many scholars turn for the most elaborate and self-conscious expression of the idea of Europe. "By the beginning of the eighteenth century," Hay argues, "it is in terms of Europe that Europeans view the world."[31] Agnes Heller and Peter Burke agree, and while Delanty privileges the nineteenth century as the definitive moment, in all instances there is a recognition of the fact that to speak of Europe before the 1700s is to recognize its appeal as limited to the vocabulary of a small elite.[32] From the eighteenth century on, Burke argues, "Europeans were more ready to talk about Europe, to see it as a whole, and to contrast it with the rest of the world than they had been in 1500, let alone the Middle Ages. Consciousness of being European was now an important social and political fact."[33] It was so not only for a cosmopolitan elite but also for "ordinary people," at least in towns, for whom by the late eighteenth century an awareness of Europe can be surmised from the increased popularization of the idea of Europe encountered in ballads and street theater.[34]

By the nineteenth century, Europe could be conceived of not only as an identity but as a tradition—a tradition that, Heller and Delanty argue, was constituted retrospectively with the popularization of the novel, the influence of a romantic sensibility, and the mass production of historical texts: "Medieval cathedrals, Renaissance cities, secret oratorios, and lay sonnets became codified and arranged side by side as manifestations of an entity called Europe or the West."[35]

To borrow and reformulate Benedict Anderson's thesis, Europe by the late eighteenth century had emerged as an imagined community. And yet if this is the case, if to speak of Europe before the 1700s is to evoke an identity that was fraught, tenuous, and fractured, it follows that any attempt to render the early European interaction with the New World as constitutive of a self–other construction is as fraught as the a priori idea it seeks to evoke. It permits us to ask the question: Who precisely is the self being posited in relation to the American other?

"*Modernity, the creation of Europe, itself created Europe,*" and it did so, in part, through the carpentry skills of the historical narrative.[36] Seeing the early contact between Europe and the New World as mediated through categories of self and otherness risks imbibing the a-historical historicism of the nineteenth century within which the discovery of the New World can be represented as a defining moment in European history precisely because the identity of "Europe" is rendered self-evident. In other words, the very history of Europe—or, for my purposes, the history of Europe's discovery of the Americas—risks positing Europe itself as an a priori subject.

Many scholars have, of course, recognized the extent to which Europe's arrival at a sense of self emerged in tandem with colonial expansion. Thus, in representing Europe's relations with the New World as one of self and otherness, one is acknowledging the fact that the self is not an a priori entity but one that comes to be constructed through the very process of interaction with the other.

Yet the very nature of the self–other thesis could conceivably be a circular one. To argue that the self comes to be constructed through identification with otherness assumes a self ready for definition; the self, in other words, is implicitly already there, it requires an a priori existence to be posited for otherness to be constituted.

What could render such an objection invalid is the fact that, in any given society, infinite possibilities exist from which particular selves come to be privileged. The privileging of particular selves over others depends in turn on that which is invested as a site of otherness. Thus, the very categories that constitute the sites of difference are themselves historically and culturally contingent. For the early Spanish colonists, it was not the color of Indian skin that was invested with significance (it is arguable whether race as a category had yet come to figure in colonial representations) but the pagan nature of Indian religion.[37] For the ancient Greeks, the eclectic forms of worship observed by their neighbors were less a signifier of barbarism than the fact that they did not speak Greek. It was language, not religion, that was constitutive of difference.

Consequently, even if we assume that the self–other binary informed European interaction with the New World in the sixteenth century (an assumption this chapter seeks to challenge), we should question why in the context of Spanish, English, French, and Portuguese interaction with the New World, it is assumed that the Self being posited is Europe when it is apparent that Europe was not only a nascent identity in the early years of the Renaissance, but an identity competing for recognition against far more powerful rivals such as Christendom, city-states, and secularized kingdoms. Europe as a confident, self-conscious, self-defining entity is an eighteenth-century phenomenon, and hence we should be wary not only of presuming the presence of such a figure in the sixteenth century but of seeing the 1500s as the inevitable prelude to the nineteenth century; a teleological retrospection that ignores the tenuous and historically contingent nature within which particular selves and their oppositional counterparts come to be privileged sites of differentiation.

It is true, as I have already noted, that by the time of Columbus's discovery of the New World the idea of Europe was already emerging. Yet while

Europe was taking on a form that was absent in ancient times—while it was, perhaps, a self ready for definition—Burke is right to warn us against over-emphasizing Europe's presence in the minds of its inhabitants in the sixteenth century and seventeenth century. It is significant that when Columbus boasted of the "temporal benefits" his discovery would bring, it was not to Europe that he spoke but to Spain and Christendom.[38]

If the decline of Christendom, the discovery of new worlds, and Renaissance humanism all offered possibilities for the construction of a European identity, the realization of these possibilities was neither inevitable nor immediate. As Heller argues: "The sixteenth and seventeenth centuries were characterized neither by the unification nor by the establishment of a common integration termed 'Europe.' In lieu of the survival of a universalizing humanity, there was rather a nascent, and quickly emerging, diversification and differentiation."[39]

The immediate effect of the breakdown of Christendom was that of greater fragmentation—a fragmentation that could be witnessed not only in terms of domestic discord, but also in Europe's interaction with the East and the newly discovered lands.

The most challenging testimony, that which most reveals the highly dubious nature of the category "Europe," is offered in Patricia Seed's account of English, French, Spanish, Portuguese, and Dutch rituals of colonial conquest and possession in the New World. For brevity and because of the late arrival of the Dutch as colonial explorers, I will not be reiterating Seed's discussion of Dutch exploration. However, a summary of her accounts of English, French, Spanish, and Portuguese expansion is useful, as it provokes an immediate challenge to any representation of Europe as a monolithic self during the epoch of discovery.

As Seed explains, the distinctive nature of English, French, Spanish, Portuguese and Dutch rituals of establishing authority in the New World were assumed by each to be self-evident assertions of possession, yet the basis of their claims to dominion were often unintelligible to their colonizing rivals. The stated objective of Seed's study, therefore, is to "render explicit the often unstated yet distinctly embedded histories and locally significant systems of meaning behind the symbolic actions and statements creating overseas authority."[40]

Turning first to the English, Seed provides an account of the landing at Plymouth and the subsequent assertion of political authority over the newfound territory. What is striking and distinctive in the English claim to dominion (as seen at Plymouth and repeated in other parts of the New World) is the absence of any ceremonial gestures, whether in the form of planting a cross, hurling a banner, pronouncing solemn speeches, or enacting symbolic rituals to mark possession. Rather, the English distinguished themselves from their rivals by conveying political authority through the establishment of dwellings, the construction of fences, the planting of gardens, the clearing of land, and the sowing and harvesting of crops. The fixture of physical, immovable objects as symbolic of possession had its roots, Seed explains, in an equally English specific interpretation of Genesis 1:28. Whereas on the continent "Be fruitful, multiply and replenish the earth" was understood to refer to human reproduction, in England it was identified with agricultural production: subduing and cultivating the land (31–35).

The English-specific rendering of this passage in Genesis as a divine command instructing man to sow and harvest the land as well as to graze livestock was itself inherited not from ecclesiastical tradition, but from Anglo-Saxon folklore (34). From these medieval origins, the passage from Genesis came repeatedly to be invoked as the legal foundation of English possession in the New World, cited by such notable figures as John Locke and William Blackstone (33).

In sharp contrast to the material matter-of-factness evident in English possession, Seed describes the highly formalized nature of French acquisition. The two most notable features marking French dominion resided in the elaborate ritualized ceremonies of possession and in the perceived necessity of acquiring native consent. A religious procession followed by a political ceremony marked French possession of an island near the mouth of the Amazon. While both ceremonies invoked distinct rituals, music, official pronouncements, and props, each required the involvement of the indigenous peoples either as participants in the procession or as spectators. Participation coupled with Indian gestures, signs, sounds, and movements were interpreted as Indians' willingness to embrace the Christian faith and native consent to have their land appropriated and governed by the French (41–46).

Again, as with the English, both elements of French possession—that of ceremony and that of consent—can be rendered intelligible only when referred back to French political culture. Seed traces back the elaborate nature of French ceremonies, as witnessed in the rituals of possession in the New World, to the system of royal succession in France itself, where hereditary kingship was not "automatic"; instead, "The new princes' power had to be established by public rituals of consecration" (50). Appropriate to the French conception of "ceremony" (which required the following of prescribed rules and did not simply denote, as in English, Dutch, and Spanish, a slightly pejorative overtone of affectation and outward formality), the rituals involved in the anointing of the king were not mere formality (55). Rather, "The coronation ritual actually legitimated political power" (51).

It is in this context that body language and gestures were a critical part of ceremonial possession, for the shouting and gestures of the crowd at the coronation of a king were interpreted as consent for the new political ruler. That such behavior was deemed to hold universal meaning led the French to assume that, on witnessing apparently similar gestures among the Amerindians, French dominion had been legitimated (55).

Spanish claims to possession marked themselves off as radically different to those of the English and the French, requiring neither structures nor ceremonies but the observance of protocol. More specifically, Spanish political authority resided in reading aloud, to the New World natives, a written speech known as the "Requirement (*Regimento*)," which called on the Amerindians to accept the superiority of Christ or be warred upon. This remarkable document that legitimized Spanish territorial claims on the basis of conquest "was one of the most distinctive features of Spanish colonialism, [for no] other European state created a fully ritualized protocol for declaring war against indigenous people" (70).

The expression of Spanish authority whereby religious and political rights were fused together traces its heritage back to Islamic jurisprudence, which had left its legacy on the political and religious practices of the Iberian Peninsula even after the re-conquest of Christian rule. It was the Maliki tradition, a specific school of jurisprudence among Sunni Muslims that was embraced by Muslim Spain, and it is from this school of thought, Seed argues, that one can trace the origins of the "Requirement" (74).

Based on Averroes's legal handbook, the notion of *jihad* (summons) in Maliki jurisprudence involved a highly stylized public ritual, which summoned non-believers to submit themselves to the superiority of Islam. It is significant to note that this pronouncement called on non-Islamic rulers to submit (if necessary, by war) to Islam, as distinct from calling on them to profess belief—a recognition that immediate conversion would be incredulous, that belief would occur over time (77).

In this context the role of the messenger, who in Western warfare was merely a runner, carried a special significance in Islamic tradition. Muhammad, after all, described himself as the messenger of God. The role of the messenger was to bear the news of the new religion to non-Muslim rulers. A refusal to submit to the jihad was a justified cause for declaring war (77).

In all instances, the Spanish "Requirement" was a re-enactment of the Muslim jihad. It was a declaration of war read by a messenger who began by summoning the Amerindians to "recognize the church as lord" and to submit to the superiority of the faith. A willingness to submit would ensure that Christian soldiers would leave "your women and children free" and not compel anyone to turn Christian. Yet a failure to acknowledge the superiority of Christianity justified war "everywhere and however possible" (quoted on 69). A document read in sixteenth-century Spanish to Amerindians at the point of a sword calling on them to submit to Christianity or be warred upon appeared as the height of absurdity to other European monarchs. Yet it becomes less mystifying when one recognizes in it the imprint of Islam on the once Muslim-ruled Iberian Peninsula.

If the Spanish declaration of war as embodied in the "Requirement" seemed incomprehensible to the other powers within Europe, the Portuguese explorers fared little better in convincing their rivals of their right to the sole monopoly of the sea routes they had discovered. In 1562, a bizarre exchange between the Portuguese ambassador and Queen Elizabeth revealed the political premise of Portuguese claims to possession. Calling on the English sovereign to acknowledge Portuguese sovereignty over all of the land discovered by the Crown of Portugal, the queen replied, "In all places *discovered* . . . he had no superiority at all," to which the irritated ambassador responded, "His master *has* absolute *dominion* . . . over all those lands already *discovered*" (quoted on 101–2).

Neither fences, elaborate ceremonies, nor speeches marked Portuguese territorial claims. Furthermore, it was not in reference to land (as was the case with the English) or in reference to the indigenous people (as was true of the Spanish and French) that the Portuguese articulated their objective. To appreciate the peculiarity of Portuguese claims necessitates an appreciation of Arabic and Hebrew influence.

The importance of Arabic knowledge through the course of the late Middle Ages had provided the Portuguese with a sophisticated knowledge of navigation unrivalled by any other European power. Such knowledge allowed for early success in exploration; it also made possible detailed calculations regarding sea routes and locations of the lands discovered, thereby permitting repeated journeys. Hence, on first landing, in April 1500, on the coast of present-day Brazil, the Portuguese fleet did not engage in any form of ritual to denote its political authority. Rather, the marker pilot, John, wrote to the king first informing him of the discovery of land and then proceeding to elaborate on the precise height of the midday sun and the mathematical details of the fleet's exact location in degrees of longitude and latitude (101). Inheriting Arabic mathematical techniques and navigational technologies allowed Portuguese political rights to be invested in the claim that, if their knowledge resulted in the discovery of sea routes previously unknown and unknowable, this was cause and justification for their exclusive monopoly of these same sea routes. Portuguese claims to monopoly of sea and trade routes were not that different from modern-day patenting laws, for their political claims rested on the premise that it was through their financial investment, physical labor, and navigational knowledge that the discovery of sea routes and new territories was made possible. The Portuguese claims, however, were largely incomprehensible to their rivals precisely because they spoke to the specificity of a *Portuguese* history—not a European one (100–30).

And that is precisely the point. The significance of Seed's study, particularly in the context of this work, is that it problematizes and destabilizes the extent to which Europe as a collective entity can be legitimately appealed to in any discussion of the fifteenth century and sixteenth century. Illustrating the marked differences by which the English, French, Spanish, and Portuguese articulated their political authority overseas necessitates recognition of the cultural heterogeneity that existed within Europe itself. That heterogeneity, in turn, reflected both domestic conditions and, in some instances, a telling reminder of the pervasive legacy of Islamic and Arabic traditions on the continent.

Hence, the establishment of English dwellings in the New World spoke to a peculiar Anglo-Saxon reading of Genesis 1:28; elaborate ceremonies and attention to native gestures reflected the distinctive nature of French political culture; the Spanish "Requirement" was testimony to the enduring influence of Islamic jurisprudence; and Portuguese pioneering discoveries revealed the debt owed to Arabic and Hebrew mathematics and navigational knowledge.

Seed's account points to the fact that, not only were there enormous cultural gaps between different European states that often made them unintelligible to one another, but these differences were carried overseas in the conquest of America. In the context of my argument, the significance of Seed's thesis lies in the fact that, while the discovery of the New World may eventually have proved to be an important factor in the construction and secularization of a European identity, the early years of conquest had the immediate effect of *fragmenting* Europe by both dramatizing the cultural and political disparities between the different states and further undermining papal authority. The peculiar English rendering of Genesis 1:28 and the expression of Spanish evangelicalism through an Islamic-style jihad indicate that cultural variations within Christianity already existed.

The rise of Protestantism offered a far more self-conscious break from the Roman church. In the representations of the New World offered by Theodor de Bry's woodcuts, one finds not only depictions of Indian cannibalism but Protestant accounts of the atrocities committed by Catholic Spain against its subject peoples.[41] Lucrative trade with the East ensured that while Christianity, whether Catholic or Protestant, shared an abhorrence of Islam, the Christian faith was not always a deterrent to entering into favorable treaties with the Ottoman Empire. Various alliances, at different times, saw relations established between the Turkish empire and the states of Milan, Venice, France, and England.[42] Even within Catholicism, state rivalries for territorial and trade monopolies in the New World and the East undermined the authority of the church in temporal matters. For example, the Spanish philosopher Francisco de Vitoria (c. 1485–1546) questioned the legitimacy of the papal bulls, which had rendered much of the non-European world the exclusive domain of Spain and Portugal.[43] Vitoria's philosophical skepticism acquired political expression not only in the objections of the Anglican queen of England, but in the sarcastic request of the Catholic king of France (to the Iberian ambassador) to see the last will and testament of Adam and Eve before agreeing to observe the church-sanctioned monopoly rights of Spain and Portugal.[44]

Given the embryonic, if not highly fragmented, state in which one finds the idea of Europe in the fifteenth century and sixteenth century, is it legitimate to speak of European representations of the New World as a discourse of self and otherness? I have sought to question the legitimacy of this interpretation, to challenge the implicit assumption that during the Age of Discovery, to speak of the self was to speak of Europe. I have attempted to illustrate that such a thesis relies for its legitimacy on an assumption that Europe was always already there; it attributes to Europe an a priori homogenous identity that is difficult to substantiate. Through the works of historians on the idea of Europe, it is possible to recognize in the emergence of a European identity both a historically contingent subject and a highly self-conscious invention. Europe as an identity and a tradition cannot be legitimately defended or appealed to until at least the eighteenth century. My appropriation and summary of Seed's thesis allows one to appreciate the extent to which a European consciousness was continually arrested by cultural disparities that rendered the discovery of the New World as a site not for the cultivation of a European identity, but as a battleground for conflicting political claims and religious interpretations. Pre-empting the possible objection that not a secular but a Christian European identity can be appealed to as far back as the Middle Ages, I have suggested that, far from being equal partners, the ambitions of Christendom often undermined the idea of Europe and that the immediate consequence of the decline of Christendom and discovery of the New World heralded not a secular European consciousness but the fragmentation of any monolithic identity.

It has not been my objective to deny the presence of an emerging sense of Europe in the fifteenth century and sixteenth century but to question how large it loomed in the imagination of the Renaissance. Through the discovery of the New World, numerous selves were articulated, of which Europe was only one expression—and not always the most significant. And as for the Other . . .

## The New World: Representations of Otherness or the Politics of Indifference?

If it is a dubious exercise to posit Europe as representative of the self in the fifteenth and sixteenth centuries, equally problematic is the theoretical rendition of the New World as having been constituted through the trope of otherness. The most striking feature that marks the first sixty years (roughly until 1550) after Columbus's discovery of hitherto unknown lands is the surprising indifference with which Europe received the news. This is not to say that when Columbus returned to the Old World after his first voyage he was not met with much fanfare—Columbus, as well as later discoverers, held processions down the main streets of European cities and towns, displaying to the crowds that gathered the exotic produce acquired from their discoveries and parading the strangely painted figures of the Indian slaves they had captured and brought back with them.[45] Furthermore, it was in the first half of the sixteenth century that some of the most notable early texts on the New World were published. Amerigo Vespucci's letters announcing the discovery of a New World (the first popular recognition that America was not an extension of Asia), Hernán Cortés's *Cartas de relación* (1522), Peter Martyr's *De Orbe Novo* (the first complete "history" of the New World published in 1530), Francisco de Jerez's *Verdadera relación de la conquista del Peru* (1534), Gonzalo Fernández de Oviedo's *Historia general y natural de las Indias* (1535), and Vitoria's treatise *On the Indies* (1539) were all published within the half-century following the initial discovery.[46]

And yet despite these publications, and despite the exploration of more than three thousand miles of South America's coastline before 1502, "The discovery of the New World," Margaret Hodgen points out, "made relatively little impression on Europe."[47] With the exception perhaps of Oviedo's *General and Natural History*, it is notable that there were few detailed accounts of either the indigenous inhabitants or the natural environment of the Americas. Kirkpatrick Sale notes that the absence of ministers, ambassadors, naturalists, and artists on Columbus's first voyage ensured that any descriptive accounts of the New World would be limited in scope.[48] Indeed, Columbus's letters are revealing for how little they do say regarding the indigenous Americans. Not only, as David Traboulay observes, was little effort made to differentiate between native cultures, but there was a marked lack of interest in the indigenous peoples altogether.[49]

Given the preoccupation with gold among Spanish discoverers and the absence of extended interaction with the indigenous inhabitants, this marked lack of interest and consequent lack of detailed ethnological accounts need not surprise us. What is striking, however, is the extent to which the very existence of America failed to capture the European imagination. It could, of course, be argued that at least in the first decade after discovery, the New World was not recognized as such—that Columbus died thinking he had voyaged to the East. Yet by the close of the fifteenth century, knowledge of a New World had been made public through the letters of Amerigo Vespucci, whose fame came to be immortalized in the naming of the continent.[50] While we can attribute an early lack of interest in the discovery of America to a failure to grasp the magnitude of that discovery, this explanation does not account for the lethargic European reaction following Vespucci's pronouncement.

Despite the publication of some notable works such as those already cited, the quantity of manuscripts published on the Americas was remarkably small. In sixteenth-century France, there were twice as many publications on Muslim ways as on Africa and America put together.[51] Similarly, Henry Elliott quotes the figure that between 1480 and 1609, four times as many works were devoted to Asia and Turkey as to America—a ratio that actually increased in size in the final decades of the 1600s.[52] The constancy and immediacy of the Islamic threat may account for this discrepancy; however, it does not explain why it took fifteen years before an account of Columbus's discovery was published in English, or why the first published *Encyclopedia* in 1751 should devote only fifty lines (a quarter of a page) to the "Americas" when "Alsace" was given eighteen times that space.[53] And while it is not surprising (given the level of illiteracy in, and insularity of, European towns and countryside) that the majority of the population "did not even suspect the existence of another continent," it is remarkable that America does not even figure in the memoirs of Spain's King Charles V.[54]

*It is difficult to speak the language of otherness when the other is virtually absent from the discourses of the self.*

Numerous scholars have sought to explain this early European ambivalence toward the New World by suggesting that the sheer immensity of the challenge the New World represented to established canonical thought ensured a measure of resistance to including America "within [Europe's] field of vision."[55] In a similar vein, Anthony Grafton argues that, prior to Baconian science, the foundation of knowledge was not predicated on empiricism and experimentation but on the a priori value placed on a limited number of canonical texts. The writings of ancient scholars and medieval saints constituted the boundaries of knowledge and the repertoire of facts. Hence, to be a man of letters required a familiarity with Ptolemy's geography; Euclid's geometry; Aristotle's politics, ethics, logic, and science; Peter Lombard's theology; and Galen's treatise on anatomy.[56]

Michael Ryan provides a somewhat different, though not necessarily contradictory, thesis when he suggests that the failure of the discovery of America to produce an intellectual crisis within Europe was not predicated on any confrontation with a radical other but was, rather, the consequence of a process of assimilation that "tended to rob [the Amerindians] of their difference and blunt the force of their impact."[57] Testimony to the truth of this argument is nowhere more evident than in Columbus's observation that the Amerindians he encountered were not human monstrosities but "of fine appearance."[58] Columbus's observation was given further legitimacy when sanctified by church authority: Pope Paul III's Papal Bull of 1537 pronounced that "the Indians are true men."[59] Even Sepúlveda, who was keen to prove the inferiority (and thus justify the enslavement) of the Indians, nevertheless deemed them suitable for conversion—a possibility available only to the human subject. Finally, the charge of cannibalism itself, leveled as it was against the Indians by Columbus and most who succeeded him, was by necessity an a priori recognition of the humanness of the native inhabitants—thus, the horror it implied.

Is it possible, therefore, that the very humanness of the indigenous Americans diffused their enthusiastic reception among Renaissance thinkers? It is well documented in the works of Hodgen, Roger Barta, and Richard Bernheimer that the wild man and his monstrous brethren, having loomed large in the literature and images of the Middle Ages, were embraced by the Renaissance with no less credulity.[60] Indeed, it is notable that the three books Columbus carried with him on his first voyage were Pierre d'Ailley's *Imago Mundi*, Marco Polo's *Travels*, and Pliny's *Natural History*.[61] Having thus been well acquainted with the hordes of semi-human "monstrosities" as engraved on the arches of Gothic churches, depicted in the works of ancient scholars, and recorded as the eyewitness testimony of travelers, it is of little surprise that Columbus should have expected to encounter more than just the human form. With the possibility of confronting Cyclopes, nymphs, satyrs, and other "fabled freaks,"[62] encountering an Amerindian may well have proved a reassuring, yet uninspiring, outcome.

Yet I would suggest two further reasons that the discovery of the New World received only belated interest. If otherness is predicated on the desire of the self to know the other, it is equally predicated on the ability to produce knowledge about the other.

First, for knowledge to be produced, the object of that knowledge has to be made commensurable. It is in this context that Greenblatt's *Marvelous Possessions* is an important contribution to the existing literature, for it alerts us to the simple, yet heavily encoded, expression of wonder. The wondrous or marvelous testifies to an inability to articulate that being observed, or experienced, into a language that is accessibly familiar.[63]

Hence, Columbus's *Journal*, littered as it is with references to the marvelous (particularly notable in his descriptions of the natural environment), testifies to a sensory experience that he is ill equipped to translate into words.[64] Columbus was not alone in this regard. Greenblatt cites numerous other examples,[65] yet all point to the fact that inspiring interest in the discovery of the New World was severely impaired by an inability to convert the sights, sounds, and smells experienced by discoverers into a readily available language accessible to domestic audiences.

The second point to note is that even when commensurability is possible, knowledge requires certain conditions for its production. While Ryan, like myself, argues the case for extending Foucault's thesis on similitude to a reading of Europe's interaction with the New World (an argument I will elaborate on in the next section), he does not engage with the fact that the production of knowledge on the Americas was inherently limited precisely because colonial rule was administered through configurations of power that were themselves fundamentally pre-modern. Power, in other words, was not instituted through the labyrinth of power–knowledge relations— that which Foucault identified with the nineteenth century. Absent, therefore, were modern forms of governmentality, population surveillance and disciplinary techniques, as well as the mounds of literature that informed these discourses, such as colonial reports, anthropological studies, police files, anthropometrical statistics, and so on.[66] Absent also in the early years of Spanish contact were the representational forms of power identified by Said and Rana Kabbani,[67] where otherness found full expression through myriad literary and artistic works. What was absent, in short, was a modern formulation of the political.

It is in this context that the work of Carl Schmitt is particularly relevant. Schmitt argues that the emergence of modern politics can be discerned at the moment when a friend–enemy distinction is born.[68] The friend–enemy binary, in turn, relied on a reformulation of the enemy that was grounded no longer in personal animosity and personal gain but in "disinterested intensity"—the ability to kill without hate.[69] As Michael Dutton argues in his interpretation of Schmitt:

> In elaborating upon this idea of friend, enemy and the nature of the po-
> litical, Schmitt would end up concluding that what set politics apart from
> other domains (be they economics, aesthetics or morality), what made
> it "authoritative" as opposed to just being "superior," was that it was the
> only domain that produced a *public* enemy whom one could kill without
> hate.[70]

The nature of Spanish power witnessed in the first sixty years after discovery was experienced through coercion, through naked violence. It was
a violence that reduced the indigenous population from twenty-five million
to one million in central Mexico alone.[71] Such violence was graphically described and passionately denounced by Bartolomé de las Casas, lamented
by Vitoria, described in Bernal Díaz's chronicle on the fall of the Aztec
Empire, and even observed by Oveido, one of the harshest commentators
on the indigenous Americans.[72] It was a violence that, while justified by the
"Requirement," had no method, no rules of conduct, no ritualistic obser-
vances or legal codes. Even war, Vitoria noted, necessitated the observance
of international and natural law.[73]

If we map self–other over Schmitt's conception of the friend–enemy, it
is possible to argue that what inspired the violence cited above was not the
"authoritative" voice of the modern state—a subject conceptualized as the
self. Rather, it was religious fervor, the quest for riches, and the cultural
repulsion expressed toward indigenous practices that were the motivating
factors governing the rules of behavior and justifying the magnitude of destruction, pillaging, and murder within the Spanish colonies. The public
other–enemy was neither present nor necessary in this pre-modern configuration of power.

For all of the cruelty and violence that were being witnessed, the political imperative to know the Indian, to govern over him, to impose a rule
of law on him, and to define oneself against him, were configurations of
power that had yet to come into sharp relief. If Schmitt is right to argue,
following from Theodore Daübler, that the "enemy is our question in a
figure"[74]—that is, the enemy is the necessary conduit for self-definition—
the initial years of Spanish conquest become illustrative of absence: an absence of desire to define the self through reference to the other.

It is precisely in the absence of what Schmitt takes to be the birth of modern politics (culminating in the friend–enemy distinction) that goes some way toward explaining the lethargic continental reception to the discovery of a new world. The absence of a motivating drive to construct and know the other—the public enemy—to arrive at self-definition ensured a colonial climate that was not conducive to the systematic study of Indian societies and institutions. Indeed, it hindered the production of such knowledge—a fact lamented by the Dominican Fray Diego Durán, who insisted that the task of eradicating paganism was severely frustrated by "those who, with much zeal but little prudence, burnt and destroyed at the beginning, all their ancient pictures. This left us so much in the dark that they can practice idolatry before our very eyes."[75]

The fundamental lack of interest in the New World among European scholars needs therefore to be seen as not only a resistance to absorbing information that radically contradicted canonical texts. Rather, the lack of interest in the Americas in the first sixty years after discovery speaks to an inability on the part of the Spanish to formulate the figure of the other. This is due to the fact that the Spanish were unable to translate incommensurability into otherness and because power was exercised as an extension of personal enmity and personal gain rather than in concert with knowledge production and the formulation of a public enemy. Constructing otherness requires both the desire to know and the ability, the conditions, to produce that knowledge. The much discussed and debated European lack of interest in the New World is testimony to the absence of both these prerequisites.

The absence of the figure of the other speaks not only to the initial period of European ambivalence toward the Americas. The effort to read sixteenth-century European interactions with the New World as emblematic of self and otherness remains a questionable exercise even when a growing enthusiasm for the Atlantic continent is finding expression in the publication of an increasing number of ethnological texts and political treatises concerned with the indigenous Americans. As I will go on to argue, it was not the language of radical opposition but that of similitude that navigated European representations of the New World. It is, of course, true that to make alterity familiar, intelligible, it needs to be translated into categories that are commensurable. Yet while in the nineteenth century such categories increasingly relied on opposition—through discursive strategies such as history and racial science (the subject of chapters 3 and 4)—the categories of the Renaissance sought commensurability through the lexicon of resemblance. Thus, it was not an oppositional paradigm that informed Renaissance knowledge but an assimilationist one.

It is in this context that a very peculiar event emerges as a significant and revealing source of information. It was a distinctive (and much written) moment in Spanish history when Charles V, King of Castile, called for an immediate halt to trade with the New World until such time as his appointed jury of fourteen learned men could hear the respective arguments of Las Casas and Juan Ginés de Sepúlveda on the legitimacy or otherwise of warring on and enslaving the colonial subjects of the Americas.[76]

If the Valladolid debate of 1550 was, as Lewis Hanke argues, an expression of Christian morality on the part of the Spanish king ("Probably never before or since has a mighty emperor . . . ordered his conquests to cease until it could be decided whether they were just"),[77] its significance also resides in the fact that this royal-sanctioned debate between Las Casas and Sepúlveda was an effort to codify the king's laws for implementation within his New World colonies. The nature of pre-modern power, made representationally famous through Foucault's visual appeal to the pyramid, relied on the ritualistic and public display of power exercised as testimony to the king's authority and witnessed as fearful warnings by his subjects.

It was, I would suggest, precisely the absence of the king's legitimating power, his legal edicts and governing gaze in the New World colonies, that goes some way toward explaining the phenomenal debate at Valladolid. The outcome of the debate would determine the nature of Spanish rule and thereby render tangible the body of the king through the systematic imposition of royal decrees defining and limiting the economic, legal, political, and moral boundaries of Spanish interaction with the indigenous inhabitants of the Americas. And yet, while the Valladolid debate of 1550 offered the first systematic engagement with the question of Spanish rule in the New World and its treatment of indigenous inhabitants, it also revealed the process by which the world of the Indian could be translated into the language of the Renaissance.

In so saying, it is important to note that when I speak of Renaissance knowledge, I refer not to a quantifiable commodity; nor is it my intention to measure the truth and falsity embedded in sixteenth-century Spanish impressions of the New World. Rather, the debate at Valladolid is revealing as a testimony to the very mechanics of Renaissance knowledge: the components that constituted its structure, the questions it posed, the boundaries it drew, and the legitimation it derived from the sources it evoked.

The overriding objective of the Valladolid debate was to determine the legitimacy of warring on, and consequently enslaving, the Indians. Sepúlveda appealed to Thomas Aquinas's definition that a war is just if the cause is just. The justness of waging war and enslaving the Indians was in turn defended through appeal to Aristotle's doctrine of natural slavery. The Indians were natural slaves, Sepúlveda argued, because they lacked reason—a "fact" that much of his thesis sought to prove through reference to idolatry, cannibalism, and the general barbarity of the indigenous peoples. Las Casas, in turn, also appealed to Aquinas when arguing that a distinction needed to be made between those infidels who had heard the true faith and failed to embrace it: "vincibly" ignorant such as the Jews, Muslims, and Moors, and the "invincibly" ignorant who, through no fault of their own, had never received the Word and thus never rejected it. The Amerindians, Las Casas argued, were of this second category; thus, waging war against them was inherently unjust. So, too, was enslaving them. However, Las Casas defends this position not by challenging the legitimacy of Aristotelian thought, but by celebrating the inherent mildness and material achievements of the Indian as proof of their rational and moral character.[78]

What stands out as significant, even in this brief summary of the debate, is the fact that while Las Casas could boast fifty years of experience in the Americas, thirty-five of which were spent championing the cause of the Indians (Sepúlveda, on the other hand, had never left European shores), it was less experience than textual authority that conferred weight and legitimacy to their respective arguments. Furthermore, following from Grafton's thesis that the world of the text was a chaotic, contradictory, and far from homogenous source of knowledge,[79] it is not unreasonable or surprising that the same canonical authorities could be appealed to by both Las Casas and Sepúlveda to support and defend radically opposing arguments.

Yet as much as the canonical texts were appealed to in order to authorize the legitimacy of the contrary positions offered by Las Casas and Sepúlveda concerning the Amerindians, it could equally be argued that the aboriginals constituted a site on which to confer legitimacy and reconfirm the authority of canonical knowledge. Does not the cannibalism of the Indians speak to a rich tapestry of sources that have testified to the existence of anthropophagy? Is not the existence of a Golden Age such as that so eloquently described in the works of Hesiod, Virgil, and Ovid proved to be true in the very life of the indigenous Americans?[80]

Whether it be the case that the texts find confirmation in the Amerindians or the other way around, what is significant is that, in spite of the discovery of a new world, the orthodoxy of the canon was left largely unscarred. The *fact* of America did not lead to a revision of the facts. In other words, there was no discursive space within which to produce the figure of the other as a figure estranged from the self.

## Signatures of Similitude

If it is the case, as I have argued, that Europe's first contact with, and subsequent representation of, the New World was not mediated through the oppositional frame of self–other, how was this strange new land rendered familiar? *The difference of the Indian was simply made compatible with that which was already known.* That which was observed could be grafted onto that which was written. Thus, the native American was not constructed as the radical other but, rather, translated into a familiar archetype who conformed to the strange but comforting worlds already immortalized in ancient texts and more recent travel narratives.

While such translations between the eye and the text have been recognized as a peculiar feature of Renaissance thought,[81] what allowed or made possible the act of translation in the first instance is a question that has largely been ignored. Ryan offers an important insight when he argues that the Americans as well as the Asians and Africans were rendered familiar through the organizing category of paganism. Paganism, Ryan elaborates, not only denoted religious practices, but was gradually extended to signify the entire cultural apparatus of non-Christian societies,[82] thereby rendering all that was potentially unintelligible into that which was immediately commensurable. In other words, once indigenous societies were made familiar, they were also made translatable and, thus, exposed to canonical interpretations.

Ryan's thesis appropriates two significant features underlying Foucault's reconstruction of Renaissance knowledge. First, explicit in Ryan's argument is the recognition that within the conceptual framework of similitude we can locate the organizing categories that "made sense" of the New

World, categories that relied on the essential premise that the world was constituted through an endless web of resemblances.

Foucault points to four conceptual grids that rendered the world familiar. *Conventientia* (convenience), "which pertains less to things themselves than to the world in which they exist," has the effect of rendering the world perfectly symmetrical. The number of fish in the sea is equal to beasts on the land and beings in the sky, and thus everything is made to correspond with the other.[83] *Aemulatio* (emulation) speaks to those things that are similar enough that they duplicate one another, are mirrored in each other, yet the "two reflected figures [are not in] a merely inert state of opposition" but, rather, one is weaker and thus malleable to the influence of the stronger (20). Next there is *analogy*, which is not dependent and thus limited to the visible similarities between properties but, rather, identifies commonality through "subtle resemblances of relations" (21). Finally, *sympathy* risks rendering objects the same. "It will not rest content to be merely one of the forms of likeness" (23) but, rather, threatens the individuality of objects by collapsing them into a homogenous whole, "thus rendering . . . them foreign to what they were before" (24). An extension and counterpart to *sympathy*, therefore, is *antipathy*. Whereas sympathy transforms objects in the direction of sameness, antipathy "maintains the isolation of things and prevents their assimilation." It jealously guards against similitude enclosing "every species within its impenetrable difference and its propensity to continue being what it is" (24).

Similitude offers a conceptual scheme premised on the familiar, a scheme that weaves the world into a complex tapestry where every thread intertwines and complements the whole: "Convenientia, ameulatio, analogy and sympathy tell us how the world must fold in upon itself, duplicate itself, reflect itself, or form a chain with itself so that things can resemble one another" (25–26).

The second insight, albeit implicit, offered in Ryan's thesis is the recognition that similitude is to be distinguished from sameness; that Renaissance knowledge did not collapse the world in on itself, reducing all difference into a single homogenous mass. Rather, as with the example of paganism, difference (in this context, the distinction between Christians and non-Christians) was constituted within the conceptual framework of the familiar. Paganism was, as Ryan argues, made analogous to, and at times made to sympathize with, the heathenism of the ancients. Yet while this logic is implicit in Ryan's argument, his overarching thesis works to collapse similitude into a homogenous whole. In arguing that it was the single organizing trope of paganism that rendered the non-European world familiar to its explorers and European audience, he implies that Renaissance thinkers reduced all the new lands discovered—whether they were in Asia, Africa, or America—into an undistinguished mass recognized and defined only in reference to their non-Christianity. Yet there is much to suggest that this was not the case. Columbus was well aware when first encountering the Amerindians of the Bahamas that he had not yet arrived at the land of the Great Khan. Both Vitoria and Las Casas argued for Indian slavery to be replaced by importing the stronger, hardier natives of Africa,[84] while even within the Americas, the kingdoms of the Aztecs and Incas were eventually identified as different from the presumed simplicity of the Taínos.

Paganism alone simply does not account for the myriad and often contradictory representations of the New World, let alone Asia and Africa. What is absent from Ryan's thesis is the third and fundamentally important feature of Foucault's analysis, which is that similitude is impossible without signatures:

> This is why the face of the world is covered with blazons, with characters, with ciphers and obscure words. . . . And the space inhabited by immediate resemblance become like a vast open book; it bristles with written signs, every page is seen to be filled with strange figures that intertwine and in some places repeat themselves. (26–27)

The chaotic world of the text is not merely that which is written; it is also that which is signified on the surface of things and thus interpretable through the conventions of convenience, emulation, analogy, and sympathy. Yet the closed body of the written text and the signatures that mark external, material objects should not be deemed one and the same. It is signatures that allow that which is observed to be grafted on the world of the text; it is signatures that make translation possible, for the recognition of signs in the inhabited world allows that which is observed to enfold, replicate, conform to, and confirm the authority of canonical knowledge. The written text, in turn, ensures that the act of seeing, touching, hearing, and smelling are not undisciplined senses threatening unpredictable responses; rather, both the experience and the description they inspire are already circumscribed by the authority of the canons. In a potentially frightening and chaotic array of signs, discrimination is possible, reading is selective, and the conclusions are predetermined precisely because the written text mingles with a world of signs, each pre-empting, drawing on, deferring to, and reconfirming the other. Resemblance speaks not only to a likeness between things but also to the referential reverence of the written word.

One finds this at the very moment of discovery. Many authors have commented on the extent to which Columbus, in hopeful expectation of sighting land, appealed to signs for confirmation. The appearance of a large cloud mass from the north, the spotting of dolphins, the drizzling of rain without wind, the approaching of "two boobies" toward the ship, and the recording of "much more vegetation" were all signs prophesying land—prophesies heralded as early as a month before the coast of the Caribbean was sighted.[85]

Yet while Kirkpatrick Sale expresses surprise and disdain at Columbus's ignorance,[86] the value of signs for the admiral can be better appreciated if the natural world is recognized as a text offering confirmation of a pre-established set of beliefs themselves encoded with the authority of canonical literature and travel tales. As Tzvetan Todorov argues, Columbus "knows in advance what he will find; the concrete experience is there to illustrate a truth already possessed, not to be interrogated according to pre-established rules in order to seek the truth."[87]

And the truth was that months into his first voyage, Columbus was adamant that the land of the Great Khan was surely within reach. "It was after all," Greenblatt notes, "the known world that Columbus had set out to discover by an unknown route: that was the point of reading Marco Polo and John Mandeville."[88]

Hence, it should be of little surprise that when encountering the natives of Trinidad, Columbus's immediate observation was the nature of their headgear: "They had their heads wrapped in scarves of cotton . . . which I believe were *almaizares*."[89] In the apparel of the indigenous Americans, Columbus recognized the veils of the Spanish Moors. Was this not sufficient proof that he had arrived on the fringes of Asia? Evidently, Columbus's appeal to signs not only applied to the natural world (in his increasingly desperate search for land), but provided the medium by which to interpret the physical and social body of the Amerindians.

But perhaps one of the most significant observations Columbus records in his first voyage is that which I have already alluded to—namely, his observation concerning the human corporeality of the Indians he encounters. "In these islands," Columbus writes, "I have so far found no human monstrosities, but on the contrary all the people are of a fine appearance."[90] The significance of this observation lies in its most categorical recognition of likeness. The natives are analogous to "us"—that is, they mirror the Spanish conquerors in the very humanness of their constitution, and yet, as Columbus goes on to describe, they are the weaker reflection, a fact evident by their lack of religion and their nudity, timidity, and primitive weaponry.

Yet the humanness of the indigenous people he encounters does not undermine Columbus's certainty that monsters do inhabit the surrounding islands—a fact that he was able to ascertain through communication with the Indians, whose gestures and signs confirmed (with remarkable accuracy) the existence of those very same creatures cited by the ancients, the saints, and the travelers. Thus, Columbus reports of an island inhabited only by warring women, one in which reside men who feast on human flesh, another where people have no hair, and yet another by the name of Avon, which is reported to be populated with human beings equipped with tails—and all of this is recorded in a single letter.[91]

Columbus's narrative, therefore, envelops this foreign land and its strange inhabitants into a reassuring embrace. The discriminate observance of a multiplicity of signs, themselves ageless and universal, enfolded the novelty of discovery into a familiar repertoire of resemblances. Yet the sphere of resemblances that enclosed the indigenous inhabitants of the Americas into the Renaissance world of similitude were predicated on signs that were often radically distinct from those observed by Western travelers in the East.

Consequently, while paganism was undoubtedly a central motif within European representations of the New World, it was so under the rubric of the "savage." It was the savage—noble or otherwise—that distinguished Renaissance representations of the Americas from that of the other worlds discovered.

While, as Lucien Febvre argues, the idea of civilization has a very recent history, the category of the savage can trace its origins back to the ancient Greeks. It is precisely in this iconography of the wild man / savage that Renaissance travelers sought inspiration.[92] Yet the signatory marks of the "savage," like that of Grafton's chaotic world of the text, allowed for disparate and contested representations—the two most significant being that of the Golden Age and that of savagery.

Vasco de Quiroga, the nominated member of the royal Audiencia in Mexico, argued that the New World is thus called not only because it was newly discovered but because "in almost everything it is like that of the first and Golden Age."[93] Such sentiments as that expressed by Quiroga were an echo of ancient authors—the poetic reminiscences of a Hesiod, a Virgil, and an Ovid. From these literary heights, the Golden Age motif became part of the imaginative currency of European travel writers. Thus, it is of little surprise that Vespucci's description of the indigenous American virtually duplicates the earlier account Mandeville provides of the people of Sumatra. Yet while Vespucci does not acknowledge his debt, Peter Martyr and Montaigne both begin by paying homage to the "old wryters"[94] before recording, for imaginative posterity, the discovery of a new continent suspended in a youthful world. Montaigne provides his famous rendition of the Americas through a literary engagement with Plato:

> This is a nation, I should say to Plato, in which there is no kind of commerce, no knowledge of letters, no science of numbers, no title of magistrate or of political superior, no habit of service, riches or poverty, no contracts, no inheritance, no divisions of property . . . no respect for any kinship but the common ties, no clothes, no agriculture, no metals. . . . The very words denoting lying, treason, deceit, greed, envy, slander, and forgiveness have never been heard. How far from such perfection would he find the republic that he imagined: "men fresh from the hands of the gods."[95]

Sale makes an astute observation when he argues that the Americas were particularly malleable to representations of Golden Age innocence because the landscape of open spaces, exotic birds, and lush greens offered such a sharp contrast to the open sewers, fortified walls, and densely populated cities of Europe.[96] Peter Martyr's description of the New World is revealing in this regard, arguing as he does that the "Indians seeme to live in the golden worlde without toyle, lyvyne in open gardens, not intrenced with dyches, divided with hedges or defende with walles."[97] In a similar vein, Vespucci notes the absence of disease in the New World, describing a landscape free of pests and a people unscarred by epidemics.[98]

While much is made of the language of lack in European representations of the New World (as exemplified by the earlier quote from Montaigne), superlatives denoting abundance inspired equally provocative images—hence the reason that Columbus was so effusive in his praise of the wealth and diversity of the natural world; that Vespucci argued that the Indians live up to one hundred fifty years; and that Montaigne's Indians (paraded as part of a street procession for Charles IX) are purported to observe, without hesitation, the poverty, hunger, and beggary surrounding them on the streets of Rouen.[99] The litanies of absence were similarly countered by the physical presence of the New World: the elaborate arrangement of flora in the newly emerging botanical gardens, the exotic life encaged in municipal zoos, the curiosity cabinets of amateur collectors, and the artifacts clothing the walls of sober university lecture halls.[100]

Nevertheless, it is true that the representational trope of absence (the lack of government, laws, commerce, writing, religion, morals, clothes, etc.) constituted an integral feature of Golden Age mythology. The language of lack was, however, equally conducive to harboring representations of a very different order: that of the savagery of the "savage." The distinction between savage life and the lived experience of the *polis* evoked a heritage dating back to the ancient Greeks. When the societal institutions and ethics of the *polis* were identified with the false trappings of an artificial existence (exemplified by Montaigne), absence conferred high praise. Yet Sepúlveda offered an alternative rendition of the world of the Indian that echoed sentiments more akin to Herodotus's savage and Aristotle's slave than to the ideal world immortalized by Plato's Atlantic and Ovid's Golden Age:

> You will scarcely find even vestiges of humanity, who not only possess no science but who lack letters and preserve no monument of their history except certain vague and obscure reminiscences of some things in certain paintings. Neither do they have written laws but barbaric institutions and customs. They do not even have private property.[101]

Central to the invocation of savagery (as opposed to the noble savage) in European writings about the New World was the trope of cannibalism. It is impossible when studying European representations of the New World to ignore the pervasive presence of the cannibal. Devoted to precisely this feature of Renaissance literature, Peter Hulme's book *Colonial Encounters* attempts to charter the emergence and powerful resilience of the cannibal motif in the context of the Americas from when it first appeared in Columbus's *Journal* to its imaginative deployment in Defoe's *Robinson Crusoe*.[102]

While the Greek word denoting the practice of eating human flesh—a practice Herodotus ascribed to the Black Sea tribes—was *anthropophagi*, the present-day term "cannibalism" has its etymological roots in the pronoun "Carib," the Indian inhabitants of the Antilles who were widely recorded to eat the flesh not only of their enemies but of their children.[103] As Hulme describes, "Through the connection made between the people and the practice of eating the flesh of their fellow creatures, the name cannibal appeared into Spanish and then the other European languages."[104]

Columbus, on his first voyage, identified the practice of anthropophagi with a monstrous race purported to inhabit the (as yet unvisited) island of the Caribs. While the Caribs, when finally encountered, proved to be human in form, Columbus was nevertheless confirmed in his view that some "savage" tribes practiced anthropophagi by the report of Dr. Chanca, the King's surgeon, who accompanied Columbus on his second voyage. Dr. Chanca recorded the presence of human bones sheltered in the houses of the Indians (reportedly Caribs) on the island of Guadalyse, deducing from this discovery the ethnological conclusions that:

> the customs of these Carib people are beastly. . . .
>
> The Caribs eat the male children [of their female captives] and only bring up the children of their own women; and as for the men they are able to capture they bring those who are alive home to be slaughtered and eat those who are dead on the spot. . . . They castrate the boys they capture and use them as servants until they are men. Then when they want to make a feast they kill and eat them. For they say the flesh of boys and women is not good to eat.[105]

Thus, from the first moment of contact, cannibalism became part of the representational diet fed to domestic audiences by European travelers. However, while cannibalism was the necessary ingredient of tabloid travel tales, it was also placed under philosophical scrutiny by Vitoria, appealed to by Sepúlveda as the penultimate evidence of Indian savagery, figured in the engravings produced by de Bry, and was the subject of Montaigne's relativism.

The ubiquitous presence of the cannibal/Carib motif could be offered as testimony to the presence of a self–other narrative in sixteenth-century representations of the indigenous American. In the charge of cannibalism, the very fusing of the Carib subject with the practice of cannibalism itself could be interpreted as one of the most potent constructions of radical otherness. Did not Columbus identify the practice of anthropophagi with monstrous races?

Yet I would argue that the representation of "savage" peoples feasting on the culinary delights of the human flesh is indelibly encoded within the grammar of similitude. Cannibalism maps the European imagination onto the social geography of the New World, enveloping the Indian into a repertoire of images that long preceded their discovery—images that roamed over the surfaces of travel writings, scholarly dissertations, poetic verse, artistic canvases, and religious treatises traversing a history from ancient times to the sixteenth century, from the sixteenth century to the present day.

Among the myriad signs offering disparate interpretations, it was the savage / cannibal that came to be privileged. As Hulme argues, Columbus shifts from an Oriental trope to a savage one, from a discourse on the Great Khan as immortalized by Marco Polo to the competing signifier of the savage as identified by Herodotus. In Columbus's *Journal*,

> each discourse can be identified by the presence of key words: in one case "gold," "Cathay," "Grand Khan," "intelligent soldiers," "large buildings," "merchant ships"; in the other "gold," "savagery," "monstrosity," "*anthropophagi*." Even more boldly, each discourse can be traced to a single textual origin, Marco Polo and Herodotus respectively.[106]

The figure of the cannibal became both the necessary prerequisite and obvious consequence of Columbus's decision to privilege the motif of the "savage" over the "Orient." The fact was that the practice of cannibalism did not require observation to testify to its presence. Columbus, when he first reported the presence of anthropophagi, had not even visited the islands of the "Caribs." Dr. Chanca never thought to consider alternative explanations for the presence of Indian bones on the island of Guadalyse; their very existence was testimony to cannibalism.[107] Similarly, Vespucci's letter to the Soderinis, reporting the events of his third voyage to the New World, recounted in graphic detail the capture of three "Christians" from among the ship's crew whom the natives then promptly murdered, roasted, and feasted on—events that unfolded, we are told, in front of the very eyes of the author.[108] It is interesting to note, however, that in a subsequent letter to the Medici family, Vespucci purports to record the same voyage. Among the numerous disparities between the two accounts, the most striking is the fact that, while the shadowy figure of the Indian cannibal remains, the gruesome encounter reported by Vespucci in his first letter is nowhere to be found.[109] Judging from the contents of the Medici letter, it is possible that the author thought the Medicis were an audience more susceptible to the Golden Age motif than that of the Indian as cannibal.

Whatever the Medicis' narrative preferences may have been, the fact is that once the motif of the cannibal had gained wide currency in Renaissance representations of the New World, any contrary evidence, while noted with surprise, never constituted a challenge or forced a reassessment of indigenous cultural practices. Hence, the fact that the "captain" had lost his way when exploring the island of Guadelupe came as a surprise to the ship's crew, who had concluded that the poor man had become a victim of the Indian appetite. His sudden reappearance, a week later, was nothing short of a welcome but unexpected outcome.[110]

It was the cannibal and, almost by extension, the practice of human sacrifice that offered the organizing trope of the savage with its second distinctive feature: paganism. Despite the fact that Vitoria and Las Casas could argue, with references to the Aztecs and Incas, that the Amerindians had "some order in their affairs," and even Díaz could pause in *Conquest of the New Spain* to record the awe-inspiring magnificence of the Aztec capital,[111] such testimonies to Indian civilization were not a sufficient rebuttal of Sepúlveda's denunciations or Cortés's indiscriminate destruction, for both the theologian and the conquistador found legitimation of their theory and practice in the trans-historical figure of the pagan.

Ryan's detailed exposition of the European fixation with paganism requires that only a limited discussion be provided here. Three features of his argument are notable. First, the all-embracing charge of pagan worship provided a means by which the inexplicable could be transformed into the familiar by translating Indian gods into the very personification of the Devil himself. Religious statues and icons, entire belief systems, and ceremonial practices could be made commensurable at the very moment that they were made contemptible: when they were identified as evil. Hence, Jean de Léry's account of a nocturnal ceremony he witnessed when among the natives of Brazil is revealing less for its descriptive value than for the fact that the response of horror and confusion the spectacle evoked was immediately allayed by the comforting recognition that he was in the presence of a familiar foe.[112] As Ryan observes, there was something reassuring in recognizing the Devil in foreign and distant lands: "His behavior had an aspect of predictability, his presence confirmed the status of the observer, and there were formulae and rituals, which Catholics at least could employ to deal with him. If you can't meet an old friend in a strange country an old enemy is the next best thing."[113]

If the presence of the Devil enveloped the indigenous American into the conceptual world of Christian theology, parallels between the Amerindians and the ancient pagans of Greece and Rome promised the possibility of a comparative ethnology whereby temporal distances and cultural disparities could be transcended. Thus, in his *Apologetic History*, described by Pagden as "an expansive piece of comparative ethnology," Las Casas provided an extensive comparison between the Greeks, Romans, Egyptians, ancient Gauls, and ancient Britons alongside that of the Aztecs and Incas.[114] Montaigne saw similarities between the Indian languages and that of ancient Greek; John White appeared to find nothing incongruous in using natives of Virginia as the models for his depiction of the ancient Picts and Britons.[115] Nor did the author of *Cosmographie*, Sebastian Münster, find any incompatibility in recycling the woodcuts illustrating Mandeville's voyage to Asia (over a hundred years prior) in his pictorial representation of the Americas.[116] José de Acosta argued for the necessity of recognizing and compiling such similarities as existed between the Gods of the Indians and those of the ancients to effect a more general strategy of eradicating pagan practices.[117] Lorenzo Pignoria assisted such efforts by observing the similarities between the gods of Mexico and those of the ancient Egyptians.[118] Finally, the Franciscan Juan de Torquemada "found that virtually the entire Greco-Roman pantheon was worshipped in America."[119]

Attempting to draw Indian religious practices into the specter of European antiquity speaks to the third notable feature identified by Ryan under the rubric of paganism: the Renaissance obsession with genealogy. However, in merging genealogy into the meta-narrative of paganism, applicable to Europe's interaction with the entire non-Christian world, Ryan fails to emphasize the peculiar rendering of the genealogical project as it came to be constituted in the context of the Americas. The peoples of Europe, Africa, and Asia could be accounted for within the biblical tradition by tracing their lineage back to the three sons of Noah: Japhet, Ham, and Shem, respectively. Explaining how the vast terrain of America came to be populated, however, required a more imaginative hypothesis.

Hence, while Raleigh may have argued that the Indian are "men without ancestors" and Isaac La Peyrere voiced, and later retracted, the blasphemous possibility that the indigenous Americans were not descendants of Adam and while the Christian Fathers themselves left no guiding principles on the subject of the Americas, the overwhelming preoccupation of many Renaissance writers concerned with the New World centered on the quest for origins.[120] The significance of this fact cannot be understated. Perhaps no other device speaks more to the language of similitude than that of genealogy—the effort to embrace the Indian within the familial, to identify in his history a shared heritage dating back to biblical origins.

Hence, for Acosta the Indians of America were the descendants of the Jews; the historian Francisco López de Gómara recognized in the New World the lost city of Plato's Atlantis, and the similarly lost Israelites of the Babylonian exile offered an alternative ancestral possibility; while Grotius identified a Viking connection and thus introduced Iceland and Greenland as privileged contenders.[121] Grotius did, however, qualify his thesis by offering three exceptions. Hence the Yucatan Amerindians, the South Americans, and the Peruvians did not draw their lineage from the Vikings but were, rather, descendants of Ethiopians, Southeast Asians, and the Chinese, respectively.[122] The genealogical project of tracing indigenous American lineage back to the Old World, and thus rendering it malleable to Christian interpretations, resulted in the identification of some twenty possible nations as the ancestral forefathers of the New World's inhabitants.[123]

Such effort to establish genealogies alerts us not only to the mechanisms of Renaissance knowledge. It also gestures to a possible explanation of how an epistemology predicated on similitude sustained itself in the presence of a new and, for Europeans, a hitherto unknown world. In its conventional usage, genealogy, it must be noted, is not history. While the sixteenth-century preoccupation with weaving the New World's inhabitants into a biblical narrative that failed to account for them gave impetus to extensive genealogical maps, such ancestral lineages were fundamentally a-historical, "for it mattered less which particular ancestor or set of ancestors was proposed than that the problem was understood in genealogical, not developmental terms. The upshot of these fantastic forays into exotic pasts was to make the New World into very old worlds, to reduce their uniqueness to similarity."[124]

In a similar vein, when Vitoria compared the Indians to Spanish peasants, and when Montaigne saw in the simplicity of his servant the innocence of the indigenous Americans,[125] they were arguing, quite simply, that the "savages" who were "out there" were like the "savages" we have here at home. Under the canopy of similitude, Vitoria and Montaigne were enfolding the world of the native Americans into the world of the familiar.

Such complex genealogies (that sought to account for that which was glaringly absent) and such simple translations (that comfortably slipped between "savages" and "servants") were feasible because secular, historical time—that which rendered cultures and people measurable and distinctive—was not a conceptual framework available to Renaissance Europe. Thus, we find innumerable illustrations in Grafton's *New World, Ancient Texts* of history being demarcated into seven stages to correspond with a Christian teleology, of books in which engravings of biblical figures came complete with fifteenth-century German costume and hair dressing, and of texts where expansive surveys of customs and manners find their taxonomic medium through geography but not time.[126] Indeed, even contemporary events found their meaning and narrative structure through reference to a biblical past. As Gruzinski describes, the devastation unleashed in the wake of the conquest of Mexico in the sixteenth century was chronicled by the Franciscan monk Fray Toribio de Benavente (better known as Motolinía) through imagery borrowed from Exodus and Revelation (Apocalypse):

> His rhetoric of catastrophe and chastisement was first of all designed to anchor the events of the Conquest in a metaphysical and providentialist context. The recollection of the plagues of Egypt and the evocation of the second, sixth, and seventh angels of the Apocalypse lent universal scope to his account and underscored the singularity of the events. Putrid waters, rivers of blood, foul stenches issuing from the mouths of dragon and beast, thunder and lightening, historical parallels with the fall of Jerusalem and its destruction by Titus—everything was employed to convey the confusion at the time, to paint the ravages of disease and war, to describe the corruption of social relationships and the unchallenged reign of gold and silver.[127]

Such disregard for secular, developmental history was to become inconceivable in the nineteenth century. When Darwin wrote in the latter part of the 1800s of the savages "out there," commensurability no longer relied on self-referencing—the appeal to analogy that was itself predicated on the familiar. The savage out there was rendered commensurable precisely because historicism enveloped the savage into the folds of human history while simultaneously asserting historical distance and, thus, cultural disparity. And if Europe once occupied that same historical moment Darwin identified with the Fuegians, the emphasis was on the "once"—a historical stage that had long since been departed.[128]

Precisely because the organizing principle of Renaissance knowledge was predicated on assimilation, the categories that constituted that knowledge were of a very different order to that of the seventeenth century, eighteenth century, and nineteenth century. It was not that cannibalism, paganism, or savagery disappeared from the iconography of early modern and modern thought, but that these categories were no longer articulated through the language of similitude, through the interpretation of signs and reverence for ancient texts.

Through the organizing category of the savage, the Americas were made not simply commensurable but familiar. A New World was made to mirror a very old and, in the reflection, could be identified the signatures of similitude. The vast repository of medieval monsters, pagan practices, cannibal feasts, and Golden Age innocence offered a self-referential medium between the new continent and the Christian canons, indigenous cultures, and ancient commentaries.

## Conclusion

This chapter has sought to argue that the conceptual grid of self–otherness is a questionable lens through which to appreciate Europe's interaction with the New World during the Age of Discovery, the age commonly referred to as the Renaissance. Three observations can be offered by way of conclusion. First, I have argued that the idea of Europe has a relatively recent history, and while its presence can be gleaned in the light of Christianity, it is a dubious claim to offer Europe as the authorial self in the context of Renaissance interaction with the New World. This fact is made all the more evident when we consider the virtual absence of Europe in the representations of the Indian as noble savage / cannibal and pagan. It is only through a series of deductions, through the medium of educated retrospection, that we can confer Europe's presence in Montaigne's inverse social criticism, Sepúlveda's panoply of lack, or the shadows of Christian representations of paganism. The self, therefore, as it came to be constituted through European contact with the New World, was neither identifiably European nor a homogenous and monolithic entity.

It was not, furthermore, a self constituted through the medium of otherness; of radical opposition. Rather, the very mapping of difference was embedded within a cartography of resemblances. The Renaissance effort to reconcile the world into a canopy of similitude was not simply a desire to translate difference into familiar categories: it is perhaps, impossible to render alterity commensurable without drawing it within our own conceptual frames. What distinguishes the Renaissance episteme from our own is the fact that the very effort of ordering the world and rendering it commensurable was distilled through the interpretive filter of assimilation. This, then, speaks to my third and final point.

Given the argument of this chapter, it becomes evident that to transport the civilization frames of self and other to a reading of ancient texts or Renaissance discoveries is to de-historicize knowledge. Ultimately, it requires colluding uncritically with the narrative of modernity: that the past is merely a prelude to, and a veiled promise of, the present. The "present," however—that which we call modernity—was some three hundred years in the future. If in the nineteenth century a confident Europe surveyed the world from the podium of "truth," it had first to define itself, to invent its own subjectivity. Yet while in these early efforts at self-definition (through the course of the seventeenth century and eighteenth century) the logic of similitude was relinquished, it was not the mantle of opposition that came to mediate knowledge of the non-West. Rather, as I will argue with reference to the works of Thomas Hobbes, John Locke, and Jean-Jacques Rousseau, it was in an appeal to universality articulated through the figure of the individuated self (inhabiting a New World state of nature) that a particular rendering of difference—one derived through identity—came to emerge.

## 2 "Constructing" Individuals and "Creating" History

SUBJECTIVITY IN HOBBES, LOCKE, AND ROUSSEAU

IF ONCE THERE was deemed to be a natural order that constituted the world—where the lost language of God could still be gleaned in the objects of his Creation, where man and society constituted an organic relationship, where social disparities were heavenly sanctioned, the kings legitimacy divinely ordained, and where the church mediated between the sinner on earth and a vengeful god—if, in other words, the world was conceptualized as a reflecting mirror of God's attention to detail, order, symmetry, and harmony, this pre-modern imagining came to be sorely bruised with the turn of the seventeenth century.

Yet if that divine promise, which had long given solace to man's earthly existence—that promise of an ordered, meaningful, and purposeful world—had been unequivocally broken, how was order to be established? How was the guarantee of peace and purpose to be secured? What was once ascribed to God became the story of man. Possessed of little other than reason, man had to impose meaning and order where confusion and chaos existed.

Intricately bound to this changing conceptual schema was the gesturing toward two future historical possibilities: the secularization of time and the reconceptualization of man as an individualized self. Precisely because the ordering of human affairs was estranged from the creation of the cosmos, the transition from chaos to meaning is a transition made possible only through the agency of men—it is a transition within secular time. Yet in this conceptual schema, man himself is transformed from the political animal of Aristotelian thought, which presupposed a natural order and meaning in the world, to the a priori individual who is *predisposed* by his *natural* reason to *impose* meaning and order on his world. Nowhere is this narrative that privileges individual agency in the transition from chaos to order more fully expounded and comprehensively addressed than in the (albeit, radically different) writings of Thomas Hobbes, John Locke, and Jean-Jacques Rousseau.

It strikes me, therefore, as an unusual absence in the works of Stephen Greenblatt and others who have engaged with the "New Historicism" scholarship that, while debating the historical and cultural variables that informed the construction of modern individual subjectivity, and while emphasizing the significance of textual readings to an appreciation of that cultural history, this same scholarship has largely neglected those very philosophers who not only posited the primacy of the individual but have located the individual within a narrative of transitional time. It is only tangentially, however, through the works of Hobbes, Locke, and Rousseau that this chapter seeks to engage with the ongoing debate concerning the emergence of a modern individual subjectivity. I say tangentially because my own readings of the contractarians is preoccupied with a different question: To what extent, if at all, did the New World inform the European privileging of the individual as the instigator of history? From this point of departure, however, it became increasingly apparent that any effort to address this question necessitated recognizing the interrelationship between a particular rendering of time as secular and manmade and a particular rendering of human subjectivity as individuated.

From Clifford Geertz's essay "The Impact of the Concept of Culture on the Concept of Man" (1973), to Michel Foucault's historicist rendering of human subjectivity, to the emergence of the New Historicism scholarship and the debates that ensued following the publication of Greenblatt's *Renaissance Self-Fashioning*, the concept of the individual as the possessor not only of rights and property but of a peculiarly modern subjectivity has come increasingly to be recognized as a historical and cultural construction.[1] The significance of this body of literature cannot be underestimated, for it represents a long-awaited and much needed challenge to the Burckhardtian thesis that the individual—that self-expressive, self-conscious, uniquely embodied subjectivity of modern men and women—was an a priori yet latent possibility, requiring only the enlightenment of the Renaissance to awaken man's individuality from its dormant state. In other words, the Burckhardtian individual was a product of history only insofar as his evolution required a particular historical moment to be realized—that moment when the shackles of medieval feudalism, kinship ties, and religious superstition gave way to Renaissance curiosity and self-expression; that moment when docility gave way to individual subjectivity.[2] As John Martin argues, Greenblatt's work more than any other offers an alternative reading concerning the emergence of the modern individual, one that does not locate modern subjectivity within a narrative of historical evolution but, rather, posits the autonomous individual as a gradually emerging "fiction" that came to be fashioned in response to a particular set of historical and cultural conditions. In other words, the all-but-naturalized individual, for Greenblatt, is an eminently modern invention.[3]

The writings of Hobbes, Locke, and Rousseau suggest the validity of Greenblatt's thesis. Precisely because the individual is the central protagonist in their political philosophies,[4] it permits one to gauge the changing faces of individual subjectivity from Hobbes's a priori mechanistic anti-hero to the self-searching, infinitely perfectible figure of Rousseau's imagination.

Yet the significance of Hobbes's, Locke's, and Rousseau's work lies beyond its demonstrative value. While Geertz may be right in his assertion that "to say that the individual is culturally constituted has become a truism,"[5] the scholarly consensus he speaks of immediately unravels once the search for causes begins. From kinship to Protestantism, patriarchal structures to capitalist property relations,[6] new literary techniques to the emergence of new conceptual categories such as virtue and sensibility—all of these factors have been offered in an effort to identify the particular historical and cultural conditions that contributed to the construction of modern individual subjectivity. This scholarship not only has compelled us to recognize (as a truism?) that our own sense of individuality (expressive of an interiority unique to each of us) is a historical and cultural construction, but it has done so through a commitment to historicism. Yet while this literature is historically engaged, what remains absent and unexamined in it is the historical construction of history. History itself, a particular rendering of time as secular, uniform, and empty,[7] is presumed to be a-historical. History itself is rendered absolute and timeless. Yet the writings of Hobbes, Locke, and Rousseau alert us to the fact that if radically different portraits of the individual emerge out of their respective works, this is due in part to their radically different conceptions of time: The faceless, uniform, and one-dimensional figure who exists within, but is unaffected by, time in Hobbes's *Leviathan* is a very different portrait from that of Rousseau's tortured individual whose perfectibility relies on the processes of time.

Precisely because the contractarians were concerned about tracing humanity's journey from a state of nature to political society, from the individual to the collective sum, the concept of time is presupposed in their writings. That the individual is located within this time-bound narrative suggests the possibility—realized in the writings of Locke and Rousseau—that how the individual is constructed and how time is conceived constitute two interrelated and self-referential questions.

This brings me to my final concern regarding the recent scholarship, which has hitherto engaged with the history of modern individual subjectivity. For all of the differences that distinguish, for example, Greenblatt's, Martin's, and Natalie Zemon Davis's writings concerning the historical and cultural factors that went into the making of an individual sensibility, they nevertheless share a central premise: that the emergence of the individualized self can be identified only with reference to events, processes, and conditions internal to Europe. Be it religion or patriarchy, kinship or capitalism, the literary or the linguistic—whatever the myriad possibilities proffered—they presume Europe as the frame of reference and point of departure. Again, however, the writings of Hobbes, Locke, and Rousseau offer a curious insight. We first encounter the contractarian individual in the elusive temporal condition of a state of nature, an allusion to a prepolitical time. Yet in the familiar story that traces the shift from the natural realm to the political, from the individual to civil society, the New World occupies at times a shadowy and at times a pervasive presence in the writings of Hobbes, Locke, and Rousseau. Not only was the New World identified with the (un)enviable state of nature, but the natural, rational, self-preserving individual was cloaked in native American garb. The individual, that (anti)hero who resided within the nebulous temporality of nature, was no other than the indigenous Indian himself.

It is the argument of this chapter that the New World has a formative place in the history of the individual, the fiction that exists today as a sacred site. In this context, Hobbes, Locke, and Rousseau are significant less as proper names, as dignitaries in the history of ideas, than as conduits for exploring the changing face of European representations of difference. Through the presumptions unquestioned, the contradictions inherent, and the words unspoken, the works of these authors posited a universal individual among the Indians.

## Masked Men and Faceless Individuals: Hobbes on the Question of Subjectivity

### ARTIFICIAL PERSONS AND PUBLIC PERSONA

Perhaps no other work of the early seventeenth century symbolizes the epistemological shift between the pre- and early modern than the writings of Thomas Hobbes (1588–1679). Sheldon Wolin,[8] among others, has recognized the seminal nature of Hobbes's proposition that man is not social; society is not natural; meaning is not divinely inscribed; and morality, justice, and injustice are not anchored in any predetermined natural laws. For Hobbes, it was chaos that constituted the premise, and defined the natural condition, of man. Order was but an artifice constituted by the collective sum of individuals to guarantee their individual safety.

It is within this context—indeed, integral to Hobbes's narrative of chaos preceding order—that we first confront the solitary, rational, and yet ego-driven figure that is the Hobbesian individual. It is this lone anti-hero who is the subject of Hobbes's infamous state of nature: a state devoid of all social trappings, a state devoid of all civil order, a state within which "the life of man [is] solitary, nasty, brutish and short."[9]

The vivid portrayal of asocial man in both *Leviathan* and *De Homine* has prompted J. Laird to argue that, despite the seventeenth-century philosopher's aversion to Aristotle, it is in fact an echo of Aristotle that rings through Hobbes's description of natural man.[10] Indeed, in his *Politics*, Aristotle argued that "any man who by his nature . . . has no state is either . . . subhuman or superhuman—he is like the war-mad man condemned in Homer's words as 'having no family, no law, no home;' for he who is such by nature is mad on war."[11]

Yet the apparent resemblance between Hobbes's and Aristotle's accounts of asocial man is immediately overshadowed by two significant differences. First, it is apparent that for a philosopher of ancient Greece, any individual who by nature lives outside society could no longer be characterized as human: Non-social man either resided among the gods or lived among the beasts. The inhabitants of a Hobbesian state of nature, however, were unquestionably, identifiably human, thus prompting Rousseau's later critique.[12] The fact was that Hobbes's asocial man was equipped with social characteristics that included not only the possession of language, reason, imagination, and passions (pride, envy, arrogance) but also the ability to rationally calculate his own self-interest.

The second reason to be wary of the apparent resemblance between Aristotle's and Hobbes's accounts of asocial man lies in the fact that for Aristotle, such a condition was an anomaly, a perversion of man's natural, social state. While for Aristotle man was inherently social and thus defined in opposition to nature, Hobbes sought to create a definable and radically distinct spatial condition within which to relocate and reconceptualize man in terms antithetical to society:

> Out of this [civil] state, every man hath such a right to all, as yet he can enjoy nothing; in [this civil state], each one securely enjoys his limited right. Out of it, any man may rightly spoil or kill another; in it, none but one. Out of it, we are protected by our own forces; in it, by the power of all. Out of it, no man is sure of the fruit of his labors; in it, all men are. Lastly, out of it, there is a dominion of passions, war, fear, poverty, slovenliness, solitude, barbarism, ignorance, cruelty; in it, the dominion of reason, peace, security, riches, decency, society, elegancy, sciences and benevolence.[13]

Hence, Hobbes created the possibility of visualizing a condition (albeit miserable and torturous) that was simultaneously "natural" *and* in opposition to society, a condition that did not proceed through an evolutionary journey—historically, inevitably, naturally—that leads from the natural (isolated) stage to the social but that requires voluntary contractual agreement in an effort to create the artificial and oppositional body of the civil state. Ultimately, in contrast to the Aristotlean model, the Hobbesian state of nature was the residence not only of beasts but also of the natural and once universal domain of men.

Thus, it is within this natural domain that we first confront the central protagonist of *Leviathan* and *De Homine*: the individual. The individual, both as a figure and as a concept, is integral to Hobbes's political treatise, for it is the individual that is at once the source of chaos and the instigator of order. He is the source of chaos precisely because his radical individualism creates a "condition which is called Warre; and such a warre, as is of every man, against every man."[14] Yet the individual is also the instigator of peace, for he, like all other men, is equipped with reason that drives him to leave a condition that is at once natural and yet antithetical to his self-preservation.[15]

It is clearly evident, therefore, that for Hobbes the individual was the locus of all agency, whether in matters of war or pursuing peace. Yet despite the centrality of the individual in Hobbes's political treatise, what is altogether lacking in his portrait of solitary man is precisely that which accentuates and defines the modern individual: a subjectivity, an individuality. What is notably absent in the makeup of the Hobbesian individual is any reference to interiority. That which we believe distinguishes each of us, imparts in us all, the sensibility that we are self-conscious, self-defining, individualized beings.[16]

One of the hallmarks of Hobbes's political writings is the fact that even the most elementary of human traits—from laughter to blushing, from grief to hope—were accorded definitional precision.[17] Given this fact, it is both surprising and revealing that on the question of personal identity, the corpus of Hobbes's works is conspicuously silent. We encounter in Hobbes's interpretation of the popular proverb *"Read thy self,"* for example, not a call for self-reflection, an allusion to individual specificity, but an instructive tale of uniformity that "teach[es] us, that for the similitude of the thoughts, and Passions of one man, to the thoughts, and Passions of another, . . . he shall thereby read and know, what are the thoughts, and Passions of all other men, upon the like occasions."[18]

The absence of any sustained engagement with the question of personal identity is made even more acute, and yet simultaneously revealing, when we encounter in *Leviathan* Hobbes's definition of what constitutes a Person:

> A PERSON, is he whose words or actions are considered, either as his own, or as representing the words or actions of an other man. . . . When they are considered as his owne, then is he called a Naturall Person: And when

they are considered as representing the words and actions of an other, then is he a Feigned or Artificiall person. . . .

*Persona* in latine signifies the *disguise*, or *outward appearance* of a man, counterfeited on the Stage; and sometimes more particularly that part of it, which disguiseth the face, as a Mask or Visard: And from the Stage, hath been translated to any Representer of speech and action, as well in Tribunalls, as Theatres. So that a *Person*, is the same that an *Actor* is, both on the Stage and in common Conversation.[19]

In a rare reference to the contractarians, Greenblatt quotes this passage to emphasize, quite rightly, the theatrical and highly malleable constitution of the Hobbesian individual. Individuality is predicated not on an appeal to authenticity, on an inalienable subjectivity, or, for that matter, even on corporeality. Rather, the identity of the natural person as much as that of the artificial man is an identity *assumed*. All that distinguishes the natural from the artificial individual is the ownership of words and actions—of possession.[20] Thus, as Greenblatt argues, the mask is not a "veneer hiding the authentic self beneath. . . . [Rather,] for Hobbes there is no person, no coherent, enduring identity, beneath the mask; strip away the theatrical role and you reach either a chaos of unformed desire that must be tamed to ensure survival or a dangerous assembly of free thoughts."[21] Ultimately, we look in vain when we look at Hobbes's individual for any signs of a consciousness that allude to a stable, authentic self.

### COVENANTS OF GRACE, ABSOLUTE STATES, AND INDIVIDUALS

How does one explain the ironic fact that, despite the centrality of the individual in Hobbes's political treatise—despite the fact that, as Carole Pateman and W. H. Greenleaf both note,[22] the Hobbesian individual is accorded a singular and purely subjective reason in the state of nature—we are unable to glean the face of this self-same figure, the core self as opposed to his public persona?

For Greenblatt, *Leviathan* is grist to his theoretical mill; to his larger theoretical premise that the distinctive feature of the European Renaissance and early modern society was the fact that the individual was not located within a narrative of authenticity, interiority, and stability. Instead, "Identity [was] only possible as a mask, something constructed and assumed."[23] Greenblatt may well be right. However, I would suggest the relevance of three additional factors that may account for why Hobbes's radical individualism did not necessitate an individualized sensibility.

The first points to the fact that Hobbes simultaneously appealed to the political contract and eschewed its democratic implications. In an extensive work on the emergence of the modern state, Gerhard Oestreich argues that through the period of the Counter-Reformation, the religious tenor of the Covenant of Grace was increasingly accorded a populist political chord. Whereas the former was predicated on status, a contract between God and the community of the elect (namely, the king and higher echelons of the church), the latter was to evoke the authority of the people—an authority that sought to circumscribe the power of the king and church not only to the will of God but also in reference to the subjects whom they governed.[24]

Without rehearsing the details of a history that gradually reinscribed a theological covenant into a populist contract, it is important to note that interlaced with the principle of political contract was the Protestant privileging of individual conscience, which imbued each Christian subject, possessed of reason, with the authority to gain access to and interpret the Word of God and his natural laws. Invested in the people, therefore, was the ability to judge whether the rule of the king was in accordance with the spiritual covenant and thus, by extension, faithfully reflective of the will of his subjects.[25]

The political implications of a populist contract predicated on the sovereignty of individual conscience rested on the radical premise not only that the king must "promise that he will rule justly and according to the laws," but that his failure to do so could provoke, on the part of his subjects, legitimate rebellion against his authority.

It was precisely the political instability and anarchical possibilities embedded in the logic of the political contract that led Hobbes, in the "Preface" of *De Cive*, to ask rhetorically, "How many rebellions hath this opinion been the cause of, which teacheth that the knowledge whether the commands of kings be just or unjust, belongs to private men; and that before they yield obedience, they not only may, but ought to dispute them!"[26]

Hobbes's efforts to arrive at a "science . . . of *Natural Justice*" that would defend political obligation against attacks from popular dissent relied for its logic not on an appeal to the divine right of kings but on reference to a political contract.[27] Hobbes appropriated the foundational language of the populist covenant—that government was founded on consent—to deprive that very consent of its populist implications. In other words, while Hobbes presupposed the language of consent (the very language that distinguished the status-bound Covenant of Grace from the political contract of choice), he immediately arrested the radical implication presumed in its logic: the possibility of dissent.

Hobbes's defense of the absolute state is too familiar to require reiterating. However, what is significant is that, while Hobbes posits the individual as the locus of all agency (it is, after all, the individual who, with others, institutes civil society and state), it is in the very moment of contract that all individuality is denied. Thus, contrary to the mood of the Protestant Reformation—one that appealed to individual conscience, self-reflection, and interiority[28]—Hobbes's primary objective was to defend uniformity, to deny the radical individualism that constituted the source of discord in his contemporary England and his analogous state of nature.

Given the argumentative logic offered in *Leviathan* and *Man and Citizen*, it is not surprising that a Hobbesian political society does not recognize—indeed, seeks to deny—the active engagement of its citizenry in the affairs of the state. Herein lies the second explanation for the striking absence of any references to individual identity in Hobbes's work. As Sheldon Wolin rightly argues, what is notably absent in Hobbes's political treatise is:

> the basic element which writers from Plato to Machiavelli had never neglected and Rousseau was to rediscover: that the stuff of power was not to be found in the passively acquiescent subject but in the "engaged" citizen, the citizen with a capacity for public involvement and an ability to identify himself with his governors through active support.[29]

An active citizenry however, requires a particular type of citizen—one that measures his conduct in relation to a higher objective good or, alternatively, is fashioned with a particular subjectivity that both corresponds to and informs the civil society within which he lives. In regard to the former, Hobbes not only refused to entertain but wholly rejected the possibility of a preordained objective good. This is why his state of nature is devoid of any normative values: "Nothing can be Unjust. The notions of Right and Wrong, Justice and Injustice, have there no place. Where there is no common Power, there is no Law: where no Law, no Injustice. . . . They are Qualities, that relate to men in Society, not in Solitude."[30]

If Hobbes denied any appeal to an objective moral order, he also dispensed with the need to tailor a particular type of subject.[31] An absolutist state made such a precondition redundant. In contrast with Locke, for whom man's natural passions and imagination required curtailing through the pedagogical fashioning of a particular individuality that would correspond to the needs of a liberal state,[32] no such intersubjective transformation was required of the Hobbesian individual. The fact that the state was initiated by the collective consent of a sum of individuals and was imbued from that moment with an authority to be feared constituted, for Hobbes, the essential ingredients necessary to ensure political obligation and civil order.

Thus, in Hobbes's *Leviathan*, natural man's transition from the state of nature to political society was a largely uncomplicated affair. The ownership of words and actions are relinquished by all individuals and invested in the hands of the Artificial Person who henceforth is said to represent the interests of all. The radical transformation witnessed by the substitution of chaos for order bears on the individual only as an external effect: His interaction with others is now regulated by law and adhered to out of fear. What is notably absent in this transition from nature to artifice, from chaos to order, is a corresponding shift in the constitution of the individual.

Indeed, the fact that Hobbes's state of nature was analogous to the English Civil War was a none-too-subtle reminder that in the absence of the state, man could revert back to his original form. It was not man himself who had changed upon entering civil society but his relation to others—a relation that, having once been unconstrained and unmediated, was now regulated by the law and authorized by the state.

The untransformative transformation from the state of nature to civil society points to the third significant explanation accounting for the lack of individuated identities among Hobbes's individuals. That Hobbes's political treatise is fundamentally a-historical is a fact that is difficult to argue against. Like Locke, Hobbes in his narrative traces man's departure from an a-historical state of nature to the a-historical moment of contract and the subsequent "creation" of civil society and state. What distinguishes the two authors is the fact that, while for Locke the state of nature had a discernible reference to time, was constitutive of a past—however a-historical—Hobbes's state of nature had a far more ambivalent and ambiguous temporality.

At one level, Hobbes's references to the state of nature as prior to civil society presupposes a recognition of the past, but this past is posited as an ever present danger. Analogous to the English Civil War and political ferment of international politics, Hobbes's state of nature is conceptualized not as an irreparable break with the past but, rather, as a reversible condition that threatens to subsume a civilized state into a pre-political battleground of war.[33] Moreover, to be reduced to a state of nature was for Hobbes not a reversal in time but an eclipse in time, a suspension of time where all "links between the past, present and future [are] snapped."[34]

The novelty of Hobbes's thesis becomes even more acute when we consider it in the light of Dipesh Chakrabarty's interpretation of history. In his critique of historicism, Chakrabarty argues that precisely because European constructions of history conceptualized time as both secular and empty, they created the space for a universalizing particularity—a space within which any cultural history could be inscribed without reference to culturally specific conceptions of time.[35] I would suggest that what makes Hobbes's state of nature so singularly distinctive is the fact that it is not simply empty of content and thus open to inscription; it is a space that cannot be filled. In a condition of unfettered freedom, unconstrained competition, and unformed desires, not even time mediates and inflects on the human condition. Thus, at the moment of contract, the individual does not leave the past and create history. Instead, he creates history out of nothing. He creates time as the God of Genesis created man.

Indeed, in Hobbes's breathless appraisal of all that does not exist in the state of nature (and thus, by implication, all that is a measure of society), his exhaustive list posits time itself among the civilized inventions:

There is no place for Industry; because the fruit thereof is uncertain: and consequently no Culture of the Earth; no Navigation, nor use of the commodities that may be imported by Sea; no commodious Building; no Instruments of moving, and removing such things as require much force; no Knowledge of the face of the Earth; *no account of Time*; no Arts; no Letters; no Society; and which is worst of all, continuall feare, and danger of violent death.[36]

If Hobbes's narrative elaborated in *Leviathan* and *Man and Citizen* has an ambiguous relationship to time, what is unambiguous is the fact that neither the state of nature nor political society is conceptualized in terms of stages, demarcated into its various parts, and thus recognizable as a process. This fact goes a long way toward accounting for the one-dimensional generic man that is the Hobbesian individual.

What allows personality to enter into the descriptive language of the individual in the writings of Locke and Rousseau is the fact that he is indebted to a process of coming-to-be. It becomes immediately apparent—particularly when reading Locke's and Rousseau's treatises on education—that in their efforts to fashion a particular type of individual to correspond with the particularity of their imagined civil state, the figure of the child comes to be privileged. For all of the philosophical differences that underpin Locke's and Rousseau's pedagogical *magna corpus*, there is nevertheless a shared contention that the child represents the unformed and thereby malleable predecessor of the adult self.

Implied in this narrative is a sense of continuity within time, a premise that childhood experiences offer a mirror, an insight, into the specificity of the adult self. Thus, in tracing the child, one initiates the process, influences the journey by which the individual self comes into being.

No such journey, process, or continuity is accorded the Hobbesian individual. Indeed, so individualistic is Hobbes's state of nature that a mother is apt to leave her newly born infant to fend for itself (or die by itself), fearing as she does that the burden of a child might diminish her chances of survival in such war-ravaged conditions.[37]

With so little interest invested in childhood, it is little wonder that Hobbes has even less to say about education. In what he does say, it becomes apparent that, far from being a vehicle by which to fashion a particular subjectivity, education for Hobbes was a medium through which knowledge came to be imparted. It had a utility value only insofar as it communicated a sum of facts, the virtue of which allowed for external effects—the navigation of the seas, construction of buildings, and so on.[38]

Precisely because time had no bearing on Hobbes's individual, precisely because the fashioning of the individual was not conceptualized as a process, childhood and its correlate, education, held little relevance to Hobbes's political treatise. Consequently, Hobbes's individuals were denied the accoutrements of individuality. They were denied the experiential, pedagogical, psychological, and behavioral influences that would allow for the reflective, interiorized, uniquely individuated self; that would allow for the necessary link between the individual child and his adult persona.

To summarize, the Hobbesian individual was devoid of a sense of inwardness because he rejected the radical implications of the political contract, because the absolute authority of the sovereign rendered the need for a fashioned subjectivity obsolete, and because Hobbes's conception of time neither accommodated nor equipped the Natural Person with the self-conscious awareness of his individual identity.

### "THEY OF AMERICA . . ."

Yet if Hobbes's instrumental individual lacked an interiorized self, he was also spared the infliction of possessing an errant individuality—whether construed in terms of irrationality (Locke), artifice (Rousseau), or psychosis (contemporary psychology). Indeed, as I have noted, so adamant was Hobbes that morality, justice, and laws exist only by the decree of the sovereign, that in the state of nature only "private Appetite is the measure of Good, and Evill,"[39] that he refused to pass any normative judgment on natural man. If it is by nature that men are self-interested, calculating, and vain beings, it follows that it is not the nature of the individual that can be changed but the conditions within which he lives. His natural tendencies can be curtailed by ensuring a uniformity of meaning through the will of the sovereign and the fear of the sword he wields.

It is in recognition of this fact that a largely ignored passage in Hobbes's *Leviathan* and *De Homine* comes to bear a curious significance and unexpected relevance. I refer to Hobbes's identification of the state of nature with the New World and its Amerindian inhabitants. In pre-empting the clamorous denial of his critics that a state of nature had ever existed, Hobbes retorted that "they of America are examples hereof, even in this present age":[40]

> It may peradventure be thought, there was never such a time, nor condition of warre as this; and I believe it was never generally so, over all the world: but there are many places, where they live so now. For the savage people in many places of *America*, except the government of small Families, the concord whereof dependenth on naturall lust, have no government at all; and live at this day in that brutish manner, as I said before.[41]

Hobbes's scant references to the Americas indicate that the New World held little interest for him beyond the rhetorical value it provided to an otherwise thoroughly European polemic. Yet in the context of this discussion, I would argue that the positing of Hobbes's mechanistic individual in the Americas, inhabiting the supposedly miserable condition of the indigenous Indian, carries a significance that lies beyond his immediate and self-conscious objectives.

As discussed in chapter 1, earlier explorers and conquerors of the New World appealed to pre-existing philosophical and religious canons to comprehend and represent indigenous America. While much of the corpus of Christian knowledge would eventually be redefined and renegotiated through the very medium of colonial interaction, early efforts at commensurability appealed to a vocabulary of similitude whereby the unfamiliar entity that was the Americas could be rendered translatable. Thus, the wisdom of ancient authors, the scholarship of medieval saints, and the tales of travelers were metaphorically and literally carried across the Atlantic in the service of rendering America and its inhabitants commensurable. The Amerindian was absorbed within a pre-existing vocabulary of resemblances. Space was provided (not created) for him among the pantheon of "savages."

Hobbes extricated the Indian from such immersion. In identifying the New World with man's pre-political condition, Hobbes created a discursive space—the state of nature—within which the Americas could be located. If as a result the Indian was enveloped into European philosophy, he was so not through a process of absorption within pre-existing categories, but through the production of this new conceptual device. This conceptual space was to be not only the centerpiece of Hobbes's political treatise but also a lasting motif in the writings of later contractarians, as well as in the literature of the seventeenth century and eighteenth century more generally.[42]

Yet the Amerindian individual who wanders the pages of later contract theorists is an altogether different figure from the one we encounter in Hobbes's *Leviathan* and *De Homine*. Having dispensed with the need to tailor particular types of individual subjectivities, Hobbes rendered the identification of "errant" or miscreant individualities equally obsolete.

Thus, Hobbes posited the indigenous Americans in the heart of Europe's political and philosophical discourse without recourse to a vocabulary of otherness. The Indian individual, as he existed in the state of nature, was no different from his European counterpart in the event that the latter reverted back to his natural condition. Dictated by passions and possessed of a calculating reason, all individuals in the state of nature were committed to their own self-preservation, were apt to pursue their own self-interest, and were likely to strive for both at the expense of others. In other words, nothing intrinsically different existed in the nature of the Amerindian that could deny him that which was open to all men in the state of nature—that is, "to conferre all their power and strength upon one Man, or upon one Assembly of men, that may reduce all their Wills, by plurality of voices, unto one Will."[43] The indigenous American, within the logic of Hobbes's political treatise, could, like all other men in the state of nature, exit that miserable condition by agreeing through covenant to be collectively ruled by another.

A central feature of Locke's *Second Treatise* (and an enduring embarrassment for sympathetic Lockean scholars) is absent in Hobbes's political works—namely, any recourse to a "just war" defense of colonial dispossession and slavery. To recognize this fact is not to suggest that Hobbes was opposed to the acquisition of colonies. On the contrary: Hobbes argued that "a Conductor, or Governour" could "inhabit a Forraign Country either formerly voyd of Inhabitants, or made voyd then, by warre."[44]

Yet Hobbes defends conquest not by appealing to any objective morality contained within natural laws (remembering that no such morality, justice, or law exists in the state of nature), but through his now familiar logic that consent derived from conquest is consent nevertheless—it constituted a legitimate voluntary contract: "It is not . . . the Victory, that giveth the right of Dominion over the Vanquished, but his own Covenant."[45] The only feature that distinguished the government of acquisition from its alternative (that of government by institution) was "that men who choose their Soveraign, do it for fear of one another, and not of him whom they Institute: But in this case, [i.e., Acquisition] they subject themselves, to him they are afraid of."[46]

Thus, in both instances the government is constituted by covenant, which in turn is propelled by fear. Wholly absent from Hobbes's defense of war and conquest is any appeal to Thomas Aquinas's "just war" dictum or any reference to Locke's errant individuality. For this reason, Hobbes is unambiguous in his rejection of slavery and, indeed, defends the right of the slave, in view of the fact that he is not covenant-bound, to "kill, or carry away captive their Master, justly."[47]

Recourse to slavery is absent from a thesis that makes no appeal to miscreant subjectivities and, thus, just-war exceptionalism. No caveats for exclusion compromise the universal aspirations of Hobbes's political treatise when it comes to the New World colonies. An objection may be raised at this point that, in identifying the Indians with a state of nature, Hobbes was relegating them to the temporal margins of European history—a prelude to civilization. Yet such a criticism is difficult to sustain when one remembers the fluidity and ambiguity of Hobbes's conception of time. The state of nature, far from constituting Europe's prehistory, was in fact a-historical. It represented a temporal eclipse, a vacuum that consumes the American Indians but equally threatens to consume rebellious subjects in Hobbes's seventeenth-century England.

Of course, this is not to deny the Eurocentrism of Hobbes's thesis. His very understanding of the civilized state counterpoised against nomadic communities is telling. It is my contention, however, that while Hobbes represented the Indians as savage, this spoke not to an unstable, irrational, or errant subjectivity but to what was deemed the lack of material effects bought on by the absence of state and society. For example, when in *De Corpore* Hobbes argues that some continents are less advanced in their knowledge of science, he accounts for this deficiency not through reference to natural inferiority or even irrationality but to the flaws in the teaching methods.[48]

Ultimately, the fact that Hobbes did not imbue his individual with the accoutrements of an interiorized self and did not require a particular subjectivity to ensure political obedience permits the accommodating of the indigenous American within the logic of his political treatise.

While much of Hobbes's thesis came to be challenged or condemned by many of his successors—particularly Locke and Rousseau—the debt owed him by even modern liberal theory is in the enduring conceptual framework of the state of nature and the civil society born of it. Although the international arena and English Civil War may well have provided the primary inspiration for Hobbes's state of nature,[49] it was to the indigenous Americans that future contractarians continually returned in their representations of pre-political society.

The subsequent privileging of the New World corresponded with the emergence of a new concept of the individual as an individuated self. Precisely that which was absent in Hobbes's political treatise can be recognized in the writings of Locke. What was lost, however, was the inclusiveness that this neglect provided.

## Patriarchal Chiefdoms and Industrious Individuals: Locke on the Question of Subjectivity

### FASHIONING INDIVIDUALS . . . AND MISCREANT OTHERS

The Hobbesian individual who emerged from the battleground of a state of nature into the authoritarian realm of civil society did so without incurring any inflictions to his individual identity. Indeed, it was not the psychology of the mind that demanded redressing but simply the face that required re-masking.

In contrast, John Locke's writings on personal identity have long been regarded as central to both his own philosophical and political thought, and our modern conception of the individual. As Gary Fuller, Robert Stecker, and John P. Wright argue, "Locke's discussion of the topics of personal identity . . . in the *Essay* . . . is the first systematic treatment of the topic in the history of modern philosophy and the source of most present day writings on the subject."[50] Thus, in *An Essay Concerning Human Understanding*, Locke argues that "Person" is a "forensic term, appropriating actions, and their merit, and so belongs only to intelligent agents, capable of a law, and happiness and misery."[51]

This sterile definition of the self, which locates the individual within a judicial framework of responsibility and culpability, is caressed with gentler brushstrokes in *A Letter Concerning Toleration*, where, in the context of religious faith, and clearly informed by the Puritan emphasis on individual consciousness, Locke enlarged his portrait of the individual by suggesting that "faith only and inward sincerity, are the things that produce acceptance with God" and "liberty of conscience is every man's natural right."[52]

Thus, what we encounter in Locke's writings—most notably, in *A Letter Concerning Toleration*—are not the multiple masks of the Hobbesian individual but, rather, an appeal to inwardness, to an individuated sense of interiority and uniqueness. It becomes apparent that for Locke, individual identity lay not only in the corporeal desire to preserve one's life, but also in a moral sense of self, a psychological anchor that located the individual subject within his own consciousness.

Yet while it has long been recognized that Locke was among the first to theorize the question of individual identity, the works that address this concern (most notably, *An Essay Concerning Human Understanding*, *Some Thoughts Concerning Education*, and *A Letter Concerning Toleration*) are often bracketed from Locke's most influential thesis: his *Two Treatises of Government*. It is not difficult to understand why. The detailed prescription Locke provides for the tailoring of individual subjectivity in his other writings appears altogether absent from—indeed, irrelevant to—his polemic against Robert Filmer and the subsequent account of the origins of political society.

Indeed, the heroic figure in Locke's *Second Treatise* is not that of a fractured subject but, rather, an agent who possesses the uncomplicated identity of a free, rational, equal individual who relies on his a priori status to depart from his natural condition. He does so, furthermore, without reference to any subjective transformation beyond that of the external directive that his freedom be constrained within, and submitted to, the civil laws of the artificial state.

Yet a closer reading of Locke's *Two Treatises* suggests that his philosophical concerns on the limitations of individual reason and the fashioning of subjectivity are not irrelevant to his political doctrine. One need only begin by recognizing the ambitious nature of Locke's project—namely, his objective to guarantee political obligation and social order without recourse to absolute government, to Hobbes's Leviathan. In other words, in his efforts to defend parliamentary government and preserve the possibility and legitimacy of dissent, Locke by necessity had to condone and guarantee individual freedom even within civil society. However, such measured freedom was conditioned on the assumption that the vast majority of individuals were not only capable of, but inclined toward, privileging and exercising rational thought. Locke's own convictions in this respect are open to question. Take, for example, the anxious doubt that underlies his insistence that "the *State of Nature* has a Law of Nature to govern it, which obliges every one: And Reason, which is that Law, teaches all Mankind, *who will but consult it.*"[53]

Reflected in this passage is Locke's ambivalence regarding man's capacity to safeguard the sovereignty of reason. In other words, man may be capable of reason, but this does not ensure, ipso facto, that reason will prevail. Herein lies the significance of Uday Singh Mehta's novel rereading of Locke's political and philosophical writings.[54]

Mehta revisits the large body of Locke's writings and much larger body of Lockean scholarship to argue a case for problematizing the taken-for-granted given of the infamous rational, free, and equal individual that professes to represent man in his natural state. Mehta's contention is that much of the academic engagement with Locke's writings has tended toward accepting as given the characterization of natural man as rational, free, and equal. From this position, the logic of liberal government and civil society can thus be rationalized as that best suited to the interests and natural rights of the rational individual. Thus, Locke's objective as elaborated in his *Second Treatise* can be taken at face value: The inconveniences of a state of nature emanate from the intra-subjective relations between individuals—an inconvenience that contract and political society can alleviate.

Against this interpretation, Mehta's rereading of Locke's work reveals not the assumption of the rational individual but a deep anxiety that this individual, in fact, needs to be constituted: "For Locke, as for liberalism, individuality is an aspiration a process of coming-to-be and not a foundational given that liberal political institutions are merely designed to regulate and secure."[55]

Mehta elaborates his thesis through specific reference to Locke's conception of madness and his writings on education. Significantly for Locke, Mehta argues, madness was not only the consequence of physical deformity or divine infliction but an ailment brought on by the passions and imagination. Thus, madness lurked in the minds of all men, threatening the sovereignty of an individual self not trained to subdue the mind to the government of reason.

If man is prone to being wayward, if reason can be compromised by the seduction of the passions and imagination, then the political stability of liberalism—which presupposes the rational predictability of individuals—would be constantly under threat. It is precisely for this reason that Mehta emphasizes the centrality of Locke's writings on education to his overall political project. The strict pedagogical regime that Locke elaborates in *Some Thoughts Concerning Education* is underscored by the imperative to privilege childhood as a site for the production of a particular type of subjectivity: a subjectivity that must be tailored to conform to the expectations of a liberal society and state. Thus, as Mehta argues, Locke's work on education is ultimately preoccupied with ensuring that the child be trained to subvert his passions to the will of reason; that from the early years of bowing to external authority (personified by the parent), the child should eventually internalize that authority and thus subjugate his mind to a self-regulated discipline predicated on the dictates of reason.

Mehta's thesis, while both novel and persuasive, must nevertheless be situated within a larger body of scholarship that has sought to interrogate Locke's free, rational, and equal subject. Some fifty years ago, C. B. Macpherson argued in his now classic *The Political Theory of Possessive Individualism* that Locke's free, equal, and rational individual, far from being a generic representation of all men, was a specific reference to one type of individual: he who owned property beyond that of his own labor. The working classes and the poor could not partake in the affairs of the state or be full members of civil society because, Macpherson argues, Locke did not allow for the possibility that the laboring poor were capable of fully rational thought—capable, that is, "of ordering their lives by the law of nature or reason."[56]

Some twenty years later, Locke's rational, free, and equal individual was again the subject of critique, in Pateman's *The Sexual Contract*. While Macpherson had argued that the Lockean individual was in fact a propertied individual, Pateman argued that presupposed in Locke's political contract was a sexual contract. More specifically, Pateman maintained that the political contract was in fact a fraternal contract—a contract between free, equal, and rational *men* that signaled the end of paternal dominion while simultaneously heralding a modern form of patriarchal relations. Like Macpherson's laboring poor, women, Pateman argued, never entirely departed the state of nature.[57]

Collectively, the work of Mehta, Macpherson, and Pateman has forced the recognition that Locke's free, equal, and rational individual is a far more complex, fractured, and ambivalent figure than sympathetic Lockean scholarship has cared to admit. Precisely because of this critical and sophisticated engagement with Locke's writings, it appears somewhat surprising that none of the authors thus far mentioned attribute any significance to Locke's copious references, in the *Second Treatise*, to the Americas and its New World inhabitants. Put another way, while Macpherson, Pateman, and Mehta recognize that in seeking to fashion the rational individual Locke had to fabricate its "miscreant" other, they fail to engage with the fact that Locke's free, equal, and rational individual was first encountered in the "woods of *America*" (14.277). This omission denies the possibility that the New World may have had some bearing on the type of subjectivity Locke envisioned for his liberal state. It is this possibility that I explore.

Before proceeding, however, it is important to note that if none of the commentators quoted thus far adequately acknowledge the pervasive presence of the Amerindian in Locke's account of the state of nature, this neglect cannot be rendered into a general criticism of Lockean scholarship. Locke's engagement with the Americas has received extended commentary. This same scholarship has sought to understand why, in a political polemic so fundamentally engaged with events in Europe, Locke's *Second Treatise* should be so extensively littered with references to the Americas and its inhabitants. Emerging out of this literature is an interesting set of facts: Locke held considerable financial interest in the slave trade, investing money in the Royal African Company and the Company of Merchant Adventurers, which was formed to develop the Bahama Islands;[58] he owned thousands of acres of undeveloped land in the province of Carolina;[59] he was the (unofficial) secretary to the Lord Proprietors of Carolina (1668–75), secretary to the Council of Trade and Plantations (1673–76), and commissioner of the Board of Trade (1696–1700); he co-drafted (with his patron Lord Ashley) the Carolina Constitution;[60] he held an extensive library of travel narratives, historical treatises, and ethnological works on the Americas;[61] and, according to Herman Lebovics, he was regarded by his contemporaries as one of the most knowledgeable men in England on matters concerning the colonies.[62]

Emerging from this wealth of information, Lockean scholars have attributed two primary reasons for Locke's extensive use of the Americas in his *Second Treatise*. Perhaps the most common explanation (indeed, the most contentious debate) has focused on Locke's financial pragmatism: that Locke's own financial interests in the New World provoked highly elaborate efforts to reconcile slavery with natural freedom and the right to private property alongside the appropriation of indigenous land. In the former Locke appealed to the just-law dictum that slavery was the legitimate compensation in a just war (23.284), and in the latter he appealed to no other than God himself (31.290, 34.291).

The centrality of the New World in Locke's political treatise has also been attributed to the fact that he, like Hobbes before him, appealed to the

Indians for legitimation, for his evidential defense of the state of nature. Whether one agrees with Barbara Arneil's thesis that the Americas offered Locke a historical trope,[63] what is true is that the New World imbued the abstraction of Locke's state of nature with a familiarity that would not be lost on his contemporary readers.

The large body of work that has concerned itself with Locke's engagement with the Americas has done much to restore the centrality of the New World as it figures in the *Second Treatise*. Certainly, financial pragmatism and evidential necessity go some way in accounting for Locke's extensive ethnological commentary. While acknowledging this fact, however, I would argue that reducing Locke's preoccupation with the New World to these two factors alone, tends to accord the Americas, in Locke's imagination, only instrumental significance: The New World either occupies a rhetorical space or was an opportunistic financial investment.

A closer reading of Locke's state of nature suggests that the Amerindian occupies a privileged space in Locke's polemic that should be accorded more than just instrumental value. While Greenblatt identifies the individual-as-self as a construction born out of, and shaped by, the history, religion, and social dynamics of a geographically bounded Europe, the location of Locke's state of nature in the New World engages the possibility that the equal, free, and rational individual to which liberal theory and politics aspire owes a measure of debt to the indigenous Americans.

### INDIVIDUALS, PATRIARCHS, AND STRANGERS

Locke, as is well known, posits a very different interpretation of the state of nature from that of Hobbes.[64] While both appealed to a natural realm, the moral vacuum of Hobbes's war-torn state gives way, in Locke's reformulation, to a morally and socially regulated sphere that is nevertheless pre-political.

Locke's state of nature not only provides for social arrangements (e.g., the family), hierarchical relations, ("*Father* over his Children, a *Master* over his Servant, a *Husband* over Wife, and a *Lord* over his Slave" [2.286]), private property, and a monetary economy, but it was equally equipped with a set of natural laws—namely, "That being all equal and independent, no one ought to harm another in his Life, Health, Liberty or Possessions" (6.271).

Moreover, while Locke, like Hobbes before him, identified the state of nature with free, equal, and rational individuals, Pateman is right to argue that Locke's pre-political state is one grounded in patriarchal authority.[65] Having dispensed with Hobbes's asocial individual, Locke's state of nature came equipped with the family (or tribal clan), where dominion was located in the father/chief—the patriarch.

Locating patriarchal authority within the state of nature enabled Locke to both appropriate and refute Filmer's doctrine of divine right. Locke's contention was that Filmer had confused the natural state of men with their contemporary political reality. In the former, Locke conceded, men were indeed prepared to accept the authority of the father: "Thus 'twas easie, and almost natural for Children by a tacit, and scarce avoidable consent, to make way for the *Father's Authority and Government*. They had been accustomed in their Childhood to follow his Direction, and to refer their little differences to him; and when they were Men, who was fitter to rule them?" (75.317).[66]

We find that Locke returns to and reiterates this theme in his chapter on the beginnings of political society, but this time he does so in reference to the Amerindians. Specifically, Locke argues that as society gets larger, extending beyond the confines of family, patriarchal dominion continues in the form of a monarchy. The limited needs of this society and the familial nature of government ensures that the rule of chiefs is fairly benign: "Thus we see, that the *Kings* of the *Indians*, in *America*, . . . are little more than *Generals of their Armies*; and though they command absolutely in War, yet at home and in time of Peace they exercise very little Dominion, and have but a very moderate Sovereignty" (108.339–40).

These few quotes (to which could be added more) point to the fact that, for Locke, the state of nature was a state of paternal dominion—a condition personified in the social body of the indigenous Americans. I have labored this point for the simple reason that if the state of nature, and the American Indian who embodied it, were identified with a distinct social system—one characterized by paternal dominion—the self that must be presumed to inhabit this space needs to be of a very different "type" from that of Locke's free, equal, and rational individual who engages in the anonymity of the market and the laws of contract. Paternal dominion, as Locke himself acknowledges, was a legitimate form of government in the state of nature because it was predicated on "paternal affection" (105.337); the father of the family came naturally to be the monarch because he was the "fittest to be trusted" (105.337); and his authority was recognized precisely because he exercised it with "Care and Skill, with Affection and Love" (107.338).

Yet because Locke's state of nature (as distinct from that of Hobbes) is demarcated by "stages,"[67] the limited society of family, Locke argues, does gradually grow to encompass non-family members, thus increasing both the family's numbers and its complexity. It is important to note, however, that even when familial society comes to be extended beyond the limits of family, it does so, Locke argues, because "those, who liked one another so well as to joyn into Society, cannot but be supposed to have some Acquaintance and Friendship together, and some Trust one in another; they could not but have greater Apprehensions of others, than of one another" (107.339).

Unstated in Locke's narrative of patriarchal government is a fact that is essential to it: that personal identity, in this social context, can be conceptualized only in relational terms. Far from being constitutive of concrete individuated identities, Locke's pre-political society locates its members within an inseparable collective whole. Within this whole, relationships are not the consequence of individual choice or momentary transaction but, rather, are expressive of a process within which kinship, friendship, and mutual recognition evolve and rely for their legitimacy on the presumption of continuity.

If society, in the state of nature, was embedded within a language of familiarity, relied on a relational conceptualization of personhood, and implied a continuity of engagement between its members, then it is logical to assume that any system of exchange, loosely understood as economics, would need to correspond to and reflect the societal structure within which it operates.

It is precisely the recognition of this fact that underwrites Marcel Mauss's detailed study of the potlatch system among the Haida and Tlingit peoples of North America, in which the self is constituted through a competitive system of gift giving that underpins and reinforces the relationship between the donor and the recipient.[68] While the scholarship on gift economies has centered on non-Western societies,[69] European medieval feudalism was equally predicated on relational conceptions of self in which the language of status, rather than free contractual relations, mediated social interaction. As Oestreich argues, following from the work of Otto Hintze:

The contract based on status, which was the medieval norm, was the foundation for "a permanent life-time relationship involving a person and his whole existence," allotting him a place in the total order which could not be freely revoked or set aside. The modern free contract, by contrast, can be dissolved and terminated. It does not indissolubly bind the whole person, as was the case with the feudal contracts, brotherhoods, betrothal and marriage.[70]

In short, in societies where an individuated conception of the self is not the organizing principle, the economic premise of that society necessitates an altogether different logic from that of bourgeois capitalism. It speaks to non-alienated, pre-contractual relations. Locke, however, was not prepared to concede the economic implications in the patriarchal society he identified with the state of nature. Indeed, if anything, Locke was at pains to argue that market relations, covenants, and binding obligations were a feature of pre-political society operating within a logic that was independent of social conventions. Men, he argued, were naturally free "to order their Actions, and dispose of their Possessions, and Persons as they think fit, within the bounds of the Law of Nature, without asking leave, or depending upon the Will of any other Man" (4.269).

As Arneil rightly points out, the radical individualism and autonomy Locke accorded the free, equal, and rational individual represented a significant departure from the more traditional view of his seventeenth-century European counterparts. Neither Hugo Groitus nor Samuel von Pufendorf went so far as to entirely detach property rights from any reference to social mores; both presupposed that the origins of private property rested on an initial agreement or compact that thereby legitimated private acquisition and the accumulation of land and goods. No such consent was required of the Lockean individual. Private property was an abstract right that had no other reference point beyond that of individual labor. As Arneil argues, "Locke categorically denies Pufendorf's, and to a certain extent Groitus's, claim that consent is essential to the right of property."[71]

### TRUSTING STRANGERS

In his chapter on the "Beginnings of Political Society," Locke emphasizes that a contract—in this instance, a political contract—presumes and necessitates certain obligations on the part of those who participate:

Every Man, by consenting with others to make one Body politick under one Government, puts himself under an Obligation to every one of that Society, to submit to the determination of the *majority*, and to be concluded by it; or else this *original Compact*, whereby he with others incorporates into *one Society*, would signifie nothing, and be no Compact, if he be left free, and under no ties, than he was in before in the State of Nature. (97.332)

As Macpherson points out:

To postulate, as Locke does, that men are by nature rational enough—both in the sense of seeing their own interest and in the sense of acknowledging moral obligation—to make the more difficult agreement to enter civil society, is to presume that men are rational enough to make the less difficult agreement required to enter into commerce.[72]

Yet regardless of the nature of the contract—be it civil or commercial—the question Macpherson fails to ask—and that Locke, in fact, sought to answer—is why anyone should feel obligated to abide by the contract he or she has entered. As James Gordley argues, despite Locke's efforts to ground moral ideas in reason, the spurious nature of his deductive logic was not lost on David Hume. As is well known, Hume was to dispense with the possibility that moral obligations could be derived from deductive logic; that morality was predicated on reason. Taking this fateful step, however, did not resolve the obvious fact that people did enter into contracts and did feel obliged to be bound by their contractual promises. As Gordley points out, Hume, somewhat unconvincingly, sought to explain this conundrum by arguing that in the early moments of human society, when settlements were very small, people maintained their contracts out of self-interest, fearing that to do otherwise would jeopardize their future contractual opportunities. People thus became accustomed over time to regard contracts as binding, and the practice continued even when society became larger.[73]

What is notably absent in Locke's and Hume's efforts to defend contractual obligation is any recognition that the very idea of the modern contract—commercial or civil—presupposes a particular type of subjectivity. As many commentators have pointed out, contractual law as it existed in antiquity and during the Middle Ages was located within an epistemological framework in which meaning and order were posited as pre-existing and predetermining values external to the agency of men.[74] Thus, contract and contractual obligations required for their legitimation an external reference—that of a morally ordered, divinely inscribed, and inherently purposeful and meaningful world.

As we have seen, it was precisely this philosophical premise that Hobbes—and, later, Locke and Hume—were to reject. When Hume posited self-interest as the compelling explanatory reason that people keep contractual obligations, he was assuming precisely that which needed to be explained: that modern contract presumes an individuated subjectivity, wherein the free, equal, and rational individual becomes the locus of agency and culpability. In the absence of a preordained and morally regulated order, the question of why individuals are bound by their contractual obligations has first to assume the autonomous, self-regulating individual.

The answer to why people should abide by contracts is, in fact, more readily comprehensible when addressed to the writings of Hobbes. Simply put, nothing (except slavery) could be worse than Hobbes's state of nature—a condition of all-consuming war. Fear, in other words, will drive men to embrace and abide by the absolutist contract when natural freedom is understood to be the source of their misery.

Because Locke located property rights and contractual transactions in the state of nature as natural to men and without reference to society, it is evident that, unlike for Hobbes, the enforcement of such moral economic responsibility was not invested in an external authority but in the individual himself. In so doing, however, Locke's state of nature had to presume the existence of an a priori identity, a particular subjectivity that could correspond to the nascent bourgeois market of pre-political society. Locke in fact had to conceive of an individual subjectivity that was indispensable to capitalist market relations—one that allowed individuals to engage in the marketplace without reference to societal expectations, social needs, or relational obligations. Such an identity, however, sat in contradiction to the relational self that occupied Locke's patriarchal chiefdom. What becomes apparent is that Locke's state of nature was home to two radically distinct subjectivities.

The Indian whom we earlier encountered—tied as he was to mutual obligations and affections; located within kinship structures; and responsive to moral codes of duty, respect, and obedience—possesses an altogether different subjectivity from that of Locke's free, equal, and rational individual, for whom both labor and goods are alienable property that has no source of reference or legitimacy beyond that of individual right. It is this latter figure—the free, equal, and rational individual—who occupies the central stage of Locke's narrative. It is this figure who, even in the state of nature, engages in contract and the market economy. It is this figure who, alongside others like him, covenants to establish the artificial structure of state and civil society.

These free, equal, and rational individuals constitute autonomous, socially abstracted agents when they engage in the anonymity of the marketplace. Capitalism does not require that the individual intimately know the person with whom he engages in a contractual transaction; it simply requires that any contractual obligations be met. That such obligations should be met even in the state of nature is a fact that Locke insists on not through reference to social expectations but because "Truth, and keeping of Faith belongs to Men, as Men, and not as Members of Society" (14.277).

Yet in the absence of social bonds, in the absence of personal relations, how can one trust the stranger of the free market? It becomes apparent that the question we should be asking is not why an individual should adhere to contractual obligations, but why an individual would contract with someone with whom he shares no history and with whom he shares no language of socially inscribed reciprocity. After all, Locke himself argued that a person was likely to "have greater apprehensions of others than of one another" (107.357).

In the absence of a social reference in which trust and confidence are predicated on the familiarity and continuity of relationships, the individual engaged in the capitalist marketplace has to presume that the stranger is indeed like himself. The relational economy also presumes on the participants; its logic relies on the recognition of mutual obligation—that the donor will one day be the recipient. However, integral to the system of gift giving is the investment in personal, ongoing relationships. It is not the judicial language of culpability but a relational vocabulary of honor that drives the gift economy. In contrast, within a contractual economy, personal relations are dispensable when anonymity is predictable, when one can assume that the market is constituted by individuals who share in the same accoutrements of individuality. Why an individual should adhere to his contractual obligations is a question that must first presume recognition of a familiar and interpretable subjectivity. It is only once a particular subjectivity is presupposed—that of the autonomous self-regulating, rational individual—that reason, self-interest, or morality can be appealed to in defense of contractual obligations.

For all of Locke's anxiety regarding the imagination, it is ultimately imaginative trust, an imagined economic community (to reconfigure Benedict Anderson's trope), that permits the successful working of capitalist relations. Given that the tangibility of interpersonal relationships (reliant as they are on a process in time) is made redundant under capitalism (time being compressed in the moment of transaction), the participants in the market have to presuppose trust without grounding it in the reality of concrete relationships. It is precisely in the presumption of trust that men through "Fancy or Agreement" (46.300) give "Gold, Silver and Diamonds" (46.300) "a Phantastical imaginary value" (184.391)—a value that makes possible the accumulation of property beyond that required for personal subsistence.

In the context of seventeenth-century England, the "phantastical" and "imaginary" extended itself to incorporate credit. In a language far too erotic for Locke, Daniel Defoe, Locke's contemporary, makes it all too apparent that the anonymity of capitalist relations does not dispense with the need for trust and honor, but it does require that such virtues be constantly reiterated, that such virtues be extolled as timeless and ethereal rather than as social and relative:

> Credit is too wary, too coy a Lady, to stay with any People upon such mean conditions; if you will entertain this Virgin you must Act upon the nice Principles of Honor, and Justice; you must preserve Sacred all the Foundations, and build regular structures upon them; you must answer all Demands, with a respect to the solemnity, and Value of the Engagement, with respect to Justice and Honor, and without any respect to Parties.[75]

In circumstances where credit mechanisms were increasingly defining economic fortunes and financial devastation, concepts such as trust, honor, respect, and justice had to be tailored to an economy that no longer presupposed relational intimacy. Indeed, the capitalist marketplace required, for its continued existence, a constant interaction between strangers in which trust had to be presumed.

Whereas for the patriarchal family of Locke's state of nature the stranger is literally that person who is unknown to the group, that person who is not part of the economy of familial recognition, for the market-oriented figure who constitutes Locke's free, equal, and rational individual, the stranger came to signify not he who was unknown but he who was unknowable—he who was equipped with a subjectivity that was not governed by the predictability presumed of a rational choice, self-interested, and autonomous individual. As Mehta argues, the necessity of conceptualizing the individual as reasoned and self-interested was a political and social imperative:

> The preference for self-interest arose because it gave human actions a predictable and stable course in contrast to the passions with their characteristically elusive underpinnings and volatile effects. Whereas the former encouraged a cautious attitude of calculation—balancing risks and benefits—the latter typically involved single-minded behavior with ruinous side effects. Similarly, whereas behavior governed by the interests was characteristically "cool and deliberate," the passions were widely disparaged as leading to impulsive, heated, and irrational acts.[76]

Against the rational stranger, therefore, was posited an irrational strangeness, a miscreant subjectivity that was not calculable and thus not reasoned. Within this conceptual economy, a socially disembodied trust necessitates recognizing the stranger in the moment of transaction as a familiar subjective figure—a self-interested, autonomous, rationally predictable individual. It is in this context that Locke's identification of the state of nature with the Americas has a significance that has largely gone unnoticed.

### STRANGERS AND ENEMIES

If we are to believe John Dunn, America is incidental to Locke's state of nature, which, reliant as it is on the theological narrative of Eden and the Fall, requires geography only as an imaginative trope.[77] I would suggest, however, that Locke's frequent references to ethnological and travel literature on the New World and his dramatic pronouncement, "Thus in the beginning all the World was *America*" (49.301), needs to be accorded more significance than Dunn allows. If Locke alludes to Genesis, he is explicit in his reference to the New World; if he calls on biblical authority, he equally appeals to the indigenous Americans. What is more, Locke locates both his patriarchal society and his free, equal, and rational individual in the New World state of nature. Within this natural realm he identifies a relational economy and contractual property relations. The patriarchal chiefdom offers the necessary distinction between pre- and post-political society. The rational, free, and equal individual, however, is essential if that prior state is to be transcended. After all, contract presupposes freedom, equality, and rationality.

Locke's positioning of two such incongruous figures in the state of nature is revealing not for its apparent contradiction but, rather, for the extent to which colonial conquest in the New World defined and tailored Locke's narrative. While J. G. A. Pocock may be right to argue that Macpherson exaggerated the pervasiveness of capitalist relations in seventeenth-century England,[78] what he (and, for that matter, Macpherson) ignores is the extent to which the conquest and colonization of the Americas offered—indeed, compelled—the fashioning and privileging of a particular type of subjectivity: that of the free, equal, and rational individual.

In a detailed study of early English (pre-Cromwellian) expansion in the New World, Robert Brenner reveals the extent to which the profitability of English colonization in the Americas necessitated a very different economic logic. Brenner argues that whereas the East Indian Company was a classic example of mercantile economics, "operated under restricted, corporately controlled conditions designed to regulate competition, to minimize risk and to ensure profits,"[79] that economic logic could not be extended to include trade with the New World.

It quickly became apparent to the Merchant Adventurers of London in the seventeenth century that if America was to be a source of imports, and thus of personal and national wealth, it would become so as a consequence of aggressive colonization: the appropriation and cultivation of land and the establishment of English settlements. The absence of immediate gains and the extensive level of investment output required to sustain the English colonies in the New World led to the failure and eventual demise of the Virginia Company's monopoly venture. With the collapse of mercantile colonialism, according to Brenner, "Individual entrepreneurs, operating through a variety of partnership forms, now took responsibility for colonial growth."[80]

Brenner argues that in 1614, the first lot of indentured servants, having completed a seven-year contract, were not only set free but provided with company plots to own and cultivate. By 1616, in the hope of expanding permanent settlement, individual settlers were provided with fifty acres of land on the condition that they financed their own passage across the Atlantic.[81] Thus, in the far-flung colonies of the New World, outside the rigidity of English class structures and aristocratic traditions and encouraged by the economic incentives and potential economic prosperity offered in the newfound colony, men of relatively low socioeconomic status began to make their fortunes in long-term, risk-laden investments: the establishment of tobacco and sugar plantations that would yield profits many years later.

What Brenner's history reveals is the extent to which English colonization of the Americas spurred a twofold development. It signified a transition from mercantile monopoly economics to a capitalism predicated on the commodification of land, the establishment of freehold title, and the beginnings of long-term settlement. Corresponding with this economic transformation—indeed, necessitated by it—was the emergence of an altogether different economic actor. The Mercantile Adventurers were part of the English elite, if not members of the aristocracy; the New World settlers, by contrast, were often men of low financial means and low social status.[82] A slave-based economy would later turn these actors into gentlemen farmers, but the initial imperative in the early years of colonization still recognized a measure of white labor in the cultivation of land.

The potential profitability of the New World relied on the economic "rationality" of the settler community. The free, equal, and rational individual was precisely what was needed. Yet, as Arneil describes, the apparent absence of such individuals appears to have been a source of anxiety for the Lord Proprietors. Accusations of idleness, debauchery, laziness, and the desire for immediate economic gain over long-term commitment to the land figured large in the letters and memoranda sent back and forth between the Carolina investors.[83] It is not surprising, therefore, that in his capacity as secretary to the Lords Proprietors, Locke repeatedly argued that the low returns on their investments in Carolina were due to an insufficient number of "industrious people" and that the "Governor and planters there [were] somewhat sluggish."[84]

Given the early history of English colonization in the Americas, and given his own financial interests in the New World, Locke's efforts to tailor a particular type of subjectivity to correspond with a nascent bourgeois economy was not without historical relevance—a relevance that is particularly illuminating in the context of the New World. That we should encounter two incongruous figures in Locke's state of nature—the free, rational, and equal individual and the relational self—may well have been informed by Locke's understanding of colonial settlement.

It is in this context that Locke's caveat that any individual "is at liberty to go and . . . agree with others to begin a new one [commonwealth], *in vacuis locis*, in any part of the World, they can find free and unpossessed" (121.349) is instructive. There is little doubt that Locke was referring to the New World, where "there are still *Great Tracts of Ground* to be found, which (the Inhabitants thereof not having joyned with the rest of Mankind, in the consent of the Use of their common Money) *lie waste*, and are more than the People, who dwell on it, do, or can make use of, and so still lie in common" (45.299).

In that same part of the world where free, equal, and rational men were finding land "unpossessed," the soil lying "waste," and the earth lying "in common," the shadowy presence of the indigenous American existed as a source of apprehension for all would-be settlers and foreign creditors. Whereas for Columbus an imaginary India was transcribed on a mythical New World, for Locke—and, indeed, for the seventeenth-century English merchant—the Americas were an all too tangible reality translatable in terms of landed property; as a source for trade in furs, tobacco, and sugar; as a new avenue for credit, investments, and stocks; as a locus for international law and diplomatic treatise; and, finally, as a site of military anxiety and armed defense against rival Western powers and local Indian nations.

Within this configuration, the indigenous Americans were no longer a curiosity, an enigmatic exotic, or a hated enemy. They were a subject of concern, a figure to be investigated, a potential enemy, a political problem. Locke's America is not of Ovidian mythology or Herodotus's history but a source of political apprehension and a subject of political relevance. It requires settlements to be established, constitutions to be drafted, laws to be imposed, and profits to be extracted. As for the Indians, difference was no longer reduced to an eclectic vocabulary that expressed personalized motivations. Instead, it increasingly focused on a series of political imperatives that came to the fore. The need to appropriate land, maintain and secure territorial conquests, protect private property, and safeguard settlers' lives produced the need for a more systematic theoretical and political engagement with the New World. It gave impetus, in other words, to more clearly articulated forms of self-definition.

This self-definition was located in the positing of a particular type of subjectivity: that of the free, equal, and rational individual—an individual who conceived of himself as an autonomous self whose material existence relied not on a political state or social bonds but on the alienable disposal of his labor, the right to buy other people's labor, and the property in goods he accumulated. He was an individual who was predictable in his self-interested pursuits, was not shy about contracting with familiar strangers, was not idle but industrious, and was quick to appreciate the necessity of contractual obligations. This stranger was a friend.

In contrast, he who was identified as an enemy was, in Locke's formulation, he who was irrational—the criminal, the mad man, the "savage." The Indian was included in this motley crew; he was also, however, called on to illustrate man's natural (i.e., rational, free, equal, propertied, and prepolitical) condition. The contradiction inherent in his positing of two distinct social formations (one predicated on a relational system of exchange, and the other on contractual relations) was not a tension that Locke was prepared to acknowledge—or, for that matter, of which he was even conscious. Thus, in the context of the economic imperatives to colonize the New World, Locke's pre-political Indian, bounded by kinship relations that could not be reconciled with the autonomous individuality of the market, embodied a subjectivity that was not recognized as different, that is, reflective of a *particular* way of being in the world, but irrational—a refusal to become a *universal* individuated being.

It is not a coincidence that Locke locates the irrationality of the Indian in the sphere of economic activity—in his supposed failure to cultivate and thereby appropriate the land as his private property. The failure of the Indian to cultivate—or, having cultivated, to leave some fields fallow—was for Locke a crime against God himself. As noted in chapter 1, Genesis 1:28 was interpreted by Locke and his English contemporaries as a divine dictate ordering men to cultivate the land and domesticate the beasts. Within this logic, uncultivated, unfenced land was by definition wasteland and thus held in common until such time as an individual, through the application of his labor, appropriated that part of the earth as his own: "God gave the World to Men in Common; but since he gave it them for their benefit, . . .

it cannot be supposed he meant it should always remain common and un-cultivated. He gave it to the use of the Industrious and Rational, (and *Labor* was to be *his Title* to it;) not to the Fancy or Covetousness of the Quarrel-som and Contentious" (34.291).

Being "industrious and rational" was synonymous with the accumulation of private property. Leaving the land "waste" was precisely what the Amer-indians had done (by leaving a field fallow, if not by abstaining from cultiva-tion altogether) and could only be interpreted, following Locke's logic, as an irrationality emblematic of the "Quarrelsom and Contentious." While many scholars have argued that Locke was guilty of defending the appro-priation of native land through his appeal to Genesis 1:28, I would suggest that what is revealing is not Locke's financial pragmatism but his anxiety regarding an incommensurable subjectivity that he could only translate as a form of unreason.

For Locke, where reason is absent, as Mehta points out, madness pred-icated on the imagination and passions must prevail. Such a transgres-sive subjectivity, one that fails to adhere to "the Common Law of Reason" (16.279), cannot be permitted the free expression accorded to Locke's fa-miliar stranger—the rational, free, and equal individual. It must instead be destroyed in the same manner as one kills "a *Wolf* or a *Lyon*" (16.279). Hav-ing already transgressed "the Common Law of Reason" by their failure to cultivate the land, the Indians compounded the severity of their crime by resisting white settlement, by defending themselves against the appropria-tion of that which Locke described as "common" and "waste" land. The two-pronged nature of Indian irrationality thus becomes a source of appre-hension, an anxiety that finds expression through rendering the indigenous American into an enemy against whom war and enslavement are justified. This irrational enemy is the rationale that legitimates European planters' waging war "against the *Indians*, to seek Reparation in any Injury received from them."[85]

The kinship bounded, pre-capitalist subjectivity of the Lockean Indian allowed irrationality to be personified within the state of nature and thus operate as a contrastive foil against which the figure of the free, equal, and rational individual could find dramatic expression. Thus, while many schol-ars have interpreted Locke's patriarchal society as the source from which free, equal, and rational individuals eventually emerged, I would suggest that no such transformation took place. While Locke identified sequential stages within his state of nature, these temporal demarcations do not correspond with a similar shift in individual subjectivities—something we later recognize in the writings of Rousseau. History, in other words, has no bearing on, leaves no imprint on, individual subjectivity as a whole. Rather, the patriarchal nature of Locke's pre-political society is one that presumes relational selves where familial recognition mediates all aspects of life, including that of exchange. The free, equal, and rational individual who also inhabits Locke's state of nature—who is, in fact, always already there—possesses an altogether different subjectivity. Thus, what we encounter in Locke's state of nature is not historically bounded identities that evolve perceptibly over time but, rather, the juxtaposition of two distinct and opposed subjectivities: that of the autonomous rational individual and his irrational, miscreant counterpart, the relational self.

### A-HISTORICAL TIME

The fact that for Locke individual subjectivity is not subject to history is one of the many reasons for agreeing with Macpherson and Dunn that Locke's thesis is fundamentally a-historical. What we encounter in Locke's *Two Treatises* is the mutual agreement between a sum of individuals to institute civil society and state. With no reference to the past, the contract signals a new beginning—the zero point of history. The question that concerns me, however, is who precisely were the agents who issued in this a-historical moment?

The pre-capitalist, relational self identified with Locke's Indian personifies a strangeness/irrationality (a miscreant subjectivity) that militates against the disembodied trust presupposed in the contractual relationship. He thus remains in the state of nature, where neither law nor history is of his making. Locke's state of nature is contextualized within time; it is representative of the past, but its temporality is divinely inscribed—it is the realm of natural laws and not subject to human will, the product of individual agency. This is a state traversed by time but empty of history; a state in which men are set by God. This is the realm, therefore, that the Indians in Locke's *Second Treatise* continue to inhabit, and in so doing, they remain subjects within a time past but not agents of future possibilities and historical beginnings.

In contrast, the free, equal, and rational individual equipped with the subjectivity presupposed by modern contractual relations transcends the past through engaging in contract. Through the collective agency of these individuals political society comes into being. Through the medium of contract not only is the state of nature departed, but the past itself is abandoned. Thus, if "historical possibilities are created by reason alone,"[86] this is because reason, having been estranged from the divine moral order, is rehoused in, and central to, the individual self.

This same individual, though not the product of history, is the source both from which emerge historical beginnings and against which history comes to be constituted as meaningful: "Person is the name for this *self*. . . . This personality extends *itself* beyond present Existence to what is Past, only by consciousness; whereby it becomes concerned and accountable, owns and imputes to *itself* past actions."[87]

Presupposed in Locke's formulation of the individual is a rational agent, one whose consciousness of his own identity is predicated on a sense of continuity between his past and present self—a continuity that in turn makes him responsible and culpable for his own actions. Locke's twin emphasis that the individual is the locus of agency, culpability, and a self-regulated morality, as well as a figure whose very identity is subjected to time, opens the possibility for a malleable subjectivity—one that can be fashioned, shaped, changed, and tailored. A malleable subjectivity also creates the possibility—indeed, necessitates the recognition of—errant subjectivities.

If Mehta is right in prescribing to Locke a general anxiety pertaining to all individuals, this suggests that the individual had not yet come to be identified as the privileged subject of European culture and history. In other words, the historicism that made it possible in the nineteenth century for a Hegel or a Mill to identify individuality as a signifier of European superiority was a confidence that is remarkably absent in the writings of Locke. The fact that my own thesis locates, in Locke's state of nature, two distinct subjectivities—the free rational individual and the relational irrational self—does not negate the logical conclusion of Mehta's work. But it does add another dimension to our understanding of Locke's writings: that while Locke held a general anxiety regarding the stability of individual subjectivities, the figure of the Amerindian embodied a miscreant self precisely because the incommensurability that he represented was rendered into a form of irrationality.

The fact that the indigenous American was the personification of an unstable, unpredictable, and irrational self brought into dramatic relief the superiority of the rational, free, and equal individual. It did so, however, without the conditionality of European superiority. For while Locke located the individual within time—time reduced to an individuated unit identifiable only insofar as it was the measure of an individual's life—he did not locate the individual within cultural history. Absent from Locke's narrative was the teleological historicism that was to consume nineteenth-century thought, a narrative that permitted the measuring of European superiority by virtue of its historical progress vis-à-vis other cultures.

It is precisely for this reason that one encounters the apparent inconsistency in Locke's representation of the Indians, who are at once irrational and at other times constitute still-life portraits of pre-political, rational individuals. Thus, a reader of Locke's *Second Treatise* finds herself tripping over comments such as, "Thus this Law of reason makes the Deer, that *Indian's* who hath killed it; 'tis allowed to be his goods who hath bestowed his labor upon it, though before, it was the common right of every one" (30.289); "Conformable hereunto we find the People of *America*, who . . . enjoy'd their own natural freedom" (105.337); and, "The Promises and Bargains for Truck, etc., . . . between a *Swiss* and an *Indian*, in the Woods of *America*, are binding to them, though they are perfectly in a State of Nature, in reference to one another" (14.277).

The fact that, for Locke, the Amerindian is interchangeably represented as irrational and as the bearer of an individuated subjectivity is possible because neither cultural explanation nor historical predeterminism mediates his writings. Thus, while Locke's state of nature is conceptualized in terms of patriarchal, kinship communities, the relational self that this form of social organization presupposes is not one that Locke can conceptualize in terms other than that of irrationality.

Conversely, however, when Locke seeks to reconfigure the Indian in terms other than irrationality, the only language at his disposal is one that renders the Indian into a European—an indeterminate figure who wanders the pre-political geography of the "woods of America" while inhabiting the subjectivity of a seventeenth-century English mercantilist. Whereas Hegel, Mill, and Marx were to appeal to tribalism, caste-ism, village community, or Oriental despotism as a historically located and culturally distinguishing signifier of difference, Locke's conception of time allowed for the language of subjectivity as a process, without contextualizing the subject within cultural histories. For this very reason, an errant subjectivity or an autonomous individuality could only, in Locke's imagination, be constituted as criminally irrational or naturally reasoned, and not as culturally inferior or historically backward.

Finally, like Hobbes before him, Locke posits the free, equal, and rational individual in the New World. However, unlike Hobbes, he does not offer the indigenous American the possibility of departing the state of nature. This is so not because Locke attributes any innate inferiority to the Indian, but because he submerges the Indian within kinship relations that deny not only the possibility of individual autonomy, but also the emergence of a moneyed contractual economy. It is with contract that political society comes to be, yet it is precisely the social abstraction presupposed by contract—that obligation and trust has to be presumed between strangers—that denies the Amerindians the ability to partake in the political covenant. Denying the particular subjectivity that contract relations presuppose ensures that the indigenous inhabitants cannot be agents of history. They must remain where Locke left them—in the a-historical condition of nature.

They will not remain neglected for long, however. It is to Jean-Jacques Rousseau that we now turn to see nature transformed into the very agent of human history and history made possible through the perfectibility of human nature. The Indian and the individual may have returned to the dressing room, but the curtains will soon rise on a new (stage) of nature.

### "Rousseau until now . . . citizen of Geneva, but at present ORANG-OUTANG": Rousseau on the Question of Subjectivity

It will be remembered from chapter 1 that the discovery of the New World prompted desperate efforts to account for precisely that which had been left unaccounted—namely, a genealogy of indigenous Americans within the privileged narrative of biblical history.[88] Efforts to reconcile Christian discoveries with the Christian canon continued well into the seventeenth century. However, in the writings of Hobbes and Locke we find that the debate shifted from the subject of man's origins to the question of man's nature; from the locus of divine Creation to the agency of mortal man.

Released from the determinism of a divine debt, man was no longer simply the byproduct of Eden and the Fall but the protagonist of his own history. Presupposed in his nature was agency, and reflecting his nature was the political society he himself brought into being. Thus, when we confront a Hobbesian state of nature, absent as it is of sin and virtue and yet constrained by unrelieved misery and unfettered violence, we recognize not only the nature of man but the potential—indeed, the imperative—for human agency.

The writings of Jean-Jacques Rousseau (1712–78) can be recognized today as both the culmination of the contract-theory tradition and a radical departure from it. Rousseau distinguished himself from his predecessors by drawing together two independent yet interrelated concerns: the origin of man and the subject of man's nature. Hobbes and Locke located man in a state of nature; Rousseau brought nature to bear on man. Where Hobbes and Locke traced the emergence of political society, Rousseau sought to trace the emergence of man himself. More significant still is the fact that on the canvas of man, a category that presupposes uniformity, Rousseau sketched the singularity of the individual. It is in Rousseau's work that individuality finds its modern inscription.

This was an individuality that was not predictable (and ultimately, uniform) in its rational utilitarianism but one inherently divided. The division to which I refer, however, alludes not to Rousseau's well-known bemoaning of distorted selves born out of degenerate society, but to an a priori division that must be presupposed when we speak of modern individuality. As Huck Gutman argues:

> In order for a man or woman to be constituted as a subject, he or she must first be divided from the totality of the world, or the totality of the social body. For a "me" to emerge, a distinction must be made between "me" and the "not me." The boundaries of the self are those lines that divide the self from all that which is not the self, which is beyond the self. The first, and essential, move in the constitution of the self is division.[89]

It is precisely in this division that the individual becomes indivisible; that he is transformed into a unitary, holistic self; that he conceptualizes himself as unique and singular. The near-obsession with interiority and uniqueness permeates the pages of Rousseau's *Confessions* and *Reveries of the Solitary Walker*.[90] "I am made unlike any one I have ever met," Rousseau informs the reader in the second paragraph of *Confessions*. "I will even venture to say that I am like no one in the whole world. I may not be better but at least I am different."[91]

Yet if through his autobiographical works Rousseau made himself the object of study, *A Discourse on Inequality* fuses the portrait of individuality with a narrative of man's history.[92] "History" is the operative word. In all instances—be it *Confessions, Émile,* or *Second Discourse*—Rousseau's narrative of the self is made possible through an appeal to a temporal continuity between the "before" and the "after." Locke privileges the child as the precursor of man; Rousseau extends this motif (as it plays itself out in *Confessions* and *Émile*) to encompass the historical trajectory of humanity itself.

### SAVAGE BEGINNINGS AND MEDIEVAL WILD MEN

In *Second Discourse*, Rousseau's "before" contemporary society, like that of his contractarian predecessors, is grounded within a state of nature inhabited by savages. It was Rousseau's contention, however, that demarcating the past from the present, the before from the after, was precisely what his philosophical forebears had neglected to do—a fact immediately apparent in their insistence on "speak[ing] of savage man and depict[ing] civilized man" (78). Thus, while the "philosophers" had rightly sought to "examine the foundations of political society" by going back to the state of nature, Rousseau insisted that "none of them have succeeded in getting there" (78).

Not one for false modesty, Rousseau offered *A Discourse on Inequality* (otherwise known as the *Second Discourse*) as the necessary corrective to the work of his predecessors. Within its pages we encounter a portrait of man in the very infancy of his natural condition. In the very purity of the state of nature, he is a figure not only radically divorced from that of Hobbes's warmonger or Locke's patriarch; he is almost unrecognizable from the humanity he is meant to represent. Not only is this figure oblivious to familial ties, a nomadic wanderer, but he is equally devoid of any human attributes beyond that of a biological resemblance. He lacks speech, imagination, foresight, reason, and self-reflection. Indeed, like the other beasts he occasionally encounters, and with which he competes for food and avoids through fear, the savage man shares an instinctual sense of self-preservation and an uncultivated empathy with the suffering of other creatures. The savage man, while human in form, is not identifiably human in faculty. Ultimately, the independence, freedom, and self-sufficiency of savage man constitute an accidental instinct necessary to his physical existence rather than a conscious individuated sense of being.

As the reader has no doubt come to expect, it was the "savages" of America and Africa that Rousseau would evoke as illustrative of man at his dawn. What we ultimately witness in the *Second Discourse* is a "philosophical anthropology" located within a temporal schema[93]—one that locates man within a universal, a-historical history.

What is of interest, however, is that the bizarre and wondrous had not entirely migrated off-shore, that Europe had not been entirely emptied of all that which was later to be displaced on the exotic landscapes of the New World and Africa. Thus, it was still possible for Rousseau, when speaking of the savagery that marks man's origins (the lack of language, reason, society, etc.) to evoke the wild men discovered, over centuries, in the forests of Europe, figures devoid of language and of society—indeed, devoid of a recognizable humanity beyond that of their human corporeality. Thus, the wild child found near Hiesse in 1344, the infant raised by bears and discovered in the woods of Lithuania in 1644, and the encounter recorded with "two other savages found in the Pyranees" in 1719 were all brought forth as archival witnesses testifying to the truth of Rousseau's portrait of man's original condition ("Note C."140).

Not surprisingly, such references have prompted some scholars to identify the medieval wild man as the inspirational source informing Rousseau's *Second Discourse*. Thus, Geoffrey Symcox suggests that the wild man "merely changed his name to the Noble Savage and remained at the centre of a tradition of social criticism which continued from Montaigne through Fénelon to Rousseau and Diderot."[94]

While the seductive symmetry of Symcox's thesis overstates the continuity between the wild man and the noble savage, it is nonetheless true that this wild-man figure who inhabited an ambiguous space in medieval iconography—at once human in form and animal in behavior—was the source from which emerged portraits of the New World and African "savages."[95] Yet while continuity between the medieval wild man and eighteenth-century noble savage can indeed be discerned, it is equally important to recognize the metamorphosis that underscores this transition—that as much as the representation of New World "savage" is heavily indebted to a medieval inheritance, it also represents a departure from it.

From its ancient roots to its medieval inscription, the figure of the wild man, this pre-modern embodiment of fear, desire, and envy, was the personification of *exceptionalism*. He was an animal-human aberration, a *trangressive* and *regressive* figure who had degenerated from a preconceived normality.[96] Even in those instances where the wild man was painted with a more sympathetic brush, his iconic significance nevertheless continued to reside in the rarity of the condition he personified. In other words, it was precisely his exceptionalism that ultimately made the wild man a figure to fear or eulogize.

In contrast, the proliferation of travel literature during the seventeenth century and eighteenth century—a literature with which Rousseau was familiar[97]—testified to the existence of entire societies made up of "savages." Aberration gradually gave way to archetype, degeneration to origins, and exceptionalism to a universal pre-social blueprint.

The pervasive presence of savages inhabiting distant lands might not have been significant in and of itself if it had not been for the fact that coupled with these "discoveries" was a corresponding enthusiasm for natural science during the Enlightenment. These two factors together informed a perceptible shift in the representation of savagery. If the wild man was a transgressive figure, an exceptional and unsettling freak of nature, the savage as he appeared in Enlightenment garb came gradually to "stand in" for pre-social man. If Rousseau's work continued to display a debt to the medieval wild man, the noble savage should not be rendered into a sympathetic inversion of a former self. The savage in Rousseau, as in much of the eighteenth-century literature, did not represent degeneration, an aberration inflicted on a few, but the model of universal man at the moment of his origins—humanity as it existed in the zero sum of history.

Conceptualizing savage man as a point of origin owes its debt, in large measure, to the natural sciences that flourished during Rousseau's lifetime. Rousseau's admiration of Carl Linneaus and his correspondence and debt to the Comte de Buffon are well documented. Indeed, in the *Second Discourse*, Buffon's influence looms large, for not only does Rousseau frequently cite Buffon's *Natural History* as a source of reference but, more fundamentally, as Robert Wokler has suggested, Rousseau sought to transpose "some of Buffon's arguments from the domain of natural history into that of civil history."[98]

Thus, while Rousseau's sympathetic rendering of the savage was openly contested (Buffon, for example, had little patience for Rousseau's romanticism), the differing shades of interpretation were underscored by a shared premise: that far from being an aberration, the savage was the guardian of man's origins.[99] The question was: What was man?

If against the degeneration and aberration that constituted the wild man the savage was distinguished as the locus of origins, then it became somewhat of an imperative to demarcate boundaries, to locate that marginal figure whose existence constituted the faint line signifying the transitional space where animal nature ended and human nature began. The fusion between the medieval wild man, the eighteenth-century noble savage, and Enlightenment natural science is nowhere more evident than in Rousseau's references to the orangutan. "Orangutan," a Malay word that literally translates as the "man of the woods," was in the eighteenth century a generic term that made no distinction between what we today recognize as different species of apes and monkeys.[100]

In the quest for taxonomic certainty, and in the wake of travelers' reports of encountering the generic orangutan in the jungles of Africa and Malaysia, the man of the forest became the subject of a heated dispute regarding his taxonomic placement. Thus, the Swiss naturalist Carl Linneaus earned the ridicule of his French contemporary Comte Buffon when, in the first edition of *System of Nature* (1735), he classified man as a quadruped animal, thereby coupling him with apes, sloths, and lizards. Buffon dismissed such efforts as an unhealthy obsession with classification and a tedious preoccupation with details.[101] Linneaus himself, while refusing to respond to or engage with, Buffon's mockery (though he did name a particularly odorous plant he discovered *Buffonia*[102]) was nevertheless aware of the dubious and highly arbitrary nature of his nomenclature. Efforts to extend his system of order from plants to the animal kingdom, and finally the human species, gave rise to categories, subcategories, and yet further subdivisions. Linneaus was eventually forced to respond to his critics by acknowledging that "man" seemed to elude his efforts at classification, and thus he was open to the advice of anyone who could bring to light "a generic character by which to distinguish man from the ape."[103] By the time the tenth and final edition of *System of Nature* was published, in 1758, Linneaus had revised his earlier classification of man by placing him under the nomenclature of "primate." Sheltered under this larger umbrella we find the homo sapien, a category that is further subdivided and includes within its ranks the wild man (*homo ferus*) and *homo monstruosus* (dwarfs, giants, men with elongated necks, eunuchs), as well as the more familiar listing of Europeans, Africans, Americans, and Asians.[104]

Rousseau entered into an already feverish debate when he questioned the testimony of travelers who defined as beasts creatures they simultaneously described as uncannily human in both physique and behavior. Perhaps prompted by Linneaus's inclusion of *homo ferus* in his taxonomy of man (and thus deviating from the orthodoxy of Buffon), Rousseau encouraged his readers to entertain the possibility, until such time as human–ape sexual union could settle the matter once and for all, that the "pongo and orang-outang [were] in fact real savage man, whose race dispersed since antiquity in the forests with no opportunity to develop any of its potential faculties had not acquired any measured perfection and were still ground in the primitive state of nature" ("Note J."155).

Given the insistence of eighteenth-century naturalists that order was discernable once nature was subjected to taxonomic "systems," it is not surprising that Rousseau should have pushed the boundaries of Hobbes's and Locke's state of nature to the point that natural man was difficult to distinguish from nature itself—from all other sentient beings. While Locke had expressed disquiet at the apparent arbitrariness and thoroughly human-inscribed classification of the natural world,[105] his examples did not question the boundaries of human distinctiveness or gesture to temporally inscribed shifts in the human condition as a species.

The fact that Rousseau located a "beginning" to his state of nature within which human nature is virtually indistinguishable from nature itself has led some scholars to ascribe to him a nascent evolutionism. Wolker, for example, goes so far as to suggest that:

> never before has conjectural history so closely approximated empirical primatology. Spared the leeches and malaria of a jungle expedition, Rousseau, by laying the facts aside, came closer to a post-Darwinian understanding of man's place in nature and the evolutionary biology of our species than did most of his celebrated philosophical contemporaries.[106]

It is difficult to accept a conclusion that reads into the work of a mid-eighteenth-century philosopher the discoveries of a mid-nineteenth-century scientist. To portray Rousseau as a prophet of evolutionary theory is to ignore that which Foucault has forced us to acknowledge: that in construct-ing a "history of ideas" narrative, we risk ignoring the epistemological dis-tinctions that demarcated the Renaissance from the early modern and the early modern from modernity. Thus, to speak of an "evolutionary biol-ogy" in the context of the eighteenth century—particularly in the first half of the 1700s (Rousseau's *Second Discourse* had been written by 1754)—is to suggest a concern with life, a preoccupation with biology, that was not to emerge until the late eighteenth century and early nineteenth century:

> The eras of nature do not prescribe the internal *time* of beings and their continuity; they dictate the *intemperate* interruptions that have constantly dispersed them, destroyed them, mingled them, separated them, and interwoven them. There is not and cannot be even the suspicion of an evolutionism, or a transformism in Classical thought; for time is never conceived as a principle of development for living beings in their internal organization; it is perceived only as the possible bearer of a revolution in the external space in which they live.[107]

Natural history does not imply the history of life—that transformative process of biological evolution that Jean-Baptiste Lamarck and Charles Darwin were later to theorize. At no time does Rousseau suggest that orangutans are our evolutionary or biological ancestors. Even when, in "Note C," Rousseau maintains that wild men and Carib children had been known to walk on all fours and thus had experienced difficulties in assuming an upright position, Rousseau credits this inability with a lack of training—social neglect—and not with any biological limitation (140). The same logic, one assumes, is extended to the orangutan.

It is, perhaps, Francis Moran who comes closer to the truth when he argues that Rousseau and his Enlightenment contemporaries still operated within a taxonomic tradition modeled on the chain of being, in which all of God's creatures—from plants to angels—were positioned in a vertical scale that reached its apex in the presence of God himself. Moran argues that "in the context of mainstream eighteenth-century thought," Rousseau's posi-tioning of natural man

> as a mid point between animals and human beings . . . would probably have been read as an allusion to the chain of being rather than as an in-dication of human descent, for unlike the later evolutionist, eighteenth

century naturalists who suggested a possible relationship between primates and human beings were generally uninterested in tracing the genealogy of these populations. Instead, their claims were meant to establish the relative position of each in the chain of being.[108]

The essential premise that underscored the logic of the chain was that of continuity and vertically ascending gradations. Thus, even Buffon, who so persistently heckled the nomenclators, nevertheless argued that "nature works by unknown degrees," passing "from one species to another species, and often from one genus to another genus through imperceptible gradations."[109] While at times the distinctions are intangible in their minuteness, at other times the "gaps" are more discernible, and the "occupier" is clearly recognizable. The shrew, for example, functions as the bridge between the rat and the mole.[110] Linneaus simply extended this logic to his discussion of man: The *homo ferus* and *homo monstruosus* functioned as the intermediary, transitional link between "pure" man and "pure" ape.[111] Continuity and gradation.

Natural history, in fact, had to wait for Georges Cuvier (1769–1832) before the principle of extinction sorely tested a chain of being that was ill equipped to explain the disappearance of entire life forms and unable to accommodate disruption and *discontinuity*.[112] Recognizing this, however, does not elide the fact that eighteenth-century natural science, while continuing to find expression through the idiom of the chain of being, simultaneously undermined its grammatical structure.

Thus, while Moran is right to recognize in Rousseau's account of the orangutan the Carib and the wild man, an underlying reference to the chain of being, this medieval inheritance by the eighteenth century had lost the pervading legitimacy of its religious moorings. A purposeful world predetermined by a sovereign God in which man was both His reflection and His greatest achievement inspired a medieval taxonomy in which all of God's creatures were bounded within the fixity of their own existence and the positioning of that existence within a hierarchical scale, a scale that was conceived of in reference to metaphysics and theology rather than temporality.[113] If divine ordinance placed man below the angels (who themselves were hierarchically ordered), man was equally assured of his sovereignty, his superiority, and, most important, his distinction from the beasts.

Yet if the world is not inherently constituted with purpose and meaning, if order is in fact the consequence of human inspiration and not divine revelation, the question necessarily arises as to what distinguishes man from the sentient beast: What, to return to Rousseau, distinguishes the orangutan from the rest of humanity?

While at once conceived within the conceptual framework of the chain of being, Rousseau's *Second Discourse* is equally revealing of the fact that the religious foundations of this medieval inheritance have been irrevocably shaken: the certainty of man's distinctiveness had lost its religious anchor. Thus, when Rousseau suggested the possibility that the orangutan may well be human, this should not be interpreted as a case of taxonomic confusion wherein new discoveries prompted new theories that together with our follies constituted the history of ideas, the history of our progressivist passage toward truth. Rather, what the *Second Discourse* reveals is that while Rousseau continued to work within the taxonomic order prescribed by the chain of being, the absence of a purposeful, divinely ordained world created the possibility for Rousseau to appeal to the wild man, the Caribs, the Hottentot, and the orangutan as interchangeable examples of humanity's origins. The word "origins" is significant here, for in speaking of the wild man, Carib, or Hottentot as illustrative of mans beginnings, Rousseau, to borrow Arthur Lovejoy's phraseology, temporalized the chain of being,[114] forcing an uneasy and unresolved coexistence between the principles of rigidity and fixity, on the one hand, and a temporally induced fluidity, on the other. The union was still possible, however, because continuity was presupposed and time was organized sequentially, not developmentally.

Rousseau's *Second Discourse* explored the possibility of stripping man of all that was held to be exclusively human—language, reason, foresight, imagination, and individuality—while simultaneously asserting his humanity. In so doing, Rousseau released the very concept of man from the prescriptive authority of the chain of being. He opened it up to interrogation, thereby transforming the concept of man into a category as fluid as it was contingent. Paradoxically, it was this very fluidity and contingency inherent in the definition of man that, for Rousseau, was to become the essential feature that distinguished the human species from all other sentient beings. In blurring the boundaries, in making opaque that which was once transparent, in ultimately reducing man to animal beginnings, Rousseau elevated the human condition over that of his fellow beasts on the grounds that man had departed that very terrain in which animals continued to wander. For Rousseau, what distinguished man, what raised him above all other creatures, was his potential for perfectibility, "a faculty which with the help of circumstance, progressively develops all our other faculties and which in man is inherent in the species as much as in the individual" (88).

In denuding man of all that had once defined him, Rousseau tailored a very different conception of individuality from that of his predecessors. By investing humanity with the potentiality for perfectibility, the very definition of man was subjected to the contingencies of time. This is why it is possible, in the context of Rousseau's writings, to speak of the emergence of man as something above his anatomical form. The malleability of Rousseau's definition of humanity lies not only in the blurring of the distinction between man and orangutan, but in the interrelation between man's "almost unlimited faculty" and the "action of time," which together work to create temporally varied portraits of the individual self (88).

It is for this reason that original man—that savage / wild man / ape still encountered in Lithuanian forests and Malay jungles—is an altogether different specimen from the noble savage we encounter in Rousseau's third stage of nature, that which Rousseau explicitly identifies with the indigenous inhabitants of Africa and the New World.

It is, of course, true that Locke also posited a state of nature that was demarcated into stages: from the patriarchal family to the growth of societies, from a hunter-gather existence to the enclosure of landed property, and from subsistence economies to the introduction of monetary exchange. Yet what distinguishes Rousseau's conjectural history is the fact that the passage of time did not merely have a bearing on, or reflect, external transformations. Rather, as Arthur Melzer rightly argues, Rousseau added another dimension to man's being: "the extreme malleability of his nature over time."[115]

Rousseau traces the shift from animalistic isolation to families and settled societies, laments the decline of artisanal independence in the wake of metallurgy and agriculture, and, finally, denounces the emergence of property relations that ignited the Hobbesian state of war and the eventual institution of unjust laws and corrupt political governance. What makes the Rousseauian historical trajectory so significant is the fact that corresponding to such cataclysmic transformations in the external environment were gradual, yet no less perceptible, transformations in man himself—man as an individuated, subjective being.

From a speechless asocial self, man formed emotional bonds within familial and social relations. With society came a cultivated sense of self but also a slavish subjection to the opinion of others. Morals and virtues distinguished him, but so, too, did insincerity and imitation. He learned speech, song, and dance while surrendering himself to comparison, arrogance, and jealousy. He came to recognize beauty and love while becoming conscious of envy and hate, and, finally, while his innate sense of empathy became a conscious sensibility, so, too, did an exaggerated sense of pride. From savage beginnings, the very malleability of man, under the auspices of time, made possible both his potential for perfectibility and his susceptibility to degradation.

Within this narrative, Rousseau locates the third state of nature—that of the noble savage—as "the happiest epoch" in human history and the "most lasting" (115). Statements such as this have led to a typecasting of Rousseau's thoughts as primitivist.[116] Yet if we return to Hayden White's definition of a primitivist as someone who sets "the savage, both past and present, over against civilized man as a model and ideal"—an ideal, furthermore, that can be returned to[117]—one cannot help but think that the charge of primitivism against Rousseau is a somewhat unfair and inadequate representation of his thought. If contemporary man has become what he is over time, then he cannot unclothe himself of the history that made him, he cannot "return to live in the forests with the bears" (113). But that which is not possible is also, for Rousseau, not desirable—hence, the necessity of a social contract.[118] Rousseau celebrates savage existence in the *Second Discourse* from a vantage point of melancholic reflection on the nature of contemporary European man. But modern man's degradation is not irreversible. The knowledge of his own perfectibility ensures that he cannot and will not want to return to the forests, while conscious agency, that expression of perfectibility, offers the optimism for change, for moral renewal. Both *Émile* and the *Social Contract* are variations on this theme.

### ADAPTATION AND AGENCY

If perfectibility is exclusive to man, so are the characteristics of adaptability and agency. Adaptability and agency, however, are not interchangeable terms. Rather, they delineate two stages in man's gradual progression to perfection. The ability to adapt to a changing environment and enter a more sophisticated stage of being is a trait that even the orangutans and wild men have in their possession. How else was the stage of noble savagery possible? Thus, original man is eventually forced to adapt to society through the acquisition of language or to a cold climate through hunting and killing for fur. Adaptability, therefore, is a form of instinctual agency. Crucially, it permits the savage to meet his immediate needs without requiring of him the future-oriented consciousness of foresight.

In contrast, agency is an expression of human perfection found only later in man's moral and social development. It is true that Rousseau distinguishes between animals en masse and man *en general* when he argues that the latter is capable of free agency, but at the moment of elaboration we discover that this agency presupposes a great deal more:

> Nature commands all animals, and the beast obeys. Man receives the same impulsion, but he recognizes himself as being free to acquiesce or resist; and it is above all in this *consciousness* of his freedom that the *spirituality* of his soul reveals itself, for physics explains in a certain way the mechanism of the senses and the formation of ideas, but in the power to will, or rather to choose, and in the *feeling of that power*, we see *pure spiritual activity*, of which the laws of mechanics explain nothing. (88; emphasis added)

If agency is that which is largely an instinctual adaptation in original man, even among the noble savage agency continues to hide under necessity, continues to be barely perceptible. Although a faint pride has emerged among Rousseau's noble savages, some traces of comparison, and thus individuation, can be gleaned. Some nascent sensibilities may be distinguishable; that same savage lives his independence and freedom as an *unconscious* truth, as an *unreflective* reality, for he knows no other against which to compare.

It is not until the emergence of agriculture that human agency, a conscious will, comes to be realized, for foresight is a contemplative condition unknown to the savage "who . . . is hard pressed to imagine in the morning the needs he will have in the evening" (117). Ultimately, the condition that the noble savage finds himself in is a product of chance and not of his own making. The contingencies of time and environment bear on him: floods, volcanoes, freezing climates, the separation of continents (113). Such freak occurrences of nature gave impetus to language and produced knowledge of fire and the invention of simple tools for hunting and fishing. In short, the cumulative effect of chance created the conditions "without which man would have remained forever in his primitive condition" (106), conditions that inevitably led man to emerge from an all but animal existence to the more noble status of savagery.

Thus, the "savages, who have almost always been found at this point of development" are at once a product of history and exist within historical time, yet they are neither the authors of their history nor the architects of their temporal condition. They simply are. The empirical "fact" of the Caribs and Hottentots is testimony to the existence of this stage of nature as much as the wildman/orangutan confirms the very origins of man. It is precisely the unconditional independence, the unqualified expression of pity, the unreflective happiness, and the unaffected and largely nascent sense of self that constitute both the source of Rousseau's valorization of natural man's condition and the necessity for its transcendence if human perfectibility is to arrive at its apex.

### BOURGEOIS MAN AND THE OWNERSHIP OF HISTORY

If conscious agency and human will are assets largely unknown to the noble savages, who precisely is in possession of such precious commodities? The economic metaphors are not irrelevant, for agency, in Rousseau's *Second Discourse*, is the currency of bourgeois man:

> But from the instant one man needed the help of another, and it was found to be useful for one man to have provisions for two, equality disappeared, property was introduced, work became necessary, vast forests were transformed into pleasant fields which had to be watered with the sweat of men, and where slavery and misery were soon to germinate and flourish with the crops.
>
> Metallurgy and agriculture were the two arts whose invention produced this great revolution. (116)

Prior to this stage, the natural elements created the imperatives of man's progress, for the savage was compelled toward gradual perfectibility as he gradually adapted to the dictates of a changed and changing environment. But nature gives way to human artifice at the very instant, the oft quoted moment, when "the first man who, having enclosed a piece of land, thought of saying 'This is mine' and found people simple enough to believe him" (109). It is in that moment that conscious agency, human will, and the *profits* of foresight are born. Agency is the twin of bourgeois man.

Thus, it is not until after the third stage of nature—with the emergence of metallurgy and agriculture, the subsequent acquisition of property, the unequal distribution of wealth, and the unjust division of labor—that man, for all his degradation, also comes to be equipped with "all our faculties developed, memory and imagination bought into play, pride stimulated, reason made active and the mind almost at the point of perfection of which it is capable" (118 ).

Yet how is it possible that a philosopher so consistently recognized as a critic of bourgeois society should simultaneously uphold it as the apex of human perfectibility, the realization of human agency? What the *Second Discourse* reveals is the extent to which Rousseau was trapped within the discourse of eighteenth-century political economy; that while resisting the material reality of its economic conditions, he could not exit an economy of language wherein agency presupposed ownership, production, rational foresight, individual consciousness, and the relinquishing of natural history's reign over the history of man. If property is born at that moment someone said, "This is mine," human history, as a product of human agency, is born at the moment it can be owned, when men can say, "We created the past; it is of our making."

It is not surprising that Rousseau should collapse the beginnings of property relations with the founding of the state,[119] that nature would be assigned the task of producing the noble savage while European man would be the instigator of that historical departure from the state of nature. Ultimately, by fusing the history of nature with the history of man Rousseau privileged natural history as the maker of man. Only later, when human perfectibility could be harnessed toward human agency, did history become the object of man's making.

And yet, Rousseau lamented that this very history that drove men to perfectibility was the same journey that led them toward their degradation. The degradation that Rousseau identified with his contemporary Europe—most notably, with Paris—was paradoxically the medium through which individual perfectibility could find expression. When Rousseau argued that the "almost unlimited faculty of man [for self-improvement] is the source of all his misfortunes" (88), he was not suggesting that perfectibility and corruption represented a moral fork on a well-traveled road, two independent byways. Rather, when we consider the tutor and Émile, the Legislator and the Citizen, the Rousseauian self and society (*Émile, Social Contract, Confessions,* and *Reveries,* respectively), what becomes apparent is that man can embody the authentic simplicity of the civilized savage only by presupposing—indeed, in complicit reference to—the degeneration of society and degradation of the self.[120] It was only against the backdrop of social pretensions, the ascendance of *amour propre,* and the slavish subjection to public opinion—it was only, in other words, with the transgression from nature—that man could return to his natural (perfected) self. It was no longer for nature to issue in a new stage for man (as it had done for the noble savage). Instead, it was man's ascendance over nature that equipped him with the agency to return to it: "Forced to combat either nature or society, you must make your choice between the man and the citizen, you cannot train both."[121]

"Make your choice," "train"—it was human intervention, the economy of production, that was being appealed to—the tutor and the legislator were the personification of human agency mobilized in the task of making an individual. Nature, that which had once authorized history and made man, was now itself subject to human fashioning. Whether one made man or made a citizen was a question now open to the contemplation of (bourgeois) European man.

### CONTESTED CONCEPTS AND COMPETING CULTURES

Yet if in Rousseau's inverted social criticism we ultimately witness a privileged European self, it is of a type radically different from that of the nineteenth century. Absent from Rousseau's writings is the exuberant confidence in Western sovereignty that was to set the tone and be the trademark of Hegelian philosophy and Darwinian science.

In so saying, I am not repeating the oft made claim that in Rousseau we see the prelude to Romanticism.[122] On the contrary: I am asserting Rousseau's affinity to the Enlightenment. The very malleability Rousseau ascribed to the concept of man, which ultimately made possible the history he traced in the *Second Discourse,* was not a tribute to Rousseau's exceptionalism but, rather, a reflection of a larger philosophical milieu in which all that pertained to man was also all that resisted definition, precision, and quantitative measurement.

This may appear at odds with the age of Linneaus and Buffon, with the age of Newtonian physics and the encyclopedia, yet it is precisely in this age that we encounter Rousseau's Caribs, Diderot's Tahitians, Montesquieu's Persians, and the China of Voltaire's imagination. How was it possible that the Caribs, Tahitians, Persians, and Chinese could be offered to a European public as objects of nostalgic longing, if not as models for emulation?

The inverted social criticism that has often been associated with Enlightenment philosophy was possible because the very fluidity of definition Rousseau ascribed to man was equally evident in the larger lexicon of Enlightenment thought. Whereas in the nineteenth century Hegelian history, Marxist political economy, and Darwinian evolution made it possible to measure men and quantify civilizations, in the eighteenth century concepts such as freedom, truth, liberty, the individual, reason, imagination, equality, nature, and, indeed, civilization were still free-floating, temporally contested categories. It was still possible to locate the individual in the New World, or civilization in China; to celebrate European ideals without incontestably valorizing Europe. It was still possible to ascribe to a European universalism without necessarily presupposing European origins.

Arguing the case that eighteenth-century conceptual categories were not yet anchored in nineteenth-century historicism or racial science does not imply that there was no continuity in the writings of Hobbes, Locke, and Rousseau. Indeed, where uniformity of thought exists between these three philosophers is in their identification of the New World with a state of nature inhabited by pre-political individuals. The specificity of geographical space is offset by a historical ambiguity. Located in divinely ordained rather than temporal time, the indigenous inhabitants of the New World are, if not entirely outside history (Hobbes), certainly devoid of historical agency. This is why they remain in that state, which Europe had long since surpassed.

I return, then, to the premise that informed the introduction of this chapter: that as illuminating as some recent scholarship has been to our understanding of the historical production of modern subjectivity, it also needs to scrutinize the production of history itself. In considering the writings of Hobbes and Locke, we find that their engagement with the question of time led to different conceptions of the self. Hobbes's failure to locate the individual self within a process in time ensured the absence of any reference to individuated identities. In contrast, the centrality of time to Locke's definition of the individual allowed for malleability in an understanding of the self that offered a sense of control and self-definition, but that also permitted the fashioning of a particular type of subjectivity in accordance with the liberal society Locke sought to defend. Such malleability, however, also presupposed the existence of errant subjectivities.

It is in Rousseau that time figures as the determining factor in the formation of the modern individual—a figure whose own sense of self follows the same trajectory as the universal history Rousseau traces. Thus, while Locke recognized that the malleability of the individual found its locus in the child, a potential rationality that could be subjected to a process of fashioning, Rousseau appropriated childhood as a metaphor for humanity itself. Rousseau's history produced, in its turn, Rousseauian individuals whose sense of self was far more complex, opaque, multidimensional, and psychologically tortured than the free, equal, and rational individuals we encountered in Hobbes's and Locke's state of nature and civil society, respectively.

Despite all of the crucial differences that distinguish the thought of the three contractarians with which I have engaged in this chapter, it is fair to say in conclusion that the story of the social contract was, and continues to be, a celebration of Europe's emergence as a historical subject where the covenant of grace was displaced by a contract between men, and where order, meaning, purpose, and history were no longer deemed the gifts of divinity but the inspirational artifice of human agency.

Yet if Europe could emerge as a historical subject when positing itself in contrast to the New World, to a state where nature and man had not yet been estranged, how could it maintain the superiority of its historical authorship in the face of India? The representational foliage of the New World through the seventeenth century and much of the eighteenth century was that of a state of nature inhabited by individuals. India inspired a radically different repertoire of images. From a-historical nature to civilizational antiquity, from recent discoveries to ancient Greek sources, from individual wanderings to caste rigidity, and from unimpeded freedom to Oriental despotism, the representational tropes that demarcated the Indian of the New World from the Indian of the subcontinent necessitated not only a pluralization of difference but a reconceptualization of identity. Paradoxically, plurality was made possible through the codification of languages, the uniformity of history, and the law of racialized science. It is to these concerns that I now turn.

# 3 Traditions of History

## MAPPING INDIA'S PAST

ABBÉ RAYNAL'S five-volume *A Philosophical and Political History of the Settlement of Trade of the Europeans in the East and West Indies* is, as the title suggests, concerned with European commercial interests and interactions with the newly founded colonies. Yet through the pages of these interminable volumes, Raynal provides much in the way of description and commentary on the native Indians and indigenous Americans. The volumes abound with hyperbole on the antiquity of Indian civilization (with equal amounts of criticism regarding caste, Oriental despotism, and heathen superstitions) alongside (in the third, fourth, and fifth volumes) observations on the savagery of indigenous Americans.

Hence, while "the Indians appear to have been the first who received the rudiments of science and the Polish of civilisation," Raynal speculates on "what an interesting and constructive spectacle" the New World would have been "for a Locke, a Buffon or a Montesquieu."[1] He describes the Americas as "a vast continent entirely uncultivated, human nature reduced to the mere animal state, fields without harvests, treasure without proprietors, societies without policy, and men without manners."[2]

William Robertson, an English historian, also produced histories of India and the Americas, although unlike Raynal's they took the form of two distinct works. Robertson's *History of America* was a three-volume work that began with the discovery of the continent and ended with the settlement by the English.[3] This work was followed in 1818 by *An Historical Disquisition Concerning Ancient India*. While the two works were not necessarily written as complementary texts, the contrasting representations of the indigenous Americans and the native Indians are immediately apparent. Robertson arrived at the same conclusion as Raynal (whose work he cites with generous praise), which was to bestow immense antiquity and high civilization on India while locating the native Americans in a state of nature. In *An Historical Disquisition*, Robertson contrasts the immediate European reaction to the discovery of the New World with the sea-route discovery of Asia:

> When the Portuguese first visited the different countries of Asia, stretching from the coast of Malabar to China, they found them possessed by nations highly civilised, which had made considerable progress in elegant as well as useful arts, which were accustomed to intercourse with strangers, and well acquainted with all the advantages of commerce. But when the Spaniards began to explore the New World, which they discovered, the aspect which it presented to them was very different. The islands were inhabited by naked savages, so unacquainted with the simplest and most necessary arts of life, that they subsisted chiefly on the spontaneous productions of a fertile soil and gentle climate. The continent appeared to be a forest of immense extent, alongside the coast of which were scattered some feeble tribes, not greatly superior to the islanders in industry and improvement. Even its two large monarchies [Inca and Aztec] which have been dignified with the appellation of civilised states, had not advanced so far beyond their countrymen, as to be entitled to that name.[4]

From the work of historians, we turn to the parliamentary politics of Edmund Burke, who defended Indian civilization by contrasting it with that of the indigenous Americans:

> This multitude of men [subcontinental Indians] does not consist of an abject and barbarous populace; much less gangs of savages, like the Guaranies and Chiquitos, who wander on the waste borders of the river of Amazons . . . but a people for ages civilised and cultivated; cultivated by all the arts of polished life, whilst we were yet in the woods.[5]

So what is it that distinguishes the Indians from their American counterparts; that deems them "civilized" rather than "savage"? The Indians, Burke argues, possess an "antient and venerable priesthood . . . a nobility of great antiquity and renown; a multitude of cities," not to mention a large population, commerce, and merchant and banking houses that "once vied in capital with the Bank of England."[6]

The significance of Raynal's, Robertson's, and Burke's juxtaposition of the Americas and India lies not in the litany of characteristics said to demarcate savagery from civilization—after all, there is nothing new in Burke's privileging of the settled *polis* over nomadic society. Indeed, it could even be argued that what appears at first glance to be a series of contrasting descriptions between the New World and India offers no contrast at all. That is, the opposition presented between the inhabitants of the New World and the natives of India is somewhat deceptive when we recognize that, albeit at different times, the positive evaluation of both the Amerindians and the Indians was predicated on a belief in their respective status as a source of origins. Whereas the indigenous Americans were the embodiment of man in the state of nature, the Indians represented the civilizational antiquity of humanity. If the Amerindians offered a portrait of man as nature made him—man untouched by time, uncorrupted by false morals, and unscathed by civilization deceits—India appeared to be fast displacing the ancient Greek and Roman worlds as the watering hole of human history.

Despite the apparent continuities, something peculiarly different can be discerned in the gradual demise of the New World as the favorite son of the seventeenth century and eighteenth century and the simultaneous emergence of India as the site of European speculation and discourse. What can be discerned is a shift in European discourse that speaks to more than just the transience of philosophical fads. If, for the Classical period, the New World spoke to pre-social man, to a universal human nature that transcended time and was unencumbered by historical memory, the appeal of India lay in its temporality—time as it presented itself through the antiquity of ancient texts, the observance of ancient traditions, the ruins of ancient monuments, and the perseverance of ancient living languages.

It is, of course, true that according authority to, and acknowledging admiration for, antiquity was not a new-fangled product of the late eighteenth century. What makes such appeals to history significant is that they were being articulated within the framework of a newly emerging epistemology.

Whereas in the seventeenth century and eighteenth century, European representations of difference were articulated in relation to a predetermined typology of Man (identified through universal traits such as reason, freedom, rights, individuals, and human nature), by the late eighteenth century Man gives way to men—a breathless parade of human difference fashioned out of the particularity of history, tradition, language, and race. In other words, in the Classical period difference was construed as a deviation from the universal norm; in the nineteenth century, we witness the emergence of a style of reasoning that presumes distinction in its very categories of analysis. Thus, for example, the faith in the singularity of reason is by no means discarded, but in the nineteenth century reason is not an attribute of man *qua* man but the hard-won consequence of particular histories, races, and cultures.

It is in an effort to pursue this larger claim that leads me, in this chapter and the next, to focus on the emergence of historicism and physiological science, for history and the body proved to be two crucial sites through which difference was rendered knowable in the nineteenth century. The body is the subject of the next chapter.

This chapter is concerned with history, or, more specifically, with the production of historical discourse—in terms of its disciplining, as well as of the pervasive impact historicism was to have on European knowledge more generally—through the course of the nineteenth century. But there is an immediate problem here. As a number of postcolonial scholars have argued, tracing European representations of difference through the conduit of nineteenth-century conceptions of history reveals only that much of the colonial world was rendered history-less.[7] In other words, focusing exclusively on the production of historical discourse as a conduit for European representations of difference elides an integral part of the story—namely, the historicity of the very categories through which the non-West was rendered historically irrelevant.

One such category that helped to distinguish the historical West from its other was tradition. Whereas Europe possessed history, the colonies could claim only traditions—traditions that petrified the past and obstructed historical progress. It is neither a coincidence nor a matter of indifference that those people designated "traditional" (as opposed to "historical") were colonial subjects. Colonialism, in short, was a crucial site on which the contours of tradition and history gradually came to take their present form. Colonialism helped to inform and shape European conceptions of history and tradition while colonized societies were simultaneously being defined, organized, and distinguished through the very same categories. Consequently, to trace how history became a vehicle for European representations of difference entails pursuing a second, interrelated line of inquiry: How did tradition (a concept that is rendered meaningful only in reference to the past) come to be not only distinguished from but also radically opposed to history? Pursuing this question requires not only subjecting tradition to historical inquiry but recognizing that the very history that presumes tradition as its object relies, for its own self-definition, on distinguishing itself from tradition. It is only by untangling the shared, mutually constitutive history of history and tradition that we can appreciate the peculiar distinction that was born out of the nineteenth century: the distinction between historical subjects and traditional peoples.

Given the multiple layers of my argument, it is necessary to describe the trajectory of this chapter. Employing colonial India (for reasons I will turn to shortly) as the site for European debates about history and tradition, the first section of this chapter not only traces the emergence of a Romantic-inspired conception of both of these concepts but also argues that in the late eighteenth century and early nineteenth century, the particularity of a people's traditions was seen as essential to gaining access to and narrating a people's history. Tradition, in other words, was broadly recognized as an accomplice to historical inquiry; it was a necessary ally in the production of historical writing. This confluence between history and tradition comes to be transformed into a language of opposition from the 1820s on. Thus, the second section is concerned with the ways in which both history and tradition come to be reconceptualized so that the customs of India were posited as the source of India's lack of history. But, as I argue in the third section, if the distinction between tradition and history becomes so pervasive as to be virtually naturalized into common sense, by the late nineteenth century a curious development complicates this narrative. The disciplining of history in the 1830s may have contributed to the divorcing of history and tradition, but the pervasiveness of historicism ensured that, by the late nineteenth century, the traditions of the colonies had been imbued with a certain significance precisely because, within a graduated, progressive history, the colonial present was temporally located in the European past. The reverberations from, and familiar echoes of, the nineteenth-century distinction between history and tradition remain with us today—the subject of the conclusion.

In tracing the alliance, ambivalence, and antagonism between the discourses of history and tradition, I seek to offer more than just the history of two concepts. I hope to illustrate how a particular style of reasoning that presumed difference as its foundation of thought could, for that very reason, render history as the peculiar preserve of the West. That this is a particularly strange turn of events becomes apparent when we consider that it was partly the antiquity of India's civilization that inspired the Oriental Renaissance of the late eighteenth century and early nineteenth century.

## India and the Oriental Renaissance

While Robertson was adding an "appendix" to *Historical Disquisition* to "clearly demonstrate, that the natives of India were not only more early civilized, but had made greater progress in civilization than any other people," the French historian Abbé Raynal was bestowing on India "laws, civil government, and arts; whilst the rest of the earth was desert and savage."[8] Voltaire, in turn, was promoting the Brahmans as "the first teachers of the human race," their traditions "the most ancient thing we know on earth."[9] Wilhelm von Schlegel pronounced India the "actual source of all languages, all the thoughts and poems of the human spirit; everything, everything without exception comes from India."[10] Johann Gottfried von Herder went even further, proclaiming that "all the peoples of Europe . . . [were] [f]rom Asia;" and Edmund Burke felt it necessary to reproach the arrogance of his countrymen, for "God forbid we should pass judgment upon a people who formed their laws and institutions prior to our insect origins of yesterday."[11] For Raynal, Robertson, Burke, Schlegel, Herder, and Voltaire, antiquity and civilization were virtually interchangeable—it is as if the temporal expanse and longevity of a given culture operated as an index for measuring its civilization status. Indeed, so pervasive does this conceptual configuration appear to have been that Hegel felt obliged to insist, "We must banish from our minds the prejudice in favor of duration, as if it had any advantage as compared with transience."[12]

The recognition of India's antiquity was nothing new. India had long been part of the European imagination, a fabled land populated by gold-seeking ants and human monsters. All of this, of course, was equally true of Egypt, China, and Japan. However, what distinguished India and ensured it pride of place among European men and women of letters was the discovery, by William Jones, of Sanskrit's linguistic affinity with ancient Greek and Latin. It was not simply individual words that contained familiar echoes but the very syntax and structure of Sanskrit that promised possibilities of a shared origin somewhere in the distant past. This was the thesis that Jones laid out when he argued in *Third Discourse*:

> The *Sanscrit* language, whatever be its antiquity, is of a wonderful struc-
> ture; more perfect than the *Greek*, more copious than the *Latin* and more
> exquisitely refined than either; yet bearing to both of them a stronger af-
> finity, both in the roots of verbs, and in the forms of grammar, than
> could possibly have been produced by accident; so strong, indeed, that no
> philologer could examine them all three, without believing them to have
> sprung from some common source, which perhaps, no longer exists."[13]

It was this possibility that enthralled and captured the imagination of European philosophers, novelists, colonial officials, and the broader reading
public. In a series of articles published in *Asiatic Researches*, Jones not only
argued for the superiority of Sanskrit's linguistic structure to that of Greek
and Latin, but also insisted on the greater antiquity of Sanskrit compared
with Europe's most ancient languages. Jones's speculative history—one
that, albeit in qualified form, remained influential long after his death—was
that while the centuries-old effort to recover the lost language of Adam was
a hopeless task (God's original language having been lost to man after the
fall of the Tower of Babel), the antiquity of Sanskrit appeared to place it
as the closest living relation to, and the least corrupted of, man's original
tongue. Thus, Jones secured for India a privileged place in mosaic history:
Man may not have originated in India, but it is there that the vestiges of his
ancient origins continued to be preserved.

Coterminous with Jones's elaborate thesis and another reason for Europe's love affair with India was the discovery and translation of ancient
Sanskrit texts. From poetry to philosophy, mathematics to astronomy, the
European reading public was exposed to a literature that it hitherto had
been unaware of, provoking what Raymond Schwab has aptly described as
an "Oriental Renaissance" not dissimilar to the earlier European encounter

with ancient Greek and Roman sources.[14] Indeed, the analogy was not lost on contemporaries, with Schlegel suggesting that "Indian study and research in general should be pursued with the grander views and opinions of those able men of the fifteenth and sixteenth centuries, who first revived the study of Greek and Eastern literature."[15]

Indeed, parallels between European antiquity and that of India became part of the conversational currency of the late eighteenth century and early nineteenth century. This was true not only in the context of philology but also in the areas of literature and science. Warren Hastings, for example, described the *Mahabharata* as equal in literary status to the *Iliad* and the *Odyssey*.[16] Jones was in full agreement, suggesting further that while India had long been recognized as the source of such inventions as "the method of instruction by Apologues; the decimal scale, adopted now by all civilized nations; and the game of chess," a full inventory of Indians' works "on grammar, logic, rhetoric, music" would reveal "higher pretensions to the praise of a fertile and inventive genius."[17] Such high praise gradually came to be disseminated to a large European reading public through the establishment of the Asiatic Society of Bengal (1789) and the publication of its journal, *Asiatic Researches* (the first volume was published in 1789). It was further fueled by Charles Wilkins's translations of the *Bhagavad Gita* (1785) and Jones's publication in English (from the original Sanskrit) of Kalidas's play *Sakuntala* (1789), which, by the end of the nineteenth century, had run into twenty-one editions with more than eighty translations.[18]

Collectively, the inherited mythology surrounding the discovery of Sanskrit's linguistic ties to ancient Greek and Latin, the elaborately woven inclusion of India in Old Testament history, and the enthusiastic European reception to Sanskrit literature all worked to ensure that Asia generally, and India specifically, were a favorite subject of salon conversation, scholarly praise, and literary admiration.

All of this is not to imply that there was a complete absence of critical commentary on India's history and its people in the late eighteenth century and early nineteenth century.[19] What it does suggest is that whether the opinions of India were celebratory, favorable, or judgmental, the antiquity of Indian civilization and the extent of its early achievements were generally allowed. Even the evangelist reformer Charles Grant, one of the most formidable early critics of India's religions and customs, nevertheless felt obliged to acknowledge (albeit in a footnote) that "though the character of the Hindoos be in a moral view now low, the development of their litera-ture, their mythology, and science, has been a great desideratum in human knowledge and must prove of eminent importance to mankind."[20]

Because India's privileged status in late-eighteenth-century and early-nineteenth-century European thought was in large part due to its pro-claimed antiquity, it is a curious fact that contemporary postcolonial scholars agree, in a rare instance of academic consensus, that India in the nineteenth-century European imagination was rendered historically empty. That is, India before the British era was an India deemed to be devoid of history.

How could India be lauded for its antiquity, be recognized for its ancient traditions, and scoured for its ancient literature, while simultaneously fail-ing to have a history? The most common explanation offered by contempo-rary scholars points to the colonial distinction drawn between indigenous knowledge of the past and what was understood as history proper. The un-derwriting premise guiding their work is that Europe drew a sharp distinc-tion between that which constituted history and that which lay under the rubric of antiquity: tradition and the past. Thus, India could be recognized to possess an ancient civilization and observe longstanding customs—be permitted, in other words, to boast a past—without thereby presuming to have a history.

There is much evidence to support such a conclusion. Indeed, I will be returning to these sources later in the chapter. Yet while I am sympathetic to the thesis that nineteenth-century Europe posited history in opposition to non-Western conceptions of the past, what is in danger of being lost in this seemingly incontestable formulation is the fact that European concep-tions of history have had their own historicity. Not only had European un-derstandings of history undergone radical revisions over the centuries, but each consecutive articulation revealed how a given period configured, or-ganized, and presumed particular understandings of truth produced from within specific knowledge regimes. If India, like much of the colonial world, was pronounced a-historical, such a conclusion was possible only because nineteenth-century history was refashioned in accordance with a more fun-damental epistemological transformation. Appreciating this fact becomes possible if we posit late-eighteenth-century and early-nineteenth-century conceptions of history and the epistemology that bore it against the back-drop of that which had come before and, thus, that which it displaced.[21]

The seventeenth century and eighteenth century, no less than the Renaissance that preceded them, sought to engage with unfamiliar worlds. They did so, moreover, not through a process of estrangement (irrevocably detaching the other from the self ), but by parenthesizing difference, by reducing difference to a position that was subservient and indebted to identity.

This is not, however, to deny the fact that innumerable and radical differences existed between the sixteenth century and what, following Foucault, I will refer to as the Classical period (the seventeenth century and eighteenth century).[22] Confronted with the Americas, the Renaissance sought to absorb and absolve the differences between the New World and its own by immersing the unknown into a lexicon of familiar signs, biblical stories, ancient wisdom, and ubiquitous folklore. Through similitude, the frighteningly new was reassuringly embraced into worlds of recognition and commensurability. God's truth was left unscathed; ancient wisdom was preserved. While the discovery of an Atlantic continent exceeded familiar horizons, it did not necessitate transgressing knowledge itself. The New World was enfolded into a familiar world of textual references and biblical truths. In short, the immediate reverberations that followed the discovery of the New World neither enhanced nor undermined Renaissance forms of knowledge.

Later generations would speak of the discovery of the Americas as a defining historical moment; for the Renaissance, however, it offered itself as another surface of text abounding with the signatory marks that made recognition possible. The beings that wandered over the terrain of this newly found continent; the flora that colored its landscape; the waters, mountains, deserts, and plains that mapped its contours; and the sky that stretched toward its horizon were all bearers of familiar signs that nestled unobtrusively among a familiar repertoire of resemblances.

It was this detailed symmetry between words, objects, and beings wherein all God's Creation was interlocked and harmoniously balanced within a pre-existing and divine order that constituted the very essence of Renaissance epistemology. And it was this epistemology that governed the writing of history during the period. While the Renaissance has long been recognized as the era that introduced a new appreciation for secular time (exemplified by the invention of the clock), Anthony Grafton is right to emphasize the extent to which biblical chronology still dominated Renaissance understandings of temporality. The famous Strasbourg clock is a case in point:

> The Strasbourg clock consisted not only of modern mechanical devices, but also traditional emblems and paintings. One set of these divided time into the great scenes of Christian drama: Creation, Original Sin, Redemption, Resurrection, Last Judgement. Another cut secular time into the four empires of traditional apocalyptic prophecy: Assyria, Persia, Greece and Rome. On the top of the smaller tower, a statue of a pelican symbolized Christ, the Redeemer and eternity. Dasypodius's work, in short, was not simply a display of the powers of modern science and technology; it was also a miniature cathedral of its own, in which the pious visitor could read the most traditional lessons of the past, the present and the (rather abbreviated) future of the human race.[23]

Moreover, if it is true that merchant life in the sixteenth century was increasingly governed by an almost religious observance of secular time, it is equally true that in this same period we witness the unprecedented popularity of astrology. Scores of works by numerous authors versed in the art of reading the stars and planets sought to reveal to mortal men their futures on Earth.[24] Thus, whether one evoked the history of the world or sought to prophesize the fate of individual men, it was biblical and ancient learning that demarcated the boundaries of time—be it the past, the present, or the future.

It was precisely this way of being, seeing, engaging with, and living in the world that was to unravel through the course of the seventeenth century. The quest to discover the intricacies of God's plan through the signs He bestowed on all of Creation was gradually abandoned once arbitrary chaos, rather than a divine order, were deemed the legacy left to mortal beings following the sin of Eve and the arrogance at Babel. By the close of the seventeenth century, God had ceased to be the organizing principle that bestowed order and meaning on the world. In the debris that remained following the irrevocable break between the Word and the object, order and meaning had now to be *assigned* rather than discovered. It was no longer divine inscription that revealed meaning but the artificiality of human categories and organizing principles that *bestowed* meaning. Therein lies the significance of Hobbes, Locke, and Rousseau: It was the collective sum of individuals that could make such order possible, for it was through their agency that civil society and state would be created, and history itself invented.

Classificatory lists organized around the principle of identity and difference freed objects, words, and beings from the circular regime of resemblance, only to reconstitute them within a series of categories and subcategories of delineation. If Renaissance epistemology can be visually represented as infinite layers of spiraling rings, the spiral by the late seventeenth century had gradually been ironed out into a flat, squared table. Beings, objects, and words relinquished the privileged autonomy their individual marks had bestowed on them when in the Classical period they were reordered, tabulated, and classified within a relational economy. Identity was now relative.[25]

The most pronounced example of this classificatory-based epistemology can be observed in the literature on natural history that flourished during the seventeenth century and eighteenth century. Whereas in the sixteenth century a plant could be identified by the individual markings that were imprinted on its very being, by the late 1600s—and, most notably, in the eighteenth century—it was not signatures but comparative structures that determined the affinity or distinction between each genus and species of vegetation. Taxonomies organized around structural identities and delineation dispensed with the need for such descriptive variables as color, scent, taste, or moral/medical attributes. Thus, in 1678 the English naturalist John Ray wrote of his determination (and that of his friend and co-author, Francis Willoughby) to "wholly omit what we find in other authors concerning . . . hieroglyphics, emblems, morals, fables, presages or aught else appertaining to divinity, ethics, grammar or any sort of human learning; and present . . . only what properly relates to natural history."[26]

Some fifty years later, Linnaeus was not only espousing a universally applicable system whereby plants could be classified according to their structural affinities and variations. He was also calling for a restricted nomenclature to ensure that the identity of each plant was systematically reduced to its genus and species, to the exclusion of normative descriptions such as moral attributes and unreliable variables such as taste, scent, or color.[27]

The cryptogram had given way to the catalogue.

The catalogue had displaced the cryptogram by the late seventeenth century not only within the confines of natural history, as in the works of Ray, Linnaeus, and Buffon, but in all areas of study. Rousseau may have been a student of botany and an avid taxonomist, but he was also, more famously, a student of *humanitas*. While the act of tabulating, categorizing, classifying, differentiating, and comparing was appealed to by the naturalist, it reflected more generally on an epistemology that, having disinherited the sign of divine articulation, sought ontological expression through the act of representation—that is, through the function of naming, bestowing meaning, and ordering the world of objects, beings, and things.

As with the world of nature, taxonomies of peoples and customs were classified and tabulated during the eighteenth century. Charles de Secondat Montesquieu's *The Spirit of the Laws* is a classic case in point, in which the mores, laws, government, and environment of Europe and non-European peoples were systematically collated, listed, and classified.[28] Linnaeus's efforts to extend the limits of his taxonomy from nature to man, Buffon's subclassification of man into semi-racialized groups, and Diderot's and d'Alembert's efforts to systematize all knowledge within the pages of an *Encyclopédie* provide further illustration.[29]

Yet while Montesquieu's detailed attention to difference between nations irritated Voltaire's universalism,[30] the fact remains that Classical thought relied for its enunciation on the premise of identity, from which point shades of delineation could then be observed and noted. Whether, as with Linnaeus, one sought to extract differences by first identifying affinities,[31] or, as with Rousseau, one began by clearing the shrubbery of differences to dramatize human nature in all its totality and with its taken-for-granted assumptions,[32] the exercise was ultimately the same: It was from the threshold of identity that differences between entities could be represented and ordered.[33]

From this point of departure it was possible, then, to proceed with a compilation of lists that were both static and a-historical, such as those provided by Linnaeus in the branch of natural history and, to a large extent, by Montesquieu in the area of human geography. However, it was equally true that this same classificatory system was malleable to temporality, if temporality is understood not as a developmental or progressive history but as a sequential mapping of time.

A popular and often repeated interpretation of the Classical period is the one that regards the seventeenth century and eighteenth century as enlightened, perhaps, yet thoroughly indifferent to the study of history. Such a representation is not, of course, without justification. We need only remember the pervasive authority of mechanistic philosophy;[34] David Hume's insistence that man remains the same throughout history;[35] Voltaire's disdain for any historical period that he deemed to be "unenlightened";[36] and Burke's denunciation of first-principle philosophy in the wake of the French Revolution—the powerful sense of breaking from the past captured in such symbolic gestures as the secularization of the calendar year that marked 1789 as Year One, or the decimalization of the Parisian clock to concur with rational scientific principles.[37]

And yet, as Carl Becker argued so many decades ago, it is a strange fact that the Enlightenment so commonly associated with first-principle philosophy also housed so many historians (Gibbon, Voltaire, Herder, Hume, Raynal, and Robertson, to name only a few) and produced so many commentaries on what history was, what it should be, and why it was relevant.[38] It is not the case that the seventeenth century and eighteenth century were unfettered by a consciousness of history, but neither is it the case that in the works of Gibbon, Hume, or Voltaire we can glean an embryonic history that was to reach maturity under the nineteenth-century tutelage of Leopold von Ranke, Jules Michelet, or Thomas Babington Macaulay.

Contrary to these two representations of the Classical period, I would suggest that when the seventeenth century and eighteenth century evoked the past, it was a past temporally conceived, fashioned, and restrained within Classical epistemology. In other words, Classical history accorded with— indeed, was a temporal extension of—the taxonomic table. History offered a sequential space within which objects, words, and beings could be ordered within a series, their location determined by their spatial positioning within time. In short, Classical history bore little resemblance to the historicist turn that so deeply engraved the intellectual life of the nineteenth century.

Historicism, Georg Iggers argues, is "a comprehensive philosophy of life which views all social reality as an historical stream where no two instances are comparable and which assumes that value standards and logical categories, too, are totally immersed in the stream of history."[39]

D. D. Runes's *Dictionary of Philosophy* elaborates on this definition by expanding it to include not only the study of human society, but also a way of reasoning that enveloped, and that included, everything. Historicism is "the view that the history of anything is a sufficient explanation of it, that the values of anything can be accounted for through the discovery of its origins, that the nature of anything is entirely comprehended by its development."[40]

In the Classical period, however, the epistemological mantra was not that everything could and must be historicized but, rather, that everything could and must be classified. History no less than nature, peoples, customs, laws, or governments was malleable to tabulation. Alongside the geographical map and taxonomies of nature resided the horizontal space of the continuum within which anything, from diverse cultures to the reign of kings, was plotted not to construct a graduated history but to compare and contrast. This is why Condorcet could argue that one should collect a select body of facts "from the history of different peoples, compare them and combine them in order to extract the hypothetical history of a single people and to compose the picture of its progress."[41]

The compilation of lists, as Condorcet's preferred method of writing history, needs to be distinguished from the long-established practice of recording the past through the chronicle. Indeed, much of the disparaging commentary leveled against the subject of history during the Classical period was in reaction to this very mode of historical writing. Thus, when Voltaire coined the phrase "philosophical history," he was probably responding to the Marquise du Châtelet's complaint that the study of history seemed to demand the memorizing of much useless information. As a list of dates and facts, it was argued, history as chronicle did not discriminate between that which was relevant and informative and that which was simply an unreflective litany of kings and conquests.[42]

Thus, the common refrain of the eighteenth century was that history, no less than nature (following Buffon's critique of Linnaeus), must rise above the mediocrity of the particular to engage with the general. As a recording of reigns and dates, history had little to recommend itself as an object of inquiry. The study of history was relevant not because the past was a sacred monument to posterity or because historicism was the means to comprehension, but because, in its utilitarian garb, history could function as an index that rendered differences and similarities visible. In its new Classical guise, history had multiple uses.

First, history gave empirical expression to philosophical meditation. In other words, the study of the past was philosophy by example.[43] Most notably, one could appeal to history to demonstrate the historically resistant temerity of a priori truths. Thus, for example, Voltaire's forays into history were not simply an engagement with methodology, a conscious effort to insert certain rules of scholarship into the study of past events (accuracy of details, nonpartisan interpretation of the facts, and a discriminating distinction between the "relevant" and "inconsequential,") but an engagement with philosophy that sought beyond all else to reveal the underlying laws that the history of men bought to the surface—universal laws that persistently washed onto the sand despite the waves of historical time.[44]

Other philosophers, torn between a mechanistic philosophy devoid of moral anchorage and a humanist philosophy desperate to assert man's rational and moral agency,[45] turned to natural man (not Adam but Amerindian) for some insight into the a priori condition, and thus universal nature, of human beings. It was precisely for this reason that the language of origins loomed so large in Classical thought: Revealing man's original condition also revealed that which was intrinsic to his nature, that which resisted the fashioning of time.[46] This was not the origin that Darwin was later to evoke, which relied on a genealogical history of biological evolution, but an original (a priori) condition in which natural men, governed by natural laws, existed within natural (pre-)time.

The popularity of the "state of nature" trope, a popularity not restricted to contract theory (even the French historian Raynal and the English historian Robertson evoked the state of nature in their accounts of the Amerindians), was due in large measure to the conviction that those who resided in nature resided outside time. From this basic premise, it was then possible to argue that native Americans embodied that which was intrinsic to human nature before that nature was artificially reinscribed by the introduction of laws, government, and the intemperate moods of history.

Even philosophers who did not engage with such imaginative reconstructions foraged through history for evidence of the immutable laws that governed human nature. Even a skeptic such as Hume, who in a now famous footnote spoke so disparagingly of Africans, could on another occasion insist that "mankind are so much the same in all times and places" that history's "use is only to discover the constant and universal principles of human nature."[47] Almost counterintuitively, it was history that was appealed to in order to reveal that which it could not expunge: laws that resisted and transcended historical time.

But the study of history had a second function. Having retrieved history from the irrelevance of the chronicle, having classified and ordered the past within the broader schematic of philosophy, this revised, tabulated, and ordered history could now be cross-listed with the adjacent taxonomies of nature, nations, peoples, customs, governments, morals, and laws. Thus, if Montesquieu could cross-list nations, laws, and environments, and if, in Rousseau's oeuvre, the Golden Age could be located equally in the society of the noble savage and in the patriarchal utopia of *La Nouvelle Héloise*, then it is not unreasonable that Voltaire's Louis XIV would coexist, under the sign of rationality, with China's bureaucratic meritocracy, or that Hume could praise the superiority of the ancient Germans to contemporary Africans.[48]

"A-historical"—that academic expletive of the modern age—was not the intellectual sin in the Classical period that it was to become. Classical history accorded a certain disconnected freedom between the contemporary present and the past that preceded it. It permitted one to browse through the corridors of the past without being entangled in its webs and infused with its odors. As a vat of examples in the service of philosophy, it was not required of history to be restrained by its affiliation to the past. Rather, it was required to provide its own taxonomy, which, like those of nature, customs, or laws (and often in concert with them), offered yet another means for discerning identity and difference. Most notably, the past was evoked to distinguish between the rational and the irrational, the savage and the civilized, the free and the un-free, superstition and science, and all the shades of distinction that colored the terrain between these polar extremes. In this respect Classical history was little different from Montesquieu's cultural geography: It merely extracted from the depths of the past an echo of what contemporary governments, laws, and customs bear witness to today. Thus, if Voltaire had contempt for the Middle Ages, it was not so much a historical period that aroused his disdain as the irrationality and superstition it embodied. In truth, for Voltaire the Middle Ages and the eighteenth century Catholic church were interchangeable.

Finally, history in the Classical period performed a third function—one that sought to reconceptualize time as a continuum, a constant backdrop against which identities and differences were rendered not only visible but explicable. In this garb, time provided a circular function. It offered a sequential space on which objects and beings could be plotted within a series while, at the same time, temporality could be evoked to justify the serial location of a given object or being. Thus, for Buffon the absence of civilization and the degree of savagery among Amerindian tribes was a direct consequence of the geological "newness" (read, immaturity) of the American continent.[49] The indigenous Americans, therefore, were positioned closer to the starting point on the grid, while the purported antiquity of geographical Europe (and thus its civilization superiority) accorded it a space farther along in the sequence. Similarly, Rousseau's distinction between the first and third stage of nature—man as animal and man as noble savage—was possible through the temporalization of the chain of being. Whereas the former marked the beginning of time, the latter was plotted somewhere in the middle of the series.[50]

If it appears that this last conception of history is closer to the one we identify with nineteenth-century thought, the resemblance is more apparent than real. Living beings are imposed on the landscape of time rather than figuring as products of history, as entities capable of being historicized. Thus, when Buffon speaks of the puma as a malformed, immature version of the lion,[51] he refers to the effects of both time and geography, but time, no less than geography, is conceptualized as a spatial backdrop within which to locate the relative positioning of the puma alongside other felines. What is absent is any reference to organic transformations, to evolutionary history where life itself, and not just living beings, is subjected to—indeed, is a product of—historical time.

What ultimately underwrites the Classical engagement with history—be it natural or cultural, about plants or people—is the continued commitment to universal first-principle philosophy. While time may affect the world of objects, words, and beings, these same entities nevertheless predate history. That over time the world has come to be saturated with so many different tongues does not undermine the a priori character of speech as the utilitarian offspring of human interaction.[52] Similarly, geography, history, and customs may shape the individual, but the a priori existence of this lone figure is undisputed. It is for this very reason that the Classical period reveals no hesitation in positing the individual anywhere in the world at any point in time. It is for this reason that Hobbes, Locke, and Rousseau could posit the individual in a New World state of nature. Locke's anxiety and Rousseau's prescript of perfectibility only complicated this figure by locating him within a process. What remained a brute truth was that the brute individual had always existed.

It was this logic that began to unravel in the late eighteenth century. This is not to say that nineteenth-century thinkers simply dispensed with the familiar lexicon of universals—reason, freedom, individual, speech—but that these attributes were now subject to the forces of history. Speech may be a universal trait possessed by all of humanity, but Herder invested language with historical and cultural particularity. Faith in the singularity of reason was not diminished, but for someone like Hegel, reason was something that Man had to strive for—it was the product of, not the condition for, historical progress. So was the individual. Far from populating the distant shores of the Americas, the individual was a latent subjectivity that found expression only through the particularity of European history, whether that was the Renaissance (Jacob Burkhardt) or the history of contract-based jurisprudence (Henry Sumner Maine). The individual for Burkhardt and Maine, but also for Hegel and John Stuart Mill, was the exclusive product of European history, a figure who, in the colonies of Asia and Africa, remained servile to the group and unconscious of an individuated identity.

### ROMANTIC HISTORY

It is this attention to particularity, grounded in historical specificity, that figures as one of the defining contributions of Romanticism to nineteenth-century thought. Whereas in the Classical period, difference was the empirical residue that stained the universal principles of reason, in the nineteenth century, reason, while still posited as universal, was entirely colored by (could only find its mode of expression through) its reference to the particular. In other words, history in its modern guise was made possible because of a prior epistemic shift in which the Classical emphasis on identity was displaced by a style of reasoning that presumed difference as a condition of knowledge production. This epistemic shift could be observed over a number of different sites. Take, for example, Lorraine Daston's and Peter Galison's study of objectivity.[53]

Focusing their research on medical atlases produced through the course of the eighteenth century and nineteenth century, Daston and Galison point to the fact that eighteenth-century reproductions of the human body acquired their scientific status by how closely they emulated nature in its ideal form (the determination of which was part of the authority invested in the scientist): "In eighteenth-century atlases, 'typical' phenomena were those that hearkened back to some underlying Typus or 'archetype,' and from which individual phenomena could be derived, at least conceptually. The typical is rarely if ever embodied in a single individual; nonetheless, the researcher can intuit it from cumulative experience."[54]

In contrast, in the nineteenth-century understanding of scientific objectivity, "anatomists and paleontologists believed that only particulars were real, and that to stray from particulars was to invite distortions in the interests of dubious theories or systems."[55] Thus, in the eighteenth century Bernhard Albinus, a professor of anatomy at Leiden, instructed his artist to *not* replicate the human skeleton in front of him as it actually was but in accordance with the scientist's ideal of perfection, whereas in the late nineteenth century, paleontologists such as Henry Bowman Brady prided themselves on "represent[ing] actual specimens with all their imperfections, as they are, not what they may have been."[56] The photograph (and by extension, the X-ray) became a metaphor and a literal example of nineteenth-century scientific objectivity, for it appeared to capture the particularity of its object (warts and all), without any apparent interference from a human subject.[57]

This same shift that privileged particularity in the sciences underscored knowledge production in fields such as realist literature and ethnology. Writing on the emergence of the historical novel, Georg Lukács suggests that, while "novels with historical themes" were written before the nineteenth century, such works "are historical only as regards their purely external choice of theme and costume. Not only the psychology of the characters, but also the manners depicted are entirely those of the writers' own day." What is lacking in the historical novel prior to Sir Walter Scott "is precisely the specially historical, that is, derivation of the individuality of characters from the historical peculiarity of their age."[58] In other words, Lukács's critique of pre-nineteenth-century historical novels rests on the fact that history functioned only as a descriptive backdrop to literary themes, whereas in the nineteenth century authors sought to create characters and plots that were indebted to, and born of, what was identified as the particularity of a given historical context.

An emphasis on the nineteenth-century privileging of particularity and distinction is also explored by Tzvetan Todorov, who has argued that nineteenth-century history ("the study of variations in time") and ethnology ("the study of variations in space") is woven from the same fabric, for "both arise from the romantic spirit that enthrones difference in the place of identity."[59] Marshall Sahlins makes a similar point in regard to culture. As culture came to take on its modern definitional characteristics (leaving behind its long association with agriculture) and acquired the status of an object available to be studied by the emerging disciplines of anthropology and sociology, its explanatory force rested on the presumption of difference. Citing contemporary criticisms of anthropology and the colonially inflected history of the "culture concept," Sahlins argues that "'culture' is notably suspect insofar as it marks customary *differences* among peoples and groups. . . . Culture as the *demarcation of difference* is at issue here."[60] Culture, in other words, spoke against universality, emphasizing instead the particularity and distinctive "separateness" between peoples.

Thus, what we witness through the course of the 1800s is a shift away from emphasizing identity, wherein universal categories organize difference in terms of exceptionalism, to an emphasis on particularity, specificity, and differentiation. The consequence for history was the introduction of a new dimension to history writing: the comparative method. Comparison can be regarded as the backlash to Enlightenment. Whereas Enlightenment history, following Reinhart Koselleck, "remained an unmistakable index for an assumed constancy of human nature, accounts of which can serve an iteratable means of proof of moral, theoretical, legal or political doctrines," comparison presupposed a relational difference.[61]

Underwriting historical comparison was the view that a given society's past was, by historical necessity, distinct from the present. Thus, history, as Michel de Certeau has argued, "begins with the differentiation between the *present* and the *past*."[62] Central to this new sensibility was an emphasis on— indeed, a reification of—the historical context. In other words, to study the past was to recognize the particularity of historical conditions that framed the events, customs, practices, and actions of a given period. To impose contemporary morals, sentiments, and categories in one's reading of the past had become anathema to romantic history (the charge of anachronism continues to be one of the worst sins a historian can commit).[63] Percy Bysshe Shelley captures this sentiment in the preface to *The Cenci*, in which he writes of his effort to capture "as nearly as possible . . . the characters as they probably were, and have sought to avoid the error of making them actuated by my own conceptions of right and wrong, false and true, thus under a thin veil converting the names and actions of the sixteenth century into cold impersonations of my own mind."[64]

The romantic reinvention of history in the late eighteenth century expressed a dual sensibility: the need to sharply distinguish the past from the present (thus avoiding the sin of anachronism) while preserving a narrative of continuity between the two temporal states (the present being born out of, and integrally tied to, the past). Romanticism—or, following Charles Taylor, "Expressivist anthropology," or, as Iggers would have it, simply historicism[65]—cultivated skepticism, if not downright hostility, toward the first-principle philosophy of the Enlightenment. In contrast to what Taylor describes as the "mechanistic, atomist utilitarian picture of human life" defended by seventeenth-century and eighteenth-century thinkers,[66] the Romantic turn—captured in the writings, for example, of Burke, Herder, Schlegel, and Shelley—emphasized the organic nature of society, the particularity of a peoples, the specificity of history. In reaction to an abstract conception of man formulated out of first-principle philosophy, a Romantic sensibility was one that insisted, following Herder, that "everything earthly and human is governed by time and place, as every particular nation is by its character," and further that this "genetic spirit and character of a people" be recognized as "singular and wonderful."[67]

To understand humanity, then, was to acknowledge diversity, the variety of human values and human life. It was to study the particularity of folklore, religion, language, ancient monuments, and, indeed, traditions, for it was through these cultural sites that a people's unique spirit found expression. It is a version of this ethos that we encounter in Burke's attack on the French Revolutionaries and his defense of organic society and national institutions. We recognize it in Friedrich von Schiller's caution against permitting philosophy to obscure the details of history. A similar sensibility is found in Herder's efforts to rescue speech from utilitarian mediocrity by insisting on the particularity of language as crucial to appreciating the particularity of a people. And even Hegel felt compelled to qualify his universal history by particularizing the Spirit as the "actual embodiment" of an "actually existing people."[68]

What was becoming apparent was that the function of history had been expanded not only to refer to the past, but to account for the present. In other words, it was increasingly argued that, to fully understand and appreciate the particular cultural qualities of a people, one needed to understand their history. It is for this reason that tradition came to be such a central element of late-eighteenth-century and nineteenth-century thought. Far from being antithetical to history, tradition was to become an important vehicle for gaining access to the past.

## TRADITION

It is striking that, although an extensive literature exists that is concerned with the historical permutations of the idea of history, there is remarkably little contemporary scholarship on the subject of tradition. This is not to say that works on the "tradition of" the Catholic church, Western political thought, or particular societies (fill in the blank) are scant. Far from it. But it does suggest that tradition as a distinct concept that embraces certain practices and institutions as "traditional" while excluding others has largely failed to provoke critical scrutiny from historians, political theorists, and literary scholars (the very disciplines that have alerted us to the historicity of history). One cannot help wondering whether the prejudice born of the nineteenth century that ultimately construed tradition as a form of habitual, unreflective practices resistant to reason and change has been reinforced by a modern scholarship that presumes the a-historicity of the concept and deems it unworthy of scholarly attention. There are, of course, a few notable exceptions to this rule.

The best known, I suspect, is the collection of essays edited by Eric Hobsbawm and Terence Ranger under the title *The Invention of Tradition*. [69] As the title suggests, and as Hobsbawm's introduction to the volume confirms, the work presumes a distinction between "genuine traditions" and another body of traditions that includes "both traditions actually invented, constructed and formally instituted and those emerging in a less easily traceable manner within a brief and dateable period—a matter of a few years perhaps—and establishing themselves with great rapidity." [70] The objective of the work, as Hobsbawm also explains, is to alert historians to the value of tradition as "important symptoms and therefore indicators of problems which might not otherwise be recognized, and developments which are otherwise difficult to identify and to date. They are evidence." [71] It becomes clear when reading the essays in the collection that the evidential value of "invented traditions" lies in their factitious claims to historical legitimacy. In other words, a study of "invented traditions" (as opposed to "genuine traditions") forces the recognition that, while many contemporary practices and institutions masquerade as authentically ancient, they are in fact shamelessly modern fabrications.

A number of criticisms can be leveled at this work but for my purposes its chief weakness lies in the fact that while interrogating the historical production of tradition, it leaves its own historical methodology closed to critical reflection. History is simply a neutral tool employed to "reveal" the spuriousness of various traditions that according to the authors have historically evolved to legitimate the political aspirations of elites within national or sub-national struggles. Thus, "invented traditions" are fabrications of history rather than history proper.

But if the essays in *The Invention of Tradition* are guilty of a certain contemptuous disregard for their subject matter—reducing tradition to an ideological weapon invented by various elites—Edward Shils's and David Gross's works (*Tradition* and *The Past in Ruins*, respectively) sacrifice history in their efforts to render tradition into a complex sociological category.[72] In their efforts to "defend" tradition against the criticism and disdain of political progressives, Shils and Gross posit tradition as a self-evident, a-historical category, a conceptual vessel that has always existed, even if the contents it carries have changed over time and place. What is curiously missing in both texts is the recognition that the idea of tradition took on a significance in the eighteenth century and nineteenth century that crucially tied its fortunes to the emerging discourses of modernity. The historicity of tradition and its significance as a boundary category that delineates certain practices, institutions, and peoples from the "non-traditional" is thus left largely unexamined by both Shils and Gross.

In contemporary scholarship, then, tradition has been reduced to an object of historical inquiry in which history itself is presumed to be a neutral arbiter, or its supporters or critics posit it as an a priori category that simply "exists" to be defended or derided. My own argument deviates from both of these approaches. Tradition, I suggest, has a history, but tracing that history necessitates interrogating the presumed "neutrality" of history itself. In so saying, I am not simply suggesting that scholars writing on the history of tradition be conscious of the historicity of history, but also that, inserted into our narrative of the birth of modern historiography, we recognize the crucial function tradition played in our understanding of the historical.

As will become evident, tradition became one of the most pervasive descriptive markers identified with non-Western societies in the nineteenth century. In other words, it became one of the crucial markers of difference employed by nineteenth-century scholars and colonial officials to distinguish the natives from the colonizers. It is no coincidence, however, that the 1800s has also been widely recognized as the century that gave birth to modern historical thinking. Not only do we witness the emergence of history as an institutionalized discipline with its own set of scientifically prescribed rules of scholarship in the nineteenth century, but, more broadly, by the late 1800s historicism was underwriting intellectual work across a wide range of disciplines, including the natural sciences, philology, and anthropology. Moreover, in contrast to tradition, history through the course of the nineteenth century was increasingly identified as the preserve of European nations. If tradition was what defined colonized peoples, history was the sign of the modern West. It is this shared history that permitted the distinction to be made in the nineteenth century between historical subjects and traditional peoples and to acquire a self-evident status that would not have been so easily recognizable in the seventeenth century and eighteenth century. Thus, having briefly mapped the shifting terrain of European conceptions of history, it is necessary to offer a similar sketch regarding the fortunes of tradition.

Turning to the Oxford English Dictionary, that gospel of etymology, it becomes apparent that "tradition" is not a word "invented" in the nineteenth century, signifying through its emergence the birth of a new style of reasoning—the claim Arnold Davidson makes for the concept "sexuality."[73] Nor can it pride itself on a tumultuous history, such as the one that Raymond Williams and, more recently, Terry Eagleton associate with "culture."[74] A derivative of the Latin noun *tradere*, "tradition" was still being evoked to designate surrender or betrayal from the late fifteenth century to the mid-seventeenth century. Since the Middle Ages, however, a host of competing meanings had begun to prevail—namely, "tradition" came to be identified with delivery, the handing down of knowledge and the passing on of a doctrine. Traditions found their mode of expression through continued usage and were commonly understood to have been disseminated through oral rather than written communication.

By the late eighteenth century, the term "tradition" had undergone something of a transformation. Having once been evoked to mark specific practices, it increasingly came to be identified as a concept that was all encompassing—that spoke to, and that expressed, the particularity of a people. Moreover, tradition bore the marks of a past that continued to live and breathe in the present, thereby stressing the continuity of a people's history and the specificity of their cultural forms. It is this privileging of tradition as unbroken continuity and invariability that lies at the heart of Burke's *Reflections on the Revolution in France*, and it is this same sensibility that is captured in Herder's insistence that it is through the transmission of tradition over generations that a people come to be what they are: "One day teaches another, one century instructs another century; tradition is enriched: the muse of Time, History, herself sings with a hundred voices, speaks with a hundred tongues."[75]

Of course, seventeenth-century and eighteenth-century writers were well aware that different nations practiced very different customs or traditions (the two words often being interchangeable). Yet recognition of difference did not detract from an overriding faith in the universality of human nature. Indeed, the often disparaging Enlightenment accounts of custom and tradition were premised on the belief that such age-old, habitual, unreflective practices clouded and obstructed human rationality, a conviction that would be shared by early-nineteenth-century utilitarians and mocked in Dickens's *Hard Times*.[76] As Shils has argued, for seventeenth-century and eighteenth-century critics of the ancien régime, tradition

> was regarded as the cause or the consequence of ignorance, superstition, clerical dominance, religious intolerance, social hierarchy, inequality in the distribution of wealth, preemption of the best positions in society on grounds of birth, and other states of mind and social institutions which were the objects of rationalistic and progressivistic censure. . . . The first entry on the agenda of the Enlightenment was therefore to do away with traditionality as such; with its demise, all the particular substantive tradition would likewise go.[77]

Thus we have Locke, for example, criticizing those men "who look on opinions to gain force by growing older," thereby ensuring that claims "which found or deserved little credit from the mouths of their first authors are thought to grow venerable by age [and are thus] urged as undeniable."[78] A hundred years later, Jean le Rond d'Alembert stated the point much more bluntly: "In the matter of customs, men of good sense follow the law of fools."[79] Traditions and customs in the seventeenth century and eighteenth century were products of unreflective habit or superstition, not productive of human societies and human difference. Yet if traditions were believed to be an aggregate of practices that reason ultimately would cast off, this was because the past was observed with the same irreverence. As Becker has argued, Enlightenment philosophers were less concerned with the question of continuity between the past and present than with breaking from the past altogether: "They were looking for 'man in general' . . . [and] man in general, like the economic man, was a being that did not exist in the world of time and place, but in the conceptual world, and he could therefore be found only by abstracting from all men in all times and all places those qualities which all men shared."[80]

It is this reasoning, as Gross points out, that created the conceptual space for seventeenth-century and eighteenth-century social contract theory. The very premise that a society could be born anew without reference to that which preceded it was, as Gross rightly argues, a radically novel idea:

> The notion that something which "follows after" could surpass something that "comes before" was itself virtually without precedent. . . . The concept of a new beginning meant inaugurating something that never existed before. It meant not completing the past but initiating something wholly separate and distinct from it, and hence privileging (at least implicitly) the present over the past, and the immediate over the transmitted.[81]

Strikingly, therefore, one does not encounter in 1750 the same resigned recognition of history's ubiquitous power over the present that one confronts in Marx a hundred years later—the Marx who spoke of "the tradition of all the dead generations weigh[ing] like a nightmare on the brain of the living."[82]

While tradition ultimately would be rendered an obstacle to historical progress, and antithetical to the historical enterprise more generally, in the late eighteenth century and early nineteenth century tradition was in fact recognized as closely aligned to the subject of history. Thus, Herder could insist that "all education must spring from imitation and exercise, by means of which the model passes into the copy" and that it was this process that was most "aptly expressed . . . by the term tradition."[83] Central to Romantic historicism was the principle of continuity. If, as I have suggested, one element of historicism is the insistence that no two epochs are the same, thus equipping one to argue that there is "no need to hold onto the values and traditions of former epochs once those epochs had disappeared into history,"[84] the same historicist in turn rejected the Enlightenment premise that the present or future was entirely free of the past. The latter thesis permitted tradition to function as an accomplice of history.

The longevity of a people's traditions operated as an index to the antiquity of their civilization. Thus, tradition was not only identified with "traditional peoples"; it was appealed to by those eager to assert the antiquity of their past. It is not surprising, therefore, that, as Hobsbawm points out, tradition became crucial to the articulation of nineteenth-century European nationalism and nationhood. Moreover, as Lynn Zastoupil has argued, the defense of and opposition to tradition was a subject of intense debate within nineteenth-century Britain, prompting passionate interventions from such notable political and literary figures as James and John Stuart Mill, Samuel Coleridge, and Robert Southey. Zastoupil himself explains the stakes of these often heated exchanges in reference to ideological differences between conservatives who sought to maintain the status quo and liberals who pushed for reform and thus questioned the value of continuing to pay homage to the past through the observation of traditions.[85] Framing the debate in terms of ideological oppositions, however, begs the question of why tradition came to loom so large in nineteenth-century discourse. It presumes (as Shils and Gross have done) the self-contained "obviousness" of the category and the inclusions and exclusions that made it meaningful. Nevertheless, Zastoupil's central thesis that what was essentially a British debate about the merits or otherwise of upholding traditions came to be displaced and played out in reference to the colonies—India being one such colonial theater—is significant.[86] It is so, however, not because British debates were passively translated and mapped onto the colonies, but because the colonial context forced tradition itself to be reconfigured and reimagined.

### COLONIAL HISTORY AND NATIVE TRADITIONS

The shift from Enlightenment universalism to what often has been identified as a Romantic sensitivity toward particularity (the specificity, for example, of language, customs, folklore, the traditions of a people) found expression not only in the literature, poetry, and philosophy of British and Continental writers but also in the context of, and in response to, the colonial imperatives of governing a subject people. Indeed, the discourse on tradition took on a material urgency in British India precisely because many a colonial official saw permitting the continued observance of Hindu and Muslim traditions as the only way to ensure the natives' compliance. Despite the rancor of Christian missionaries and the demands of utilitarian reformers, the East India Company largely resisted aggressive policies of religious conversion and social reform. This hesitance was often couched in terms of respect for what was described as the ancient customs of the natives. In a letter to Lord Cornwallis, Governor-General of Bengal, for example, William Jones insisted that:

> nothing indeed could be more obviously just, than to determine private contests according to those laws, which the parties themselves had ever considered as the rules of their conduct and engagements in civil life; nor could any thing be wiser, than, by a legislative act, to assure the Hindu and Mussulman subjects of Great Britain, that the private laws which they severally held sacred, and a violation of which they would have thought the most grievous oppression, should not be superseded by a new system of which they could have no knowledge, and which they must have considered as imposed on them by a spirit of rigour and intolerance.[87]

In a similar vein, the colonial official and historian John Malcolm argued in *Notes of Instructions to Assistants and Officers* that the natives of India would be more greatly disposed to British rule by the "consideration we shew to their habit, institutions, and religion, by the moderation, temper and kindness with which we conduct ourselves towards them; and injured by every act that offends their belief or superstition, that shews disregard or neglect of individuals or communities."[88]

Whether the imperative behind indulging Hindu and Muslim traditions was predicated on genuine admiration for Indian civilization (certainly present in the writings of some Orientalists) or pragmatic concern for social stability and political legitimacy, the imperative to transform tradition into an object of study was, as Ranajit Guha has argued, inextricably tied to the needs of colonial governance.[89]

In recent years, scholarship concerned with colonial history has increasingly challenged overly simplistic accounts of colonialism as nothing more than the exercise of unmasked power operating through the binaries of colonizer–colonized, self–other, oppressor–oppressed, perpetrator–victim. In contrast, a growing body of literature has identified the many sites of ambiguity that marked colonial relations: religious conversions from Christianity, cross-cultural marriages, friendships and homoerotic relationships.[90] Moreover, as has already been noted, enthusiasm for Sanskrit literature, and for Indian civilization more generally, was shared by Europe's reading public and British colonial officials during the late eighteenth century and early nineteenth century, a fact that cannot be satisfactorily accounted for if one appeals only to the conscious political objectives of colonial subjugation and colonial power.

While this recent scholarship has added a necessary complexity to our understanding of colonial history, we should be wary of allowing it to overshadow or undermine an earlier, yet no less valid, thesis—namely, that colonial history is a history of power. Having once established that continuity rather than radical reform would be the governing principle of East India Company rule, the imperative to gain access to and translate the opaque world of native traditions was deemed crucial for the legitimacy and security of colonial governance. In other words, constant efforts to gain access to Indian traditions were far from benign. Jones, it should be noted, may have come to genuinely appreciate Sanskrit literature, but, as he testifies, the imperative to learn Sanskrit as a judge in the colonial court of Bengal was initially born of a distrust of native informants. In a letter to Cornwallis, Jones makes it clear that a failure to learn Sanskrit and Arabic would require colonial officials to depend on "the opinions of native lawyers and scholars," an unhappy consequence, given that, as Jones continues, "We can never be sure that we have not been deceived by them."[91]

Tradition in the colonial context was not simply that which required defending or disparaging. Indeed, before any political positioning was possible, the tradition of the natives had first to be *known*.[92] In the colonial context, to speak of indigenous traditions—practices, customs, laws, religious rites, institutions—necessitated ascertaining what these traditions were in the first place. As Guha illustrates, the problem the colonial official confronted was how to gain knowledge of indigenous traditions. For example, propelled by the material interests of empire, East India Company officials were keen to determine the system of land revenues (and, thus, property relations) that existed in late-eighteenth-century and early-nineteenth-century Bengal. Having sought and largely failed to ascertain this information from the natives, colonial officials turned their attention to textual sources, inspiring the production of a number of historical works (Alexander

Dow's three-volume *The History of Hindostan*; James Grant's *An Historical and Comparative Analysis of the Finances of Bengal; Chronologically arranged in different periods from the Mogul Conquest to the present time, etc.*; and James Mills's *History of British India* are among the better known). In Guha's reading, a distinction began to emerge within colonial discourse between native traditions and a colonially inspired historiography. Yet, as Guha rightly points out, if colonial conceptions of history replaced indigenous understandings of the past, they nevertheless had to rely on native material. "The material which had to be historicized, was of course the sum of all existing narratives—annals, chronicles, anecdotes, folklore, etc.—but the narratology brought to bear on such material was that of contemporary Europeans."[93] Colonial historiography relied heavily on indigenous textual sources that were invested with authority precisely because they were deemed to embody the traditions of a people. History writing, in other words, was being sculptured out of, and in reference to, tradition. What the natives refused to divulge—their oral traditions—the colonial official would acquire through other means: tradition as it was embedded in Arabic and Sanskrit texts.

The emphasis on the text as the source of native traditions ensured that if colonial histories were produced through reference to native traditions, tradition itself was reconstituted through a colonial understanding of the past. Lata Mani's work on debates around *sati* in early-nineteenth-century India is particularly instructive in this regard.[94] While Christian missionaries had long petitioned the colonial government to ban the practice of widow self-immolation, similar condemnation from some indigenous quarters forced East India Company officials to address the question of *sati*'s legality. Mani's work is dense with detail, but for our purposes, three points are of particular significance. First, the government's reluctance to intervene on an issue it had determined to be a "traditional" practice led to a convoluted and drawn-out decision-making process that involved appealing to native pundits who were instructed to scrutinize religious texts to determine whether *sati* was in fact sanctified by Hindu law. However, the fact that Hinduism had never been a codified, distinct "religion" meant that innumerable Sanskrit texts that had been written over centuries contradicted each other on the subject of *sati*. The unruliness of this process led to a second curious addition to the discourse on tradition: Confronted with multiple religious sources, it was decreed that authority would be bestowed on those texts that were most ancient. In other words, it was determined that antiquity bequeathed authority. If a more ancient text appeared to sanction or renounce *sati*, that text would bear the weight of the government's ruling. The logic underwriting this reasoning speaks to a third, oddly counterintuitive, revision of what constituted tradition within colonial narratives: the presumption that religious texts were deemed more "authoritative" than usage. Thus, when a British official was asked whether he agreed with the abolition of *sati*, he replied, "I do; it was not the Hindu law, it was merely usage."[95] In other words, irrespective of the actual practices and customs indigenous peoples might observe, bestowing the authority of tradition on a practice required deriving its legitimacy from an "ancient" textual source. It was a logic that seemed to go against the grain of tradition itself, which had been as much about an oral handing down of customs and practices over generations as about codified "rules" that were detached from usage.

*Sati* is not an "invented tradition" in the ways that Hobsbawm and Ranger understand the term. It has had a long (though often interrupted) history among Rajput (that is, upper-caste) women in Rajasthan. Having said that, however, to proceed to identify *sati* as an example of Rajasthani Hindu tradition is to miss the point; it is to repeat Shils's and Gross's mistake wherein tradition is attributed the status of a self-evident "fact." What is significant about the *sati* debate (though the remarriage of widows and the age of consent were also sites of heated exchange) is that in colonial and native efforts to determine the authenticity, or otherwise, of *sati*'s status as "tradition," tradition itself was being reconstituted as a discrete category that marked certain practices as distinct from others. Such conscious and determined efforts at classification brought tradition into the orbit of a whole other set of vocabulary, such as authenticity, duration, invariability, textual and oral authority, and, most specifically, historical continuity.

It is this gesture to historical continuity that is significant, for it suggests that, despite the peculiarly colonial inscriptions that marked colonial debates about tradition in India, such debates in the late eighteenth century and early nineteenth century were still anchored within the larger conceptual field of history. It is not the case that tradition and history were conflated as one and the same thing; however, it is also not true that tradition was viewed as antithetical to history. What we witness instead is an ambivalent relationship between tradition and history in the late eighteenth century and early nineteenth century. The antiquity of India's traditions made tradition—particularly that identified with textual sources—of primary importance to colonial productions of Indian history. It was an appeal to this history, in turn, that offered the much sought material needed to legitimize colonial rule. The British, it was argued, were simply continuing where the Mughals had left off, and preserving tradition was the link between a pre-British past and the colonial contemporary.

## The Absence of History and the "Despotism of Custom"

Thus far I have argued that in the late eighteenth century and early nineteenth century, we begin to witness a shift in European representations of difference that actually signals a foundational shift in the prerequisites and presumptions of knowledge production. Difference is no longer conceptualized in terms of a deviation from some universal norm, for such a logic presumes a thought structure that situates identity as its point of origin, that seeks to organize knowledge by establishing identities between words, objects, and beings to then engage with, and account for, difference. This describes the enabling logic of Classical thought. In the late eighteenth century and early nineteenth century, a different style of reasoning is brought to bear on European representations of difference that privileges difference, emphasizes particularity, and proceeds from specificity, for only through the recognition of distinction, only by way of examining the particularity of a given object, can more general, empirically reliable conclusions be derived. I have sought to elaborate and illustrate this shift in thought with reference to the late-eighteenth-century and early-nineteenth-century reimagining of history and tradition as valuable expressions of a people's particularity. Moreover, I have suggested that in the late eighteenth century and early nineteenth century, history and tradition were recognized as co-conspirators in the production of uniqueness that was said to define and distinguish each nation and historical period from all others.

This logic that views the present as born out of the past and views tradition as both a connecting chain to history and a crucial trope for identifying the specificity of a people in the present, is precisely what came to unravel by the second decade of the nineteenth century. By the 1830s, we begin to encounter a more familiar paradigm than the one we have been discussing. Ancient traditions may well speak to an ancient past, but they would cease to speak to what Hegel identified as "History Proper."

Thus, from Europeans' celebration of India's antiquity and colonial efforts to fathom Indian history (as a crucial means for aiding colonial governance), we confront Hegel's *Philosophy of History*, wherein India is reduced to being a "land of desire"—the paradoxically passive instigator of other people's histories.[96] But Hegel was still working within the framework of philosophical history (philosophy and history had still to be prized apart) and thus could render India relevant to the historical coming-to-be of Spirit. Ranke would have none of that. History, he famously pronounced, was about what happened.[97] But what precisely did happen that permitted Ranke to argue what was quickly becoming a self-evident "fact": that "India and China have a lengthy chronology" but, at best, have a "natural history"?[98]

A number of theories could and have been offered. However, there are three distinctive shifts in European conceptions of history that were to have a significant impact on European representations of cultural difference: the move from an aggregate-based history to world history (or, to put it another way, from the agency of God to the agency of man); the disciplining of history into an institutionalized field of study; and, finally, the emergence of anthropology.

Scholars as diverse as Iggers, Todorov, and Isaiah Berlin have recognized in the writings of Herder (particularly in *Also a Philosophy of History*) a cultural relativism that largely disappeared in the work of his successors. As Iggers argues, it is "only in Herder's early work of 1774 [that] we find the historicist position formulated in its radical form: the conception that every age must be viewed in terms of its own immediate values; that there is no progress or decline in history, but only value-filled diversity."[99] What Iggers describes as the *Antinormativität* (anti-normative) strain of historicism assumed that "whatever arises in history is per se valuable. No individual, no institution, no historical deed can be judged by standards external to the situation in which it arises, but rather must be judged in terms of its own inherent values. There are thus no rational standards of value applicable to a diversity of human institutions. Instead, all values are culture-bound."[100] Berlin's account of Herder is equally enthusiastic:

> For Herder everything is delightful. He is delighted by Babylon and he is delighted by Assyria, he is delighted by India and he is delighted by Egypt. He thinks well of the Greeks, he thinks well of the Middle Ages,

he thinks well of the eighteenth century, he thinks well of almost everything except the immediate environment of his own time and place. . . . Herder is the father, the ancestor, of all those travelers, all those amateurs, who go round ferreting out all kinds of forgotten forms of life, delighting in everything that is peculiar, everything that is odd, everything that is native, everything that is untouched.[101]

A decisive shift has therefore been traced between a Herderian history that sought to study the specificity of particular cultures without recourse to a normative yardstick and later historians who did not shy away from assuming the superiority of some peoples over others. Hegel's *Philosophy of History* would be a classic example of the latter approach to history. The distinction drawn between Herder's history and that of Hegel is that, whereas Herder emphasized the distinctiveness and uniqueness of particular cultures and eschewed a normative system of measurement, Hegel sought to rank particular cultures within a graduated, teleological history.

There is reason to be somewhat skeptical of intellectual portraits that paint Herder as an ardent relativist steadfastly eschewing Eurocentric bias and arrogant judgments against non-European peoples. Like Hegel after him, Herder could not resist the temptation, in *Outlines of a Philosophy of the History of Man*, to narrate human history through the familiar analogy of the stages of life wherein childhood, adolescence, youth, and maturity were the temporal metaphors mapped on the various nations of the indigenous New World, China, India, and so on. But my intention is not to argue for or against the consistency or lack of consistency of Herder's relativism. Even if we allow for the fact that Herder's writings distinguish themselves from Hegel's by the fact that they offered a gentler, more sympathetic, and less arrogant portrayal of cultural difference, we should be wary of reading differences in content as differences in epistemological worldviews. Ultimately, both Herder and Hegel were working within what Koselleck has referred to as the "unitary history of modernity," which simultaneously permitted "the multitude of individual histories of the entire past."[102] Unlike medieval history, Koselleck suggests, in which "history itself was claimed to derive from God" and its universal character was produced in "the form of an aggregate," modern history distinguished itself by conceiving of history as a *"plurale tantum."*[103] For all of the emphasis on archival documentation, Koselleck maintains that the modern historical narrative continued to rely on theory, for only then would a secular history (i.e., "history in and of itself"; history that no longer looked to God for its point of reference but relied instead on its own internal logic and rules) be more than an aggregate of individual events and actions. Only then could the seemingly discrete, unconnected histories of so many particulars be made to speak to something beyond them, to "world history as a system."[104]

That Hegel's *Philosophy of History* is a classic example of Koselleck's thesis is easy to discern. The distinct histories of China, India, Egypt, and so on are offered not in the form of an aggregate but in the context of an integrated system that ensured the "interdependence of events and the intersubjectivity of actions."[105] But Herder, no less than Hegel, was a modern historian, as Koselleck understands the term. After all, if Herder's cultural relativism was born out of the need to acknowledge the particularity of each people, he nevertheless did so under the auspices of a singular Man. Individual histories bore a large relevance, offered a unifying and unitary logic that found expression through the human subject.

But this human subject was not empty of all content, devoid of all meaning. That history was no longer subject to God but the consequence of human will begs the question of who exactly this heroic new figure was that presumed the role of being both the sole object of history and its only instigator. "The whole history of mankind," Herder argued, "is a pure natural history of human powers, actions and propensities, modified by time and place."[106] The fact that this figure was always presumed to be male is itself instructive. But in addition (though not unrelated) to the question of gender, Herder offered a further glimpse into the traits that went into constituting the protagonist of history. Significantly, one of the places we encounter this subject is in Herder's discussion of tradition.

If Herder offered the most cogent defense of tradition as expressing a people, there are a few significant instances where he qualifies his enthusiasm by qualifying tradition itself, such as when he speaks of "progressively operating tradition."[107] In a more elaborate passage, Herder has this to say:

Tradition in itself is an excellent institution of Nature, indispensable to the human race: but when it fetters the thinking faculty both in politics and education, and prevents all progress of the intellect, and all the improvement, that new times and circumstances demand, it is the true narcotic of the mind, as well to nations and sects, as to individuals. Asia, the mother of all the mental illumination of our habitable Earth, has drunk deep of this pleasant poison, and handed the cup to others.[108]

What is revealing in this passage is not that Herder permitted a progressive historical narrative to undermine his relativism. Rather, what is significant is that Herder's effort to draw a distinction between what can crudely be identified as "good" and "bad" traditions is born out of a particular understanding of the human subject that in its turn renders his relationship to history and tradition simultaneously productive of and detached from his being in the world. Whereas "bad" traditions "fetter . . . the thinking faculty," preventing "all progress of the intellect, and all the improvement, that new times and circumstances demand," "good" traditions, Herder implicitly suggests, are worthy of respect because they are the product of human choice, consciously indulged for reasons of sentiment but also expendable if deemed contrary to historical progress. This distinction reveals a number of tensions embedded in Herder's text.

First, if in Berlin's telling a Herderian history is put in the service of cataloguing (and celebrating) human particularity in all of its variety, if it seeks to render history into a narrative of so many particulars, it does so with an eye to achieving a higher, more elevated objective: These multiple histories intertwine and gesture back to the singularity of all histories, which is Man. In other words, tradition and history produce men in all their diversity, while at the same time Man has to be posited as the precondition enabling these traditions and histories. As much as tradition and history bear their stamp on, and are productive of, the unique specificity of a people, these same "people" are presumed to be capable of recognizing their traditions and their history as distinct from themselves—hence, the reason that tradition and history can be acted on; that Herder can chastise (in a passage immediately following the one quoted earlier) the Chinese, Indians, and ancient Greeks (among others) for failing to recognize and relinquish those traditions that impede critical thought. Man is posited simultaneously as a product of and as autonomous from his environment. The former prohibits as well as enables particular ways of living and conceptualizing the world, thus allowing for human diversity. Man's autonomy, however, equips him with the agency to act on the world—a world recognized as an object distinct from himself.

As Heidegger has argued, modernity enabled Man to represent the world as picture, as that which was detached from himself (thus rendering possible the very idea of representation; of "representing"). In so doing, however, it was not only man's relationship to the world that changed but the very subject we call Man. It is not simply the object that has been transformed but also the subject that has gazed on and affected that object.[109] In other words, despite the pretensions to universality that this figure implies, the Man being presumed is of a particular type: He is a choosing, autonomous individual who recognizes himself as a subject independent of a world of objects on which he acts. He is a being who is born of and shaped by a collective (as opposed to the asocial Enlightenment figure who existed prior to, and was the instigator of, social life), but this collective identity does not detract from his own volition, his conscious agency, his rational and emotional self.

This is the figure that defines Herder's Man—indeed, modern man—as the centerpiece of history. What distinguished Herder's writings from those of his successors was that he did not explicitly articulate or elaborate on a distinction that was to become commonplace through the course of the nineteenth century—namely, that "good" and "bad" tradition correlated with Western and non-Western subjectivities. Indeed, the tension that pervades Herder's *History of Man* is that he presumes a particular type of subject (he who has a specific relationship to the world) without explicitly naming him: Western Man. It was this unspoken presumption in Herder's writings that was to find full expression through the course of the nineteenth century. Herder's work signals a shift away from Classical thought, emphasizing as it does the particular over the general, the historical over the universal, and difference over identity. What was implicit in Herder's writings became more pronounced over the course of the nineteenth century. The thesis that would gradually emerge was that Man did not simply make his own history but was fashioned by it. It was not simply his external environment that changed; it was Man himself. His very sense of self underwent transformation. Significantly, however, all men in all cultures did not experience this transformation in human subjectivity.

Particular historical conditions in the West permitted the emergence of individual consciousness wherein Man came to recognize himself as a free, self-determining individual distinct from the group and thus capable of autonomy, choice, agency, and volition. This particular type of self was absent in the colonies, where individual expression was suppressed and smothered by the collective force of habitual, unreflective traditions and tribal, caste, and religious affiliations.

Just as the self-determining, self-knowing individuated subjects of the West modified or relinquished traditions, so, too, did they influence, affect, and shape their own history. But in the East, the very customs that suppressed man's individuality also, for that very reason, denied him the possibility to claim a historical past. It was this conclusion that John Stuart Mill defended when he pronounced in *On Liberty* that "the greater part of the world, has, properly speaking, no history because the despotism of Custom is complete. This is the case over the whole of the East."[110]

The conflation of tradition with historical lack was not present in Herder's writings, for he did not presume that the presence of traditions qualified the historicity of a people. Instead, as I have argued, for Herder history and tradition worked together to fashion the particularity of a people, and thus studying a nation's traditions was an integral element to studying its history.

It is not that Europeans lacked traditions—as Hobsbawm has documented, tradition was virtually a cottage industry in nineteenth-century Europe[111]—but that their traditions were deemed the product of thoughtful reflection, the consequence of a self-conscious desire to pay homage to the past. Observing traditions (such as those identified with the nation-state) was the expression of individual choice manifesting itself in the collective will. Even when traditions were the subject of criticism, as they often were in the nineteenth century, this simply testified to the fact that tradition was no longer simply limited to identifying a type of practice or institution but had become an object of discourse—there to be studied, celebrated, denigrated, reformed, or, following the contributions in Hobsbawm's and Ranger's edited work, "invented." It was this conscious agency that presumed an element of choice in the observation of tradition that was argued to be lacking among the natives of the colonies. Precisely because the natives did not recognize their traditions as distinct from themselves, precisely because they lacked a sense of self that was individuated, they not only failed to modify, relinquish, or reform their traditions but they ceased to be agents in the making of their own history. Whereas in the West individuals chose to observe traditions that were recognized as discrete rituals sustained through the conscious will of the observer, in the colonies the natives did not *observe* traditions but were entirely *subjected* by them.

The correlation between history and tradition that Herder's writings presumed would gradually be discarded once the traditions of the natives were offered as the primary causal explanation for their historical stagnation. Unchanging traditions corresponded with historical lack. This is the logic we encounter in Hegel's *Philosophy of History*. Hegel's *History* distinguishes itself from Herder's on two counts. The first returns us to the premise that a singular Man is the subject and instigator of history. That which had to be teased out of Herder—that the unifying subject of history was not simply man but a particular rendering of the human subject—was, in Hegel's text, posited as one of the defining achievements of human history. If history essentially traced the journey of Spirit to the full consciousness of its being, and if pivotal to that consciousness was the realization of freedom and reason, then the very point of history—revealed at the moment of its culmination—was the birth of the modern subject. What Herder presumed, Hegel sought to historicize. In short, Hegel's thesis was that the subject of history is a particular type of subject; that subject is European; and it is history that permits us to account for how and why this is the case. Hegel's conclusion, by very different means, was to be rearticulated through the course of the nineteenth century by historians such as Burkhardt and scholars-cum-British colonial servants such as John Stuart Mill and Henry Sumner Maine. The free, equal, rational individual whom Hobbes, Locke, and Rousseau had presumed universal was now a figure that owed his existence to the particularity of European history.

Related to this first point is a second. In positing the modern Western subject as the subject of history, Hegel did not relinquish the nineteenth-century concern for particularity. Particularity continued to be pivotal to Hegel's history, finding its most exalted expression in the modern individual and the modern state. However, what does become apparent in Hegel's *History* is that it is possible for a people to be so particular as to render themselves irrelevant to history. This, in fact, was the verdict Hegel passed on the civilizations of Mexico and Peru.

One expression of particularity that impeded historical progress in the non-West was tradition. Unable to recognize traditions as forms of particularity that are nevertheless malleable to change and responsive to human agency, such practices and institutions, along with the people who observed them, were effectively naturalized—they were, in other words, of no concern to history. This was the fate of India. In Hegel's formulation, India's relevance to universal history ceased once the "healthy" progression toward class formation petrified into a tradition of caste division. At this moment, historical time gave way to natural time, wherein, as Iggers argues, nature was regarded as "the science of the eternally recurring, of phenomena themselves devoid of conscious purpose." History, in contrast, was composed of "unique and unduplicated human acts filled with violation and intent."[112] In other words, whereas history spoke to the agency of men to fashion social change and propel history forward, tradition represented a relapse into the unconscious cyclical time of nature—time devoid of historical significance.

Hegel's *Philosophy of History* signals a gradual shift in European representations of India from an Orientalist thesis that asserted the centrality of India to world history (particularly, though not exclusively, in reference to philology) to a more robust defense of the West's superiority on all fronts, including that of historical agency. Central to this shift in representation was a reevaluation of tradition. Whereas for Herder tradition was history's muse, for Hegel it was history's nemesis.[113] If an earlier school of thought (articulated and defended not only by philosophers but also by colonial officials) identified tradition as a close ally of history precisely because it was recognized as expressing the particularity of a people and offered a means by which to trace the continuity of the past into the present, by the 1820s it was increasingly being argued that tradition was, in fact, an obstacle to historical progress.

What Hegel articulated through the rarefied language of Spirit within the confines of philosophical discourse was also finding expression in the much less obscure domain of colonial policy in India. By the 1830s, tradition was increasingly being viewed as anathema to historical progress and contrary to the duties and responsibilities a colonial government owed its native subjects. One of the sites upon which this shift in sentiment found most dramatic expression was in the context of debates around native education.

Prior to the 1830s, colonial policy regarding the funding of native education emphasized the need to maintain what were deemed traditional educational structures. Hence, Muslim and Hindu colleges were publicly funded; Arabic and Sanskrit texts constituted the main body of the curriculum; and instruction was conducted in vernacular languages. In the 1830s, this policy, identified with the Orientalist school of thought, came to be challenged within the East India Company administration by officials defending the Anglicization of education. The Anglicists insisted that if India was to have a future, it had to be rescued from the paralyzing effect of its past and the gripping hold of its traditions. This translated into an attack on vernacular education and a defense of English-language instruction. Thus, Macaulay, one of the main representatives of the Anglicist position and the author of the infamous "Minute on India Education," insisted that English-language instruction be the pillar of colonial education policy. He also insisted that, far from continuing to indulge the superstitious beliefs of the natives (the defining feature of native learning), the indigenous population should be introduced to Western science, literature, and history:

> The question now before us is simply whether, when it is in our power to teach this language, we shall teach languages in which, by universal confession, there are no books on any subject which deserve to be compared to our own; whether we teach European science, we shall teach systems which, by universal confession, whenever they differ from those of Europe, differ for the worse; and whether, when we can patronize sound Philosophy and true History, we shall countenance, at the public expense, medical doctrines which would disgrace an English farrier,— Astronomy, which would move laughter in girls at an English boarding school,—History, abounding with kings thirty feet high, and reigns thirty thousand years long,—and geography, made up of seas of treacle and seas of butter.[114]

The opposing Orientalist side of the debate, represented by, among others, the Sanskrit scholar H. H. Wilson, defended the continuation of vernacular education and favored an emphasis on the teaching of native Arabic and Sanskrit texts. Wilson maintained that "although the books [Sanskrit texts] may be ancient, they are the actual living literature of the country; they are the still extant authorities for the laws and for the institutions of the Hindu's."[115] Consequently, forcing English-language education on the natives risked offending their long-established religious and traditional belief systems.

As is evident, both sides in the controversy articulated their positions in terms of what was best for the "natives." Wilson's position should now be familiar: He evoked the importance of cultural particularity ("No people can ever become instructed or enlightened, except through their own language"),[116] the interests of the empire in keeping the natives on its side, and the merits of a native literature that was not, as Macaulay would have it, completely bereft of intellectual value. What underwrote Macaulay's thesis was the presumption that if the colonial government hoped to improve the condition of the natives, that could be achieved only by introducing them to Western ways of thinking. Cultural particularity—native traditions, including their system of knowledge—was precisely what impeded India's civilizational progress. To continue to publicly fund the teaching of Sanskrit and Arabic texts was to sanction "monstrous superstitions." It was an exercise in indulging "false History, false Astronomy [and] false Medicine."[117] Through European education, offered via the medium of English-language instruction, a wholly new type of native subject vastly superior to his former self would gradually be produced—one who, in Macaulay's words, would be "Indian in blood and colour, but English in taste, in opinion, in morals and in intellect."[118]

The anxiety that expressed itself in Herder's *History of Man* between the desire to value tradition and advocating historical progress ceased to be a concern once tradition itself ceased to be highly valued. In 1835, the East India Company revised its education policy. Not only did the reforms represent a victory for the Anglicists; they also hinted at the declining fortunes of tradition. In contrast to the Romantic sympathy it had once evoked, tradition was gradually to become the trope of India's historical backwardness.

While colonial officials were debating the merits (or otherwise) of indulging native traditions, history as a particular form of narration was emerging as pivotal to demarcating historical peoples from a people without history. In other words, it was increasingly argued that the historical relevance of a nation required the possession of not only a historical past but also a historical consciousness—a consciousness that was manifested in the existence of "properly" historical (as opposed to "mythological") primary source documents.

Hegel's dismissal of Africa and indigenous America and his qualified inclusion of Asia in *Philosophy of History* was in part inspired by what he understood to be the methodological premises of historical writing, which required first and foremost documentary evidence. In a direct criticism of Orientalists' enthusiasm about India's significance to history, Hegel maintained that the discovery of Sanskrit's affinity to Greek and Latin and the consequent thesis that human migration to the rest of the world first emanated from Asia was an impossible hypothesis to prove because it speaks to an "ante-historical period" that "lies beyond the pale of history; in fact precede[s] it."[119] It is not, however, Hegel but Ranke who is credited with transforming history into science. As tradition was being dethroned and its relationship to history was being annulled, history itself was being transformed into a rule-bound discipline.

Denying India a history would soon take on a double meaning. India was not only lacking a historical past (having not experienced progressive development) but, as the subject of history itself came to be systematized within the rules of a discipline, the history Indians had written was also being denied any validity. Two premises were converging that would inform the discipline of history: history as progress and history as practice, or the history we make and the history we write.

When Ranke wrote his now famous words that history is about what happened,[120] he was not simply challenging the authority of philosophy over the discipline of history. He was actually defining history *as a discipline*. As Iggers points out, it was Ranke "who introduced seminars in which future historians were trained in the critical examination of medical documents . . . [making] it an integral component of the training of historians. By 1848 all German speaking universities had adopted it."[121]

While historians were free to choose their object of interest, what constituted historical writing was increasingly determined through reference to a methodological science. Science in this context referred not to the incontestability of facts—few historians could claim such a luxury in the interpretive field of the humanities. Rather, science was understood as disciplinary practice. Historical thinking, Jorn Rusen and Friedrich Jaeger have argued, becomes "scientific when it follows definite rules which guarantee the possibility of testing its statements about the past, thus its objectivity, and assure a continuous growth in knowledge about the past, in other words a progress of knowledge."[122]

For Ranke, while historical scholarship required first and foremost the privileging of primary sources, it also required the observance on the part of the historian of strict self-censorship. The longing gaze of wishful philosophy had to be dispensed with if historical scholarship was to rank as a science, was to be predicated on the authoritative weight of disembodied objectivity.

Yet for all of the emphasis on objectivity, and for all of the outbursts against philosophy, the fact remains that for Ranke and, for that matter, Burkhardt, Wilhelm von Humboldt, and Johann Gustav Droysen, history did have a purpose, for it revealed the gradual evolution of human progress.[123] The logic of history, however, was to be uncovered not through appeal to natural law applied universally, but through the study of so many particulars from which history's general, grander design would be revealed. India, however, was in the unfortunate position of being *too* particular to have any general relevance. Thus, as we have seen, Ranke had little to say about India other than to acknowledge that it had a "lengthy chronology," which he then summarily dismissed as a form of "natural history."[124] Hegel had already covered this terrain. What distinguished Ranke's work from earlier pronouncements on history was not the historical demolition of India, but the "scientification" of history wherein the historical past was indelibly intertwined with the writing of history.

The idea that history presupposes writing, the existence of a script, was already an established premise within European thought. Walter Mignolo, for example, argues that the Spanish denied the Amerindians any claim to history because in most instances writing was unknown in the New World—the exception being Mexico, where the picto-ideographic nature of the text was largely discounted as an inferior form of written expression.[125] In the context of India, the very impetus for the Oriental Renaissance was the enthusiasm generated in Europe over Sanskrit literature. My contention, therefore, is different from that articulated by Mignolo. The formulation that I speak of is not the identification between history and writing but between history and the *writing of history*. If the historical validity of India's past was denied, so was the history that Indians wrote.

Macaulay's earlier dismissal of Indian historical accounts as fictional was a theme echoed in the *Calcutta Review*, which criticized Sanskrit literature for containing "nothing of genuine history. . . . Not a single page of pure historical matter, unmixed with monstrous and absurd fable. . . . The very principle of historical narration appears . . . never to have entered into the minds of the early writers in this language."[126]

Significantly, the same point is repeated in the preface to a five-volume work entitled *The History of British India as Told by Its Historians*, collected by the English historian Henry Elliott. In it, we read that the inspiration behind "this Index has not been constructed on account of any intrinsic value in the histories themselves. Indeed it is almost a misnomer to style them histories. They can scarcely claim to rank higher than Annals."[127] Even Max Müller, Indiology's favorite son, conceded that "there is perhaps too little of Kings and battles in the Vedas, and scarcely anything of the chronological framework of history."[128]

Given that India was increasingly condemned to marginality in the context of world history and, further, was viewed as altogether lacking in historical consciousness, it is of little surprise that, as many contemporary scholars have noted, India's past ceased to be useful even to colonial officials. Thus, the third notable shift we discern in European conceptions of history vis-à-vis India comes in the more material form of colonial policy. As Gyan Prakash has argued, "Linguistic, ethnological, archaeological, and Census surveys and the District Gazetteers emerged . . . [and] with these, the older India of Sanskrit texts and Brahmans was pushed off center by details on peasants, revenue, rent, caste, customs, tribes, popular religious practices, linguistic diversity, agroeconomic regimes, male and female populations, and other such topics."[129]

The days of scouring ancient Sanskrit and Arabic texts to gain access to India's past to formulate contemporary colonial policy had been largely dispensed with by the second half of the nineteenth century. With them went the authority of those very traditions that the ancient works were said to enshrine. Tradition was embodied no longer in texts but in contemporary practices; tradition was no longer a source for historians but the disciplinary domain of the anthropologist. "By the late nineteenth century," Nicholas Dirks argues, "Indian history had been effectively eclipsed by Indian anthropology. To understand and rule India, the British no longer felt the need to ask historical questions; instead, they thought about India anthropologically. Indians were known by their caste, their character, their custom."[130]

In so arguing, Dirks is not suggesting that colonial administrators simply shifted their allegiance from history to anthropology to arrive at a better knowledge of their colonial subjects. Rather, what underwrites his work is the recognition that history and anthropology had emerged, through the course of the nineteenth century, as two distinct disciplines that purported to study very different objects. Whereas history appropriated the past as its object of study, anthropology was concerned with contemporary populations. More significantly, while history was increasingly viewed as the preserve of Europe, for it is only there that human agency had propelled social and political change, anthropology's central purpose was the study of "primitive" peoples within the amorphous field of culture. In this context, culture spoke not to human volition and conscious will but to habitual, unconscious affiliations and practices.

Tradition, therefore, continued to be pivotal to colonial concerns. Indeed, as Dirks argues, the blind observance of "irrational" traditions was what increasingly defined British representations of its colony. But the source of information on the archaic world of native traditions now came not from archaic texts but from another source: anthropologically informed statistics on caste breakdowns, religious affiliations, population data, census questionnaires, and anthropometry.

Any bearing tradition once had on the study of history appeared to have been erased from colonial memory. Any possibility that India had a claim to history prior to British rule was summarily dismissed. The combination of India's historical inertia, the absence of historical documentation (and, thus, historical consciousness), and the ascendance of anthropology as the primary source of colonial knowledge production collectively ensured that, at least when it came to history, India was of no significance.

Yet what inevitably gets lost in these formulations is the extent to which historicism had colonized the nineteenth-century European imagination. In other words, while there is ample evidence to suggest that India was deemed history-less in all the ways identified here, we do not want to confuse the disciplining and rarification of history with, or subsume it in, a more fundamental epistemic shift that pervaded European thought—namely, the premise that everything must be accounted for with reference to history. Thus, if India itself lacked a history, if it was largely absent among the players of world history, India proved to be relevant to the understanding of other histories. In India's contemporary traditions, it so happened, was preserved Europe's past.

# Vedic Visions and Village Communities

By the late nineteenth century, it was increasingly being argued that India was nothing short of an archaeological site for European history. India's inertia, its living traditions, the very attributes that provoked the disdain of historians were, in fact, the source material for gaining access to and reconstructing the European past. India's value was proving useful on a number of fronts. Take, for example, Müller's rapture over India's Vedic past and Maine's thesis on primitive property relations.

By the time Müller came to teach at the colonial training camp of Haileybury College, he was heir to a rich tradition of Orientalist and philological study within which Sanskrit loomed large. While, as Marx once observed, the topic of India consistently cleared the seats of Parliament, the great pronouncements on Indian antiquity were both revived and reached new heights in Müller's writings. There one finds the culmination of German Romanticism and philological scholarship.

In his lectures to the students of Haileybury College, Müller reiterated time and again the significance and relevance of studying Indian literature, language, and antiquity for "everybody who cares for himself, for his ancestors, for his history, or for his intellectual development."[131] It was to India one had to go to pursue:

> that study of the history of the human mind . . . whatever sphere of the human mind you may select for your special study, whether it be language, or religion, or mythology or philosophy, whether it be laws or customs, primitive art or primitive science. . . . Some of the most valuable and most instructive materials in the history of man are treasured up in India, and in India only.[132]

It is with Müller that we come to be acquainted with the significance of India's past as embodying not only a remote antiquity but one that both precedes and reflects Europe's early history. India is relevant to Europe because within its language and ancient literature can be "revived the recollections of our childhood."[133] In encyclopedic form, India, for Müller, was the referential text for the earliest forms of human wisdom. Müller maintained that the texts Jones had translated, such as Kalidasa's *Sakutala* and the *Laws of Manu*, represented India's renaissance. The *Rg Vedas*, on the other hand, voiced the authentic words of an ancient humanity and provided within its pages the earliest rays of human history. In Vedic literature and the Sanskrit language to which it is indebted, we revive "the Education of the Human Race," the "first intellectual development of religion and mythology," the "childish age of the human mind," the "childlike state in the history of man," the "earliest deposit of Aryan speech . . . [and] the earliest deposit of Aryan faith," the "childhood of the human race," our "old forgotten home," and the preservation of words "in their most primitive state."[134]

Müller had effectively appropriated and repositioned India's past-present as a story of European beginnings. But if India's ancient texts spoke to ancient Europe, its contemporary social institutions were no less malleable to European historical retrospection. The historical archive lay not only in written texts and living languages but in life itself—life as it existed in the village communities of rural India.

The village community was an object of romantic glorification in the colonial literature. It represented a historically neutral institution, ambivalent toward and protecting its population against the tide of time and the ravages of wars and invasions. This theme of the "immemorial" village community, as Louis Dumont rightly argues, loomed large within a colonial literature that was both self-referential and self-perpetuating.[135] It was one of the signatures, alongside caste, despotism, and religion, of India's passive past, its temporal stasis. Yet it was in the very a-historicity of the village community that its historical significance lay. The historical inertness of India's village community was for that very reason to become invaluable to a history independent of India.

From the official dispatches of the colonial administration, the theme of the village community acquired new significance in the hands of the English legal scholar Henry Sumner Maine, who insisted that in the Indian village community one could observe the legal and property formations that existed in pre-feudal European history.[136]

Maine's work was situated within the larger context of European scholarship, which revealed that before the rise of feudalism, primitive forms of land ownership—identified in Europe as the *mark* and known in India as the "village community"—had existed in Germany, England, and the Scandinavian countries. These land systems consisted of a number of families who exercised "a common proprietorship over a definite tract of land, its *Mark*, cultivating its domain on a common system and sustaining itself by the produce."[137] Within this configuration, Maine argues, India becomes enormously significant, particularly "when we find that these primitive European tenures and the primitive European tillage constitute the actual working system of the Indian village communities and that they determine the whole course of Anglo-Indian administration."[138]

Maine's *Ancient Law* was published some fifteen years before the Rede Lectures, so it is not surprising that Maine expressed such enthusiasm for the village community. After all, India appeared to offer empirical validation of Maine's broader thesis that social progress can be measured by the extent to which a society has moved away from the complexity of status-based relations to the transparency of a contract economy.

In brief, it was Maine's thesis that early forms of European social organization were mediated through complex and rigidly hierarchical social relations. Within this configuration, identity was relational, familial, status-based, and governed by a logic of obligation, duty, and authority. From these early forms of social organization, where identity was subjugated to status, European history charted its course away from the intimate, opaque, and located (specific) to a contractual economy predicated on individual autonomy, individual agency, and legal and economic transparency.

As I have argued with reference to Locke, to evoke a contractual economy is to presuppose rational, free, and equal individuals. Identity does not seek sustenance in external validation; rather, it resides in interiority and is governed by judicial culpability. The problem Maine resolved was the dilemma Locke confronted: how to reconcile the familial relations Locke identified with the state of nature with a polemic that asserted the a priori status of rational, free, and equal individuals. For Locke, resolution could only take the form of rendering relational identities into "irrational" subjectivities. After all, if the figure of the individual could be found among "savage people" (Hobbes), in the "woods of America" (Locke), or among the Caribs of the New World (Rousseau), then any deviation from the universal type had to be construed as an aberration.

What Maine proceeded to do was to disentangle status-based relations from the language of individual exceptionalism (what Locke identified as "irrationality") and reinscribe it within the language of historicism.[139] In the late nineteenth century, the individual continued to be a universal concept, but it was no longer a trans-historical one.

Against the background of Maine's legal-historical thesis, the relevance of the village community becomes apparent. What occupies a place in Europe's past finds contemporary expression in British India. Or, to phrase it somewhat differently, if the modern is synonymous with contract, with European social organization, and India is emblematic of a pre-contractual, status-based society, then India is everything Europe once was but has ceased to be.

As Sanskrit is the sister of all languages and the *Vedas* are the primeval voice of humanity's childhood, the Indian village community is the prehistoric incarnation of Europe's own antiquity. "A large part of ancient Europe survives in India," Maine informs us, for while in Europe the village community belongs "chronologically to the Past," in India it "is a living and not a dead institution."[140]

### CONCLUSION

We appear to have come full circle, with tradition and history reconciled by the close of the nineteenth century. Yet if reconciliation had taken place, it had done so on very different terms from those first articulated in the late eighteenth century. For Burke and Herder, the specificity of a people's tradition was a means of gaining access to the particularity of a people's history and culture. By the time Müller and Maine were writing, India's traditions were again recognized as relevant to history, but the history that they spoke to was no longer that of India but that of the West. Tradition ceased to be posited in opposition to history because it had gradually come to be historicized in its own right. Societies governed by tradition (primitive societies that in a later age were to be redesignated "traditional") were societies that continued to reside in a particular stage of history that non-traditional societies had once experienced but had since surpassed.

That this narrative is a familiar one highlights the powerful legacy of nineteenth-century thought on our commonplace understandings of history and cultural difference today. The idea that "traditional" societies are, for that reason, historical remainders is made conceptually possible through what Johannes Fabian has termed the "denial of coevalness," by which he means *"a persistent and systematic tendency to place the referent(s) of anthropology in a Time other than the present of the producer of anthropological discourse."*[141] Presumed in this denial is a particular configuration of history as developmental, wherein time marches progressively forward, carrying some nations with it while leaving others in a state of suspension at various stages of the past.

But what is it about "traditional" societies that render them not just culturally but temporally distinct? As I have suggested in this chapter, the answer lies not simply in the fact that populations observe traditions (that, after all, is equally true of the "modern" West) but that traditional societies are *governed* by, and, critically, unreflective of, their traditions. In other words, the subject that observes traditions in the West is an altogether different subject from that found in "primitive" societies. As David Kolb argues:

> When we think about the superiority of modern individualist ways, we tend to think that we are what one becomes when one sheds traditional ways. We are the modern people who can judge and accept or reject. We are not bound by tradition. . . . Our modern individualism is a purer "human" identity that has something to do with being an "individual" before one is Italian or Swedish or Japanese. One is free to choose, free from the restraints of traditional fixed values.[142]

The Western subject is a unique product of European history—an autonomous, self-determining, self-sufficient, and individuated being who recognizes himself as an agent capable of having an impact on an external world and thereby changing that world—both historically and in the present. When it comes to traditions, therefore, the modern individuated self may observe them, but she recognizes them as discrete rituals that she chooses to follow and can equally choose to relinquish.

Such formulations were by no means self-evident.

I have argued in this chapter that in contrast to the Classical period, when knowledge was constituted through the prism of identity, in the nineteenth century it was the privileging of difference that offered the foundational premise of knowledge production. One vantage point from which to view the articulation of this epistemological shift is in the field of history. But at the same time, as history was being rarified into a discipline, was increasingly becoming sensitive to accusations of anachronism and increasingly hostile to grand philosophical narratives that obscured the particularity of historical contexts—at the same time, in other words, as the particular was elevated over the universal—much of the colonial world was being pronounced a-historical, or empty of history.

To trace European representations of difference in the nineteenth century through the discursive and disciplinary trope of history when it was the very absence of history that was to define non-Western peoples necessitated tracing the history of another concept—that of tradition—that was gaining ascendancy at the same time as the Romantic glorification of the past.

In the late eighteenth century, precisely in reaction to the universal abstractions of first-principle philosophy, philosophers such as Herder, parliamentarians such as Burke, and colonial officials such as Jones and Wilkins defended the particularity of a people's traditions as a necessary conduit for studying and gaining access to the specificity of their history. Such a thesis ceased to be hegemonic when, in the course of the 1820s and 1830s, India's antiquity ceased to be an index for India's history. Concurrent with this shift was a reevaluation of tradition. The traditions of the natives were no longer allied to history; they were, instead, the causal explanation of their historical stagnation. By the late nineteenth century, this thesis, while still pervasive, had been slightly reconfigured. Tradition ceased to be outside of, and in opposition to, history but came to be absorbed into the folds of history. In the traditions of colonial peoples was preserved Europe's past.

The various permutations that history and tradition underwent from the late eighteenth century offers one vantage point from which to trace European representations of difference. European discourses on the body—the subject of the next chapter—prove to be equally revealing.

## 4  Of Monsters and Man

THE PECULIAR HISTORY OF RACE

IT SEEMS SOMEWHAT OBLIGATORY for a book tracing European representations of difference to address the subject of race. To do so would be to enter a growing field of scholarship—edited books, journal articles, manuscripts, conference themes, and conference papers—that has, in addition to other concerns, spent much effort and time debating the origins of race. Whereas Thomas Gossett and Tzvetan Todorov have presumed the universality and trans-historicity of race,[1] other scholars have sought to identify the moment of origin in both the near and distant past. Did race exist in prototypical form, as Benjamin Isaac has suggested in *The Invention of Racism in Classical Antiquity*?[2] How much weight do we want to give to the etymological history of the word "race"—the fact that, as Ivan Hannaford argues, race entered European languages only after the thirteenth century and carried a meaning very different from that of modern understanding?[3] What of the twelfth-century Norman understanding of *gens*? Is that not an example, as Robert Bartlett has documented, of medieval racial terminology signifying biological affinities based on blood relations?[4] Turning to David Theo Goldberg, we are persuaded that the Renaissance—most particularly, the conquest of the New World—actually constitutes the origin moment,[5] but then again (though for different reasons), George Mosse and Kenan Malik offer the Enlightenment as a strong contender. I, not wishing to be left out, have posited the nineteenth century as the defining moment.[6]

Integral to periodization is the concern for identifying causes. Whereas Goldberg identifies colonialism as the central prompt for racial discourse, Hannah Arendt and Nicholas Hudson locate racial thinking in the formation of modern nation-states and nationalist thought, while George Stocking has emphasized the decisive role played by the emerging disciplines of anthropology and Darwinian science.[7] This list is by no means exhaustive. My intention, however, is not to revisit this debate here. Indeed, this chapter is only ostensibly about race.

I say "ostensibly" because what concerns me here is less the emergence of racially identified bodies per se than the birth of the human subject as the bearer of knowledge and source of meaning. Intertwined with this first point is a second: Concurrent with the birth of the subject was the rendering of the world as object, and included among these "objects" was the body. Man's historically shifting relationship to knowledge, in other words, had a crucial bearing on the possibilities and limitations attributed to the body.

Knowledge of the body and the significance attributed to it changed historically over the four hundred years that divides the Renaissance and the nineteenth century. This chapter seeks to map these broader transformations in European representations of the body to argue that nineteenth-century racial thought relied for its enunciation on particular epistemic conditions that were absent in the Renaissance and Classical Age. Specifically, nineteenth-century racial theories rested on an epistemological edifice that both recognized the body as an object *and* represented that object as transparent, intransigent, and measurable. It was precisely the rendering of the body as an immutable, passive object that transformed it into a site of discourse and accorded it a significance it had hitherto lacked.

Given the historical terrain I intend to cover, this chapter is organized in three chronological sections. In the first section, I focus on late medieval and Renaissance thought, arguing that the absence of man as subject and the presumed agency of God and other non-human actors, worked to produce an understanding of the body that endowed it with transformative and transgressive potential. Speaking meaningfully of the body in the medieval period and the Renaissance requires relinquishing modern categories of race (and, for that matter, gender or sexuality), for what we confront in this period are not races but a far more eclectic array of characters that include wild men, monsters, hermaphrodites, and lactating monks. In short, Renaissance understandings of the body as fluid and dynamic militated against fixed or stable categories of racial distinction.

The second section turns to the Classical Age (the late seventeenth century to the late eighteenth century), when man comes to recognize himself as the subject and bearer of knowledge. Concurrent with this transformation was the rendering of the body as object. Yet this object is not an immutable, fixed entity but one that was recognized as pliable and malleable to human agency. The body was an entity that could be negatively transformed by an undisciplined imagination or positively subjugated to, and transcended through, the will of reason, the influences of pedagogy, and the possibilities of science. Classical representations of the body as pliable and thus receptive to human volition, I argue, failed to accord racial physiology with an overriding and deterministic significance.

Finally, the third section is concerned with the nineteenth century and addresses, most specifically, the subject of race. It does so however, in the context of a nineteenth-century episteme that, like that of the Classical Age, recognized man as subject but, unlike in the preceding centuries, was compelled to qualify his transcendental status in the full knowledge of man's historicity. The body in this context comes to have a deterministic significance precisely because it is accorded an immutability and intransigence that is resistant to the inconstancy and variability of time. The body, in other words, becomes a stable, transparent, and measurable object of knowledge—a body that is knowable precisely through its meticulously raced, sexed, and sexualized classification. It is only in the nineteenth century, I suggest, that it becomes possible to speak of racialized bodies in any meaningful sense, because it is only at this time that the body comes to be packaged in discrete, inflexible categories of delineation. This argument will be developed in reference to nineteenth-century racial science and the policing techniques of anthropometry, and then fingerprinting, in British India. But before we turn to the world of races, criminal castes, and skull measurements, it is necessary to acquaint ourselves with Amazons and monsters.

# Bodily Antics within a Divine Order

In 1533, Charles V of Spain was informed of the imminent arrival at the ports of Santander and Laredo of sixty ships carrying some ten thousand Amazon women. Valladolid was in the throes of excited expectation when it was further rumored that the ship's crew was seeking mates to replenish its all-female population. The vaunted and widely publicized arrival of these exotic/erotic people had short-lived but significant material repercussions for the town itself. Its population soared as news spread of the impending visit, and the price of meat, vegetables, and lodgings reached astronomical heights. Needless to say, the ship never did reach its expected destination, and consequently the high hopes fueled by the prospect of an unrestrained orgy were bitterly disappointed.

This event—or, more accurately, non-event—is described by Germán Arciniegas in *America in Europe: History of the New World in Reverse*.[8] Unfortunately, Arciniegas does not cite the source of his information. But it is not important. The incident *could* have taken place, for we have learned enough about medieval and Renaissance history to know that Amazon women were only one example of the vast diversity that made up God's kingdom on Earth.

Similar stories are related in the pages of contemporary scholarship, usually followed by remonstrations at the ignorance of a bygone age. Kirkpatrick Sale, for example, appears bemused if not contemptuous of what he regards as the superstition that pervaded Renaissance thought and practices. He has little patience, for example, with Columbus's efforts to discover land by referring to natural signs such as the movements of clouds and the sighting of dolphins. In my retelling of the anticipated Amazon event, I have been conscientiously cautious to avoid the language of "belief," "imagination," "mythology," "superstition," and "fable." I am cautious not in order to persuade the modern reader of the existence of Amazon women or as some misguided effort to recuperate the voice of the subaltern but as a means to explore what it meant for European conceptions of difference when diversity included among its ranks wild men and women, ghosts, witches, and a complex array of divine prodigies and portents that came in the form of human monstrosities.

For some time now, the fabulous creatures that roamed the pages of ancient and Renaissance texts have been revived in the works of contemporary scholars. These "fabulous freaks," as Rudolf Wittkower once called them, have come to fall under the generic title of the "wild man."[9] This ambiguous nomenclature, which has included within its ranks tailed humans, witches, and reclusive Christian sages (Richard Bernheimer); centaurs, satyrs, titans, Amazons, and Cyclopes (Roger Barta); and anti-prophets, giants, and nomads (Hayden White), has, in fact, no ancient equivalent. Whereas Bernheimer justifies the nomenclature through reference to the Latin *silva* (wild), referring to both the character and the habitat of the wild man, Barta's work, which focuses specifically on antiquity, defends his use of the term through reference to the Greek word *agrios* (undomesticated and wild fields), signifying the antithesis of *hemeros* (a domesticated, docile space).[10]

Despite the etymological confusion, the wild man can be recognized as possessing some general characteristics. His existence testified to a series of transgressions that found expression in three interrelated ways: physiological confusion (anatomical disarrangement of human body parts or the intermingling of human and animal physiques), moral ambiguity (the wild man, like beasts, was often described as oblivious to social norms and ethics), and geographical displacement (the wild man often resided in the wild, whether in the forested mountain regions that skirt the *polis*, or Christian community, or on the distant and exotic shores that lay beyond its horizons).

Such transgressive characteristics ensured that the wild man and wild woman were figures to be feared. Though it is true that during the Middle Ages the wild man came to have some positive religious associations as mystics,[11] for the most part such creatures testified to the dangers of wild, unsocial spaces. When they were not eating young children, wild women were known to transform themselves into beautiful maidens to lure unguarded shepherds, only to return to their original hideous form after their passions had been satisfied.[12] More generally, not only did the close proximity of wild men and wild women—their tendency to live in the wooded margins of a village or town—ensure that these figure would pose a perennial threat to the security and stability of community life, but their very existence testified to the dangers and degradation that could befall the individual who sought to live outside the moral, social, and physical boundaries God bequeathed to mortal man.

In addition to wild men and wild women, about whom more will be said in the next section, the late medieval Christian canon, Renaissance travel tales, and medical treatises all recognize the existence of another set of beings who are generally identified as *monstraum*. As Lorraine Daston and Katharine Park argue in their exhaustive *Wonders and the Order of Nature*, monsters in medieval and Renaissance thought were often demarcated in two distinct categories.[13] There were monstrous species (the dog-headed cynocephali, the horse-bodied onocentaurs, or the double-sexed androgynes of Africa) that, particularly after the eleventh century, provoked admiration rather than fear: They spoke to the infinite diversity of God's kingdom rather than being an omen of God's displeasure. Indeed, in one fifteenth-century woodcut, the cynocephali are represented "as an urbane and productive citizen in European dress, engaged in commercial activity and flanked by a castle of French architecture and design."[14]

But if monstrous species did not provoke fear, the same could not be said of monstrous individuals. Monstrous individuals (conjoined twins, a child born with two heads, and so forth) spoke not to the benign magnificence of God but to his vengeance and anger. Monstrous individuals generated horror less because of their form than because of their signification: They were warnings, portents of the evils to come if sinful Christians did not return to the path of God. As Daston and Park elaborate, "If the marvellous races were a phenomenon of the margins, an embellishment and completion of the natural order, individual monsters erupted in the Christian centre, bought on by its corruption and sin. They were suspensions of that order, signs of God's wrath."[15]

Wild men and monsters were part of a complex cosmology that presumed God as its center. For my purposes, the medieval and Renaissance literature on wild men and monsters is significant for three interrelated reasons. First, for the medieval period and the Renaissance, wild men, marvelous races, and monstrous individuals did exist. In other words, the question that Paul Veyne answered affirmatively—"Did the Greeks believe in their myths?"[16]—elicits the same positive response when directed at medieval and Renaissance thought. Whether we consult the Christian canonical literature (e.g., the work of St. Augustine or Thomas Aquinas), the travel literature (of which John Mandeville's and Marco Polo's writings are among the most famous), the cartography of the period (such as the luscious maps reproduced from Ptolemy's *Geography* that litter the world with fabulous creatures), or the innumerable illustrations and woodcuts that the Renaissance in particular inspired, what becomes immediately apparent is that wild men, monsters, and marvelous species were not relegated to the status of myth or dismissed as the superstitious beliefs of an ignorant lay population. Rather, ecclesiastical authorities and many of the learned men of the Renaissance sanctioned the existence of this eclectic assortment of characters. Indeed, as Arnold Davidson has suggested, the existence of wild men and monsters was entirely in keeping with, and an integral feature of, medieval and Renaissance reasoning.[17]

Second, far from representing the pervasive irrationality of pre-modern ideas, Daston points to the fact that the space occupied by the figure of the monster was part of a larger theological distinction between the natural and that which lay outside its norms. In contrast to the binaries of nature–culture familiar to moderns, late medieval Christian theology—particularly the writings of Thomas Aquinas—offered a dense and complex classificatory system that recognized the non-natural as operating through multiple sites. As Daston notes, in contrast to the "natural," where nature functioned in predictable ways, the non-natural recognized within its ranks the supernatural, the preternatural, the artificial, and the unnatural.[18]

The supernatural consisted of miracles that could only be attributed to the hand of God. It is only the agency of God that could suspend the order of nature—that could allow for the parting of the Red Sea, the resurrection of the dead, and the walking on water. But if miracles were solely the work of God, according agency to preternatural events was a much more complicated affair. While in practice miracles and preternatural occurrences were rarely so clearly demarcated, Aquinas insisted on the need to distinguish miracles from marvels, the suspension of nature from the transgressions of nature. Not only were preternatural occurrences more common than miracles, they often signified portents or prodigies. In such an event, the preternatural was the work of God—a sign of his displeasure. Comets, rain of blood, monstrous births, seasonal anomalies such as snow in summer—all such events could be an omen delivered to man by God.[19] But preternatural occurrences could also be attributed to the devious work of demons, the action of angels, human sorcery, or the work of nature itself. Included in the preternatural were "figured stones, petrifying springs, the occult virtue of plants, and minerals and myriad other deviations from the ordinary course of things."[20] Thus, interpreting the preternatural and identifying its rightful source was no small concern. Witchcraft trials for example, hinged on the question of agency: Was a sudden, inexplicable illness that befell an individual the work of the devil, the sorcery of a witch, a judgment from God, or the function of nature?[21]

No such ambiguity troubled the categories of the artificial and the unnatural. Both were singularly the product of human agency and thus accorded a lower status in the hierarchy of unnatural events. The artificial was born of man's labor from the fruits of nature—the oak table was artifice; the oak tree, natural. The unnatural was similarly attributed to the actions of man. Entirely ensconced in the language of morality, unnatural acts directly contravened the order of nature and thus constituted a violation of divine law. Largely articulated through the medium of the familial and the sexual, Aquinas included among his list of unnatural acts sodomy, bestiality, and self-abuse.[22]

Within this complex configuration, monstrous species such as Amazons and androgynes were part of the larger order of nature—they reflected the awesome and immense diversity of God's Creation. Monstrous species, in other words, carried no normative significance. As Daston and Park explain, "The wonders of the East and other topographical marvels had no particular intrinsic meaning. God had made them at the beginning of time for his own reasons; they simply were, like foxes or Frenchmen or the Rock of Gibraltar, and they symbolized at most the power and wisdom of their Creator."[23]

Thus, within the context of late medieval and Renaissance conceptualizations of nature, the dual-sexed race of androgynes was not outside the natural order but an expression of it. Monstrous individuals, on the other hand, were recognizably unnatural, and their birth testified to the world of the preternatural—the complex array of prodigies and portents that were signs of God's disapproval or, alternatively, the monstrous antics of demons. There was no question in the mind of the Protestant scholar Lycosthenes that "a monster is an imposing sign of divine wrath and malediction."[24]

In either instance, whether monstrous species or monstrous individuals, what is singularly apparent—and this speaks to my third point—is that medieval and Renaissance thought attributed to nature volition and malleability that ultimately would be denied it in the nineteenth century. The complex (and for us moderns, unfamiliar) configuration of the natural and non-natural, not to mention the existence of hybrid human-and-animal populations, suggests the lack of fixity, permanency, and passivity attributed to nature. Thus, monstrous individuals spoke to the constant threat of nature's transgressions when willed by God, angels, or demons. But nature itself was also attributed with agency. As Lycosthenes makes clear, "We do not condemn natural explanations and we greatly respect astrology too. But we know that nature is God's minister in matters both favorable and unfavorable, and that through her agency, he aids the pious and punishes the impious, according to their different conditions."[25]

Consequently, even when occurrences once accorded to divine or demonic sources are increasingly, through the course of the sixteenth century, attributed to natural causes, this should not necessarily be interpreted as the gradual embracing of secular skepticism. Nature was a protagonist. In his sixteenth-century compendium of monsters, Ambroise Paré could accord some births with divine significance while identifying others as stemming from natural causes, such as the maternal imagination.[26] Indeed, in his first chapter Paré assigns thirteen causes of monsters, of which ten are attributed to nature; two, to God; and one, to demonic forces.[27] It is quite possible, Paré assures us, that a woman who delivers a monstrous child may not be witnessing the wrath of God but suffering the consequences of her own imagination. It was precisely this explanation Paré recounted to explain the birth of a white child to Ethiopia's Queen Persina and King Hidustes: It was not a case of infidelity but the consequence of the queen's imagination, which had been aroused by a painting of Andromeda that hung in her bedroom "during the embraces from which she became pregnant."[28] The image subsequently imprinted itself on the body of her newborn child.

I will have reason to speak more on the maternal imagination in the next section. For the moment, however, what is significant is that nature was capable of infinite variety (monstrous species), could be transgressed (monstrous individuals), had volition (e.g., through collusion with the maternal imagination), or could, in some instances, be suspended altogether (as in the case of miracles). Given that nature was neither mute nor immutable, it should not surprise us that the body in medieval and Renaissance literature was attributed a malleability and opacity that rendered its boundaries porous and fluid. The fixed, passive, measurable transparency accorded the body in nineteenth-century thought was not *available to thought* in the medieval and Renaissance periods.

Caroline Bynum's work on the medieval church is instructive in this regard, because the rich allegorical imagery of the period relied on gendered attributes that did not necessarily correspond to sexed distinctions.[29] For example, Bynum argues that, from the twelfth century to the fourteenth century, "Maternal imagery was applied . . . to male religious authority figures, particularly abbots, bishops and the apostles, as well to God and Christ" (112). Thus, Anselm of Canterbury (ca. 1109) appealed to Jesus as Mother: "But you, Jesus, good lord, are you not also a mother? . . . For what others have conceived and given birth to, they have received from you. . . . It is then you, above all, Lord God, who are our mother" (114). What Bynum refers to as the "feminization of religious language" (135–46) during the Middle Ages found expression through psychological references such as that of Bernard of Clairvaux (1153), who instructed abbots to combine the authority and discipline of a father with the love and gentleness of a mother (118). However, such symbolism was not confined to behavioral attributes. It also appealed to rich, often erotic, corporeal imagery. Aelred Rievaulx (1167) was not alone in employing the image of the woman's breast with the love of Jesus when he urged that Jesus's "naked breasts will feed you with the milk of sweetness to console you" (123). Such imagery was not confined to Jesus. Instructing prelates on their responsibility, Barnard urged them to "be gentle, avoid harshness, do not resort to blows, expose your breasts: let your bosoms expand with milk not swell with passion" (118).

Bernard was enamored with the imagery of divine breasts feeding the human soul. For Guerric, Abbot of Igny (ca. 1157), pregnancy and the womb, the association with birth, was the allegory to which he appealed when he wrote, "Brethren, this name of mother is not restricted to prelates. . . . It is shared by you too who do the Lord's will. Yes, you too are mothers of the child who has been born for you and in you, that is, since you conceived from the fear of the Lord and gave birth to the spirit of Salvation" (121). The maternal figure offered a powerful and emotive set of associations in the Middle Ages, for it appealed to three representations commonly identified with the feminine: the generational powers of women; mothers as loving, affectionate, and tender; and women as nurturing (feeding their newborns with their own milk [132]). That such imagery could be appropriated and applied to male authority figures—whether the abbots or Jesus himself—suggests the fluid nature of gendered imagery in the Middle Ages. As Bynum rightly argues, "The female (or woman) and the feminine (as distinct from women) are not the same. The former is a person of one gender; the latter may be an aspect of a person of either gender" (167). Indeed, if

Jesus was often represented in feminine garb from the twelfth century to the fourteenth century, in the Carolingian period, Bynum argues, it was not unusual to represent the Virgin Mary donning a beard and attributed with male characteristics (139).

The absence of a rigid correlation between gendered attributes and sexed bodies in the Middle Ages can be explained, at least partially, by the fact that, as Thomas Laqueur argues, "For several thousand years it had been a commonplace that women have the same genitals as men, except that as Nemesius, bishop of Emesa in the sixth century A.D., put it, 'Theirs are inside the body and not outside it.'"[30] The fact that women's bodies were colder than men's (attesting to women's inferiority) meant that not enough heat was generated to push their genitals out. This one-sex model, to borrow Laqueur's term, which informed European conceptions of the body from the ancient Greeks to the eighteenth century, sustained a hierarchical distinction between men and women that nevertheless did not presume radical differences between male and female anatomy. As one author put it, "Turn outward the woman's, and turn inward, so to speak, and fold double the man's, and you will find the same in both in every respect."[31]

Precisely because the female body was recognized as simply an inversion of the male body, there was little cause, Laqueur suggests, for assigning different names to female anatomy. What today would be identified as the vagina, labia, uterus, and ovaries were, for a millennium, recognized as penis, foreskin, scrotum, and testicles, respectively.[32] As for menstrual bleeding, that was no different from bleeding more generally: It was the body's way to release excess fluids (thus the pervasive practice of leeching as a curative procedure for illness). It is in this context, as well, that we can understand medieval iconography of the Savior wherein the blood of Christ did not simply bear a metaphorical resemblance to mother's milk; rather, following medical theories of the time, maternal milk was the product of the mother's own processed blood. Thus, Bynum argues, when evoking the image of "Christ the Savior feed[ing] the individual soul with his own blood," the analogy drawn was that "of the nursing mother whose milk *is* her blood, offered to the child" (133).

Whereas the two-sex model of the body that was to emerge in the late eighteenth century (and continues into our own time) presumes a radical incommensurability and distinctiveness between male and female anatomy, the one-sex model that saw little corporeal variation between men and women attributed the body with a greater degree of fluidity and transformative power. Not only were some anatomical parts accorded mobility (the womb, for example, was well known to wander), but also a sudden imbalance of heat and fluids could account for sudden changes in sex.

The fascination in the Renaissance with hermaphrodites has increasingly received the attention of contemporary scholars.[33] In the sixteenth century, one of the more famous cases, recorded by Paré, is that of a girl christened Marie-Germaine who, while chasing a swine that had escaped her care, jumped over a ditch. At that moment, "The genitalia and the male rod came to be developed in him, having ruptured the ligaments by which they had been held enclosed."[34] Michel de Montaigne, who recorded the event many years later, noted that Marie-Germaine (renamed Germain) became the subject of a song sung by village girls "in which they warn one not to stretch their legs too wide for fear of becoming males, like Marie Germaine."[35]

What becomes apparent from this literature is that the body, independent of divine or demonic intervention, was far from an immutable entity. For this reason, efforts to render the body a site of identity were necessarily complicated. As I argued in chapter 2, in his various essays and his book *Renaissance Self-Fashioning*, Stephen Greenblatt has consistently argued that individuality as an expression of a deep-seated sense of interiority was not a sensibility familiar to the men and women of the Renaissance. In attributing a much more fluid sense of self to Renaissance thought, Greenblatt has denied to the Renaissance a psychology of individuality (a cognitive sense of uniqueness and authenticity) even at the level of corporeal identity.[36]

Greenblatt dramatized his point through a Renaissance court case involving the trial of Arnaud du Tilh. For some eight years, du Tilh lived as a small farmer by the name of Martin Guerre, until the real Guerre returned to his French village of Arigat and denounced du Tilh as an imposter bent on stealing his property and carrying on adulterous relations with his wife. The significance of the case, as Greenblatt explains, rests on what was strikingly absent from the court records—namely, the failure on the part of the judge or even Guerre himself to locate identity in his body, in his corporeal individuality. Indeed, "No one bothers to invoke Martin's biological individuality or even his soul, let alone an infancy that would have seemed almost comically beside the point."[37] Efforts during the trial to corroborate Guerre's guilt or innocence made reference to his body, but it only "figured . . . as a collection of attributes—lines, curves, volumes (scars, features, clothing, shoe size, and so on)—that could be held up against anyone who claimed the name and property of Martin Guerre."[38]

For all of the commentary the body generated, for all of the fascination it provoked, medieval and Renaissance writers could not presume stable identities and rigid corporeally based typologies in part because they could not presume stable and fixed bodies. It is questionable, therefore, whether medieval and Renaissance thought could have appealed to discrete, corporally organized racial categories. I argued elsewhere that in a world where wild men and monsters exist, there is no conceptual space for race.[39] Such variations as we identify with race were simply peripheral and largely insignificant when God's Creation was so magnificently diverse as to allow for a vast array of human–animal hybrids. But even if we cede this point in deference to scholars who recognize in modern racial prejudice a pre-modern origin, what remains largely uncontroversial is the fact that nineteenth-century racism was historically distinctive from any pre-modern articulation. This is so, however, not simply because in its latter incarnation race came to be associated with science. While it is true that according race with scientific legitimacy was a novel feature of the nineteenth century, this begs the question of how the body first came to be represented as a stable, transparent, immutable, and passive object—an object available to scientific scrutiny.

The historical literature I have appealed to suggests that nineteenth-century representations of the body as transparent, measurable, and immutable would have been wholly unfamiliar to both medieval and Renaissance thought. But if the examples I have provided testify to the fluidity of medieval and Renaissance conceptions of the body, they do not in themselves account for why these historical periods could recognize in the body such transformative and eclectic possibilities. Pursuing this question necessitates identifying what the medieval period and the Renaissance share: the absence of man as the precursor to, and the agent of, knowledge.

Michel de Certeau's *The Writing of History* is instructive in this regard, for he warns us, with reference to writing religious history, that "a society that is no longer religious imposes *its* rationality, *its* own categories, *its* problems, and *its* type of organization upon religious formulations. . . . From this perspective the only possible religious history would be a history of religious *societies*."[40] It is at the very moment when "society" frames our historical enquiry—when, in other words, we appeal to sociological models in our investigation of the Middle Ages or the seventeenth century—that we effectively erase the particularity of the history we seek to write: "In this perspective, 'comprehending' religious phenomena is tantamount to repeatedly asking something else of them than what they meant to say; . . . to taking as a representation of the society, what, from their point of view, *founded* that society."[41]

In a historical context within which Amazons, human–animal hybrids, and monsters are not contained within sociological categories of "belief" but simply *are*, the recognition of difference needs to be articulated through conceptual grids that are unfamiliar to the modern. I have already discussed one such grid in the form of similitude wherein knowledge of the New World was organized through a pre-existing network of resemblances that, far from constituting the Americas as a radical other, worked to render it familiar and recognizable. Yet what was only gestured to in chapter 1 is what I now wish to speak to directly—namely, that this form of reasoning did not presume a rigid delineation between man and the rest of God's Creation.

A number of scholars have sought to trace the shift from an enchanted world where men coexisted with monsters, ghosts, and witches and was subject to the whims of God, angels, and demons to a modern era wherein the only conceivable subject came in recognizably human form and was the sole bearer of knowledge in an world otherwise devoid of meaning.

Evoking the language of disenchantment is an obvious reference to Max Weber, for it was Weber who articulated the classic historicist thesis that each era of European history had its own particularity, its own *Weltanschauung*, or worldview. With a certain nostalgic regret, Weber describes the loss of an earlier time in European history, one that permitted space for miracles and magic, for divine intervention and demonic sorcery, for nature's volition and nature's transgressions. Yet Weber's poignant description of the modern as disenchanted did not deter him from reading in modernity's loss a clearly recognizable gain: the unveiling of truth. In that melancholic moment when modern man no longer conceived of the world as purposeful, meaningful, and divinely ordained, he may have lost his innocence, but he gained reason. The superstition of earlier times had given way to the recognition that God, angels, and the devil were products of the human imagination. This, after all, had always been the case. But it was modern man who finally bequeathed to himself that which he had earlier bequeathed to the supernatural: agency, volition, meaning, knowledge, order, and Reason.[42]

Yet as historicist as Weber's evocation of *Weltanschauung* appeared to be, it was Martin Heidegger who forced us to recognize that the very idea of *Weltanschauung* had to be historically interrogated. It was not that each historical period had it own worldview but, rather, that the conceptualization of the world as picture was itself the product of modernity.[43] The world as picture was a world constituted through representation; it presumed a way of being, living, and ordering the world that necessitated a distinction between the human subject as observer and a non-human world of objects: "Hence world picture when understood essentially does not mean a picture of the world but the world conceived and grasped as a picture. What is, in its entirety, is now taken in such a way, that it first is in being and only is in being to the extent that it is set up by man, who represents and sets it forth."[44]

Representing the world as picture required man to become "the primary and only real *subiectum.*" It simultaneously necessitated a radically different relationship to "that which is as such."[45] Man now conceptualizes "that which is as such" as objects independent of himself, as representations constituted by him in reference to himself. In other words, while Weber was right to argue that a divinely ordained, purposeful universe was the distinctive feature of an enchanted age, he implicitly privileged that which he recognized to be absent: a modern epistemology wherein the world could be rendered an object (a picture) only from the vantage point that elevated the human subject an observer, as he who both was "in" the world while simultaneously able to extract himself from it.[46]

For this reason, the language of representation when applied to medieval and Renaissance thought becomes problematic. Searching for medieval and Renaissance *representations* of the body is necessarily fraught, because evoking the language of representation presumes a subject representing and a world available to being represented. It presumes a distinction between subject and object, a world that recognizes "man" as an ontological category.

Man as subject was not an ontological possibility in medieval and Renaissance thought. This becomes evident when we register three features of medieval and Renaissance thought that thus far have been only obliquely and diffusely gestured to through the histories of the body I have narrated.

First, as Certeau argued, religion as a conceptual boundary that encapsulates its subject by distinguishing it from other conceptual categories limits rather than enables our understanding of medieval and Renaissance thought. God existed not as a product of thought but as its very condition of possibility. His presence is what constituted, framed, and, indeed, enabled knowledge. It is only in the knowledge of God's presence and in the context of His Creation that wild men incited loathing, that monstrous species inspired awe, and that monstrous individuals provoked foreboding. Even when, as was increasingly the case during the Renaissance, strange occurrences were explained through reference to natural causes, the "nature" being summoned was not an objectified entity but an active agent, the handmaiden of God.

Related to this first point is a second: Man was not privileged as the sole bearer of intentionality or volition—indeed, man continually had to bow to the will of an interventionist God; guard himself against the deception of demons and witches; co-exist with spirits, ghosts, and wild men; and remain cautiously alert to the transgressive powers of nature. As I argued in chapter 1, following Foucault, Renaissance knowledge was not predicated on a binary relationship between human subjects and material objects. It relied on an intricate web of resemblances that wove words, being, and things into the fabric of Creation. In other words, man was not a subject that could be extricated from Creation; man was part of a larger cosmology that included (but did not exhaust) non-human actors—spirits, demons, wild men, monsters, and angels.

It is, finally, within this web of relations that man was not a sovereign subject gazing on a world pacified and subordinated to his reason, that the body could retain its transformative powers, could be an active agent, could transgress its porous boundaries and offer itself as a site for salvation and sacrifice, demonic convulsions, or prodigal possibilities. The body, in medieval and Renaissance thought, was opaque and elusive, fluid and mobile, malleable and unpredictable.

The three features I have identified with medieval and Renaissance thought should alert us to why any scholarship on pre-nineteenth-century racial thinking cannot afford to detach such subject matter from its epistemological bearings. Whether we turn to St. Augustine's insistence that all creatures of God are testimony to His magnificence, sixteenth-century efforts to register human differences in conformity with the attributes of the planets, the growing popularity of the Old Testament account of Ham's exile to Africa, the expulsion of Jews and Moors from Spain at the close of the fifteenth century, or the scathing denouncements of indigenous American savagery during the era of conquest, what we cannot afford to lose sight of is that, however race was conceived during these historical periods and in whatever ways racism found expression, it did so within a compass of thought conditioned and circumscribed by the knowledge of God.

Even in those instances in which race was evoked without any pronounced reference to God—think, for example, of Othello—identity, as Greenblatt suggests, cannot presume the body as an irreducible site for its enunciation. Othello's black skin is offset by his lineage, bravery, and loyalty (the play, after all, is a tragedy), a fact that is succinctly articulated by the Duke of Venice: "If virtue no delighted beauty lack / Your son-in-law is far more fair than black."[47] Othello's identity, in other words, is not reducible to his body. Instead, his physiognomy is continually complicated, qualified, destabilized, and moderated through a moral and social economy that includes lineage, religion, gender, wealth, and a host of virtues and vices. A purposeful, meaningful, and divinely ordered world is implied, for it is only with the presumption of such an order that the tragedy of Othello is rendered intelligible.

Where the body does not lend itself to stable identities and rigid classificatory systems, any scholarship on race in the medieval and Renaissance must be alert to the conceptual presumptions that can underwrite and distort the historical periods we seek to investigate. Man as the bearer of knowledge and the body as an object of representation are two such presumptions that cannot be sustained in the context of medieval and Renaissance thought.

From monstrous species to monstrous individuals, an interventionist God and malicious demons, wild men and libidinous hags, wandering wombs and lactating monks, hermaphrodites and imposters, nature's wondrous feats and unnatural transgressions, preternatural marvels and supernatural miracles—for all of the differences that distinguish medieval and Renaissance thought, the fact is that neither age accorded man the ontological status of subject. Man was not privileged as the exclusive bearer of meaning, order, and knowledge. God, wild men, monsters, demons, witches, ghosts, and, indeed, nature itself coexisted, intervened, enabled, and obstructed human ambitions. In the medieval and Renaissance periods, we neither encounter man as subject nor the body as object; neither man as transcendental observer nor the world as picture.

## Dangerous Imaginations and Pliable Bodies

In November 1726, news had reached London that the wife of Joshua Toft, a poor cloth worker residing in Godalming, had a month earlier given birth to a rabbit.[48] John Howard, the town doctor, had dismissed earlier claims by Mary Toft to have delivered monsters. When Toft was again in labor sometime in October, Howard, who approached the matter of monstrous births with the characteristic skepticism demanded of his profession, was ultimately persuaded of the truth of Toft's story on witnessing and, indeed, delivering the first of the Toft rabbits. News of the strange births had not only grabbed the attention of a curious public, but, as Lord Hervey informed a friend by letter, "All the eminent physicians, Surgeons, and Men mid-wifes in London are there Day and Night to watch her next production."[49] Their efforts were not in vain, for conveniently Toft's pregnancy was far from reaching its conclusion: She would give birth to a total litter of seventeen rabbits over a period of a month. Ultimately, however, irrespective of the eminence of the individual doctors, all testimony verifying the truth of the monstrous births was to meet with censure, ridicule, dismay, and anger when, on December 7, some two months after her first "production," Toft bowed to the pressure and threats "of several skeptical doctors and a menacing justice of the peace" and admitted that the whole story had been a cruel hoax.[50] With the assistance of her mother-in-law (who was also the local midwife) and her husband, Toft had skillfully and without detection managed to insert the rabbits into her vagina and, further, had fooled observers with her unique ability to produce the convulsions resonant with the contractions of labor.

The supernatural and preternatural had enormous explanatory appeal in the late medieval period and through the course of the Renaissance. They permitted one to account for (if not necessarily to understand) the strange events that periodically disrupted and troubled town and village life. Some

Renaissance scholars also came to recognize in unusual phenomena another explanatory possibility: natural causes.

In the context of monstrous births, the maternal imagination was one such natural cause. The explanation remained persuasive well into the eighteenth century.[51] Indeed, the story of Mary Toft is one of many in the seventeenth century and eighteenth century that testifies to the fact that monstrous births were not a thing of the past.[52]

Over the past twenty years, a growing body of literature has documented and commented on the lack of biological fixity attributed to the body in seventeenth-century and eighteenth-century writings. In addition to the work of Laqueur, the various contributors to G. S. Rousseau's and Roy Porter's edited *Sexual Underworlds of the Enlightenment* have explored the possibilities of gendered, sexual, and class transgressions that the Classical fascination with masquerading, cross-dressing, gender passing, libertinism, and the newly emerging novel permitted.[53] To these essays can be added Lynn Hunt's work on the politically and socially seditious nature of seventeenth-century and eighteenth-century French pornography and Julia V. Douthwaite's *The Wild Girl, Natural Man and the Monster* on the eighteenth-century faith in human perfectibility characterized by the century's fascination with wild children.[54] Finally, while much of this literature has focused attention on gender and sexuality, Dror Wahrman's recent work extends this scholarship to also consider Classical representations of colonial bodies—bodies that were conceived as malleable and responsive to the effects of climate, eclectic customs, and human ingenuity.[55]

I will return to this scholarship later in this section. For the moment, however, this growing body of work has persuasively demonstrated, through reference to a vast array of late-seventeenth-century and eighteenth-century travel accounts, judicial documents, medical treatises, novels, and philosophical writings, that, as Terry Castle has argued, the Classical Age presumed a "'polymorphous' subject—perverse by definition, sexually ambidextrous, and potentially unlimited in the range of its desire"—not to mention, in light of Wahrman's work, racially indeterminate.[56]

Yet what is largely absent in the midst of this copiously documented scholarship is an explanatory framework through which to account for why Classical thought accorded the body such plasticity and malleability. After all, the body in Renaissance thought was also recognized as a potentially unstable and fluid entity. Is the Classical Age, albeit with some minor variation, simply an extension of the Renaissance? While references to miracles and prodigies were to become less and less frequent (and more and more ridiculed) by the late seventeenth century, the continued appeal of the imagination as a causal explanation for monstrous births suggests that Classical representations of the body as porous and fluid were in keeping with Renaissance orthodoxy. Such seamless continuity, however, cannot be historically sustained. Indeed, as I argue, it is not historical continuity with the Renaissance that helps to account for Classical representations of the body. Rather, the malleable body of the Classical Age owes it explanatory appeal to a radically different epistemological logic from that which underwrote Renaissance thought.

The differences can be recognized in three ways that in reality are interwoven but can nevertheless be identified in the following terms. First, man's relationship to knowledge fundamentally changed. Knowledge ceased to be that which was *received* by man from God; instead, it was *acquired* by man through use of the reason God bequeathed him. Second, once knowledge was recognized as the fruit of human agency, man was accorded a significance and centrality that was denied to him during the Renaissance. Third, following from the fact that man was posited as the bearer of knowledge and the source of agency, it was not for God but for man to produce meaning, establish order, invent society, establish the political, and identify the rules governing truth.

With the emergence of man as the locus of agency and the bearer of knowledge came a corresponding shift in Classical representations of the body. What we encounter in the Classical Age is neither a body that is demonstrative of volition nor a body trapped within its own biological fixity. Rather, and somewhat counterintuitively, the body was accorded a malleability and fluidity in Classical thought precisely because it lacked any authoritative status within Classical thought. The ontological privileging of man as subject and the corresponding shift in his relationship to knowledge had the effect of minimizing the significance accorded the body. In other words, the body was either subsumed by or rendered marginal to more pressing concerns relating to human reason.

The remainder of this section is concerned with exploring this argument through reference to Classical debates on the role of the imagination, on the transformative potential of human subjectivity, and on the limitations and possibilities of corporeal fashioning.

One would expect that the controversy generated by the Toft affair would foreground and be organized around the spectacular productions of the maternal body. After all, the Toft hoax is a dramatic reminder of the gendered vocabulary that underscored Classical debates concerning the imagination and the body. Dictated by emotions and passions, as Jean-Jacques Rousseau famously argued, women possessed a lesser form of reason.[57] They were thus more susceptible to the effects of the imagination.

Yet what is immediately striking in Denis Todd's description of the controversy following the Toft affair is that, while women were viewed as more susceptible to the dangers of a wandering imagination, the danger was not confined to them. Recognizing this fact may go some way toward explaining the public agitation that followed the Toft case. The initial belief in the rabbit births and subsequent discovery of the ruse generated a popular and scholarly hysteria that was reflected not only in an avalanche of commentary, critiques, books, satires, and poetry, but also in the rich almost messianic language and imagery that the incident provoked. The Toft hoax, in other words, incited a controversy that appeared altogether disproportionate to the case itself—that of a poor illiterate woman seeking to make a profit out of a ruse.[58]

Accounting for such an excessive public reaction cannot be limited to Classical anxieties about the female body. Indeed, what is significant about the Toft affair is that a case made sensational by the remarkable feat performed by Mary's body actually helps dramatize the strangely peripheral significance accorded the body in Classical thought. This becomes evident once we recognize the extent to which Classical discussions of corporeality were consistently subsumed by what was posited as the more pressing and vexing concern regarding human cognition from which reason, agency, and free will were said to derive.

One school of thought, born out of a fusion between Cartesian dualism and Newtonian natural philosophy, essentially denied the body any significance at all.[59] The intellectual confluence between Cartesian and Newtonian philosophy relied for its foundational premise on the incommensurability of inert matter and non-material substances. Whereas consciousness (the non-material) permitted rational agency and allowed for free will, the body (matter) was a passive, unconscious machine that, in accordance with the laws of motion, carried out its functions independently of the mind.

The human body, as one seventeenth-century commentator argued, was "truly nothing else but a complex chymico-mechanical notion, depending on such principles as are purely mathematical."[60] The body so regulated to maximum efficiency by predetermined laws was incapable of conscious volition, of transformative powers. It was incapable, in short, of being influenced by the imagination.

The implications of mechanical philosophy for Classical theories of generation were significant.[61] Indeed, it was against the background of these intellectual currents that pre-existence, a theory that emerged in the last quarter of the seventeenth century, came to be the prevailing explanation for generation some thirty years later. Following from the principle that the body was a complex, mechanically regulated object, defenders of pre-existence maintained that the unborn child did not so much "grow" in the womb as "uncoil," the female body having been implanted since Eve with fully formed individuals. The power of the maternal imagination to affect the unborn child was therefore an impossibility. Not only could consciousness have no bearing on corporeality, but God had performed the task of generation some six thousand years earlier.[62]

As Porter rightly cautions, Classical medical theories were far from monolithic.[63] Indeed, as Todd demonstrates, even before—but certainly after—the Toft hoax, polemical battles ensued between defenders of dualism and those who continued to testify to the interactive relationship between the mind and body.[64] Yet in the face of such multiple theories and much contestation, advocates and critics of mechanical philosophy nevertheless shared a core ontological presumption: that the locus of agency (intentional or not) emanated from the mind. If at issue was the body's responsiveness to the will of the imagination, what was not contentious was that which was no longer available to thought—namely, the possibility that the body possessed a volition and will of its own. For the critics no less than for the advocates of dualism and pre-existence, it was the power of the imagination and not the will of the body that was the source of contestation. The explanatory efficacy of the maternal imagination rested on the premise that monstrous births were the consequence of a disturbed mind, an imagination that had subordinated and subjugated

the body to its own anarchical wanderings. Defending a correlation between the mind and body did not translate into a privileging of the body
itself. Indeed, it was the imagination, not corporeality, that acquired an
anxiety-laden significance in the late seventeenth century and eighteenth
century.

Thus, whereas Paré in the sixteenth century could diminish the significance of monstrous births by attributing them to natural causes, for Classical thought positing the imagination as a source of explanation was far
from reassuring. The imagination was recognized as essential to human
knowledge, for among the many functions it assumed was the ability to
translate an external world into images available to the higher faculties of
the mind. But the imagination's powers were not limited to this purpose,
for, as Todd rightly notes, the imagination could also "creat[e] fanciful con-
structs that corresponded to nothing in the external world."[65]

Herein lay the problem.

During the Renaissance, knowledge was antecedent to, and existed independently of, the knower (hence, the enabling poetics of similitude, the
ubiquitous presence of signatures, the tireless search for resemblances).[66] In
the Classical age, "signs are ideas (or similar representations such as percep-
tions, images, or sensation)" that are born of, derived from, and must presuppose a knowing mind.[67] Thus, Foucault argues, "There can no longer
be an unknown sign, a mute mark," because Classical signs are an arbitrary
construction, a conscious human invention that represent (as opposed
to resemble) the objects that they mark.[68] Knowledge, in other words,
is no longer derived from the *discovery* of signs; it is derived from their
*imposition*.

What we recognize in the Classical age is that which was absent in the
Renaissance: the power to represent. The foundational premise of Classical epistemology is the positing of knowledge as that which is obtained
through man's ability to represent the world to himself. Presumed in such a
logic was man's independence from the world of words, beings, and things.
The world was available to the human gaze precisely because man was posited as both in the world and, simultaneously, autonomous and detached
from it. This is why knowledge was no longer viewed as emanating directly
from God. Signs were not the divine litter that marked the objects of God's
Creation; they were, rather, the fruits of human reason that first emanated

from the human mind and only subsequently came to be identified with the external world.

The significance of this ontological distinction between the sign and the object world resides in the presumption that underwrites it: that man is the bearer of knowledge. If the Renaissance recognized in God the author of all truth—a God who bestowed on man a meaningful, ordered, and knowledge-excreting world on which He made his own presence known through prodigies and supernatural feats—in the epistemological landscape of the Classical age, it was man who posited his own existence as the necessary precondition of knowledge. Knowledge, in other words, was anthropologized. Robert Boyle's position was representative of that of many natural philosophers when he warned, "It is a dangerous thing to believe other creatures, than angels and men, to be intelligent and rational; especially to ascribe to them an architectonic, provident, and governing power."[69] Anthropomorphizing nature—attributing to nature volition or agency—was tantamount to worshiping false gods.[70] In the late seventeenth century, Boyle was prepared to share man's authority with angels. By the middle of the eighteenth century, man had usurped the sole rights to knowledge and free will. "It is the presence of man," Diderot explained in the pages of the *Encyclopédie*, "which makes the existence of things meaningful," for "man is the single place from which we must begin and to which we must refer everything."[71]

It is from his privileged status as a knowing subject that man appropriates from God the prerogative to assign signs to objects, combine signs (such as ideas) to produce complex thought, and establish identities and differences between related objects and beings, thereby discerning the order of the world. Thus, we can recognize in the writings of Hobbes and Locke a familial, epistemic resemblance, as demonstrated in their efforts to privilege linguistic signs as a product of human invention rather than as the fruit of divine magnificence.

Reason was an exclusive privilege bequeathed to man by God. But it was a privilege that was fraught with the anxiety of its loss. If knowledge, meaning, and order are the products of human ingenuity and are produced and sustained through rational thought, then the value—indeed, the necessity—of safeguarding the sovereignty of reason against the demands and deceits of lesser emotions took on an urgency and fueled an anxiety that had no parallel in the sixteenth century.

It is within this context that the imagination took on an unprecedented significance in the seventeenth century and eighteenth century. The imagination was not only a threat to the individuated corporeal self; it was also a threat to the social and political body. Even if, as François Boissier de Sauvages was to argue, "The imagination itself does not err, since it neither denies nor affirms but is fixed to so great a degree on the simple contemplation of an image," the fact that the imagination functioned as a "great leveler" unable, of its own accord, to distinguish reality from fantasy, ensured its ambiguous status as both an enabler of reason and that which aides in its deception.[72] What the imagination disregards is that which is crucial to—indeed, a condition of—Classical thought: that signs are not of the world but are born of the mind and only subsequently come to be assigned to that which they mark. Because the imagination translates the external world into the neutral singularity of a series of indiscriminate images, it does not safeguard the sovereignty of reason. Rather, it risks collapsing the ontological distinction between the knowing subject and a world of objects. It is unsurprising, then, that the imagination provoked such extensive commentary in the seventeenth century and eighteenth century.

Among the many commentators preoccupied by the dangers of the imagination was John Locke. As noted in chapter 2, the imagination for Locke was that function of the mind that required vigilant policing and strict control. This, as Uday Singh Mehta has persuasively argued, was the guiding principle underwriting much of Locke's work.[73] The problem that Locke identifies is that unreason—of which madness is an extreme form— is an immediate and ever present danger that haunts the most rational of men. Madness, Locke argues, "has its Original in very sober and rational minds;" for it is "a Weakness to which all men are . . . liable [and] which . . . universally infects mankind."[74]

Locke's anxiety concerning the imagination was not his alone. His contemporary Jonathan Swift voiced similar concerns when he argued that "the difference betwixt a madman and one in his wits consisted in this: that the former spoke out whatever came into his mind, and just in the confused manner as his *imagination* presented the ideas. The latter only expressed such thoughts as his judgment directed him to chuse."[75]

Similar observations can be found a hundred years later—when, for example, Matthey, a Genevan physician and student of Rousseau's, lampooned the deceits of civilization and its complacent presumptions to reason: "Do not glorify in your state, if you are wise and civilized men; an instant suffices to disturb and annihilate that supposed wisdom of which you are so proud; an unexpected event, a sharp and sudden emotion of the soul will abruptly change the most reasonable and intelligent man into a raving idiot."[76]

If the burden of knowledge lies, as it does in the Classical Age, on man and man alone, and if for that very reason, order and meaning are of his making, then with such responsibility came urgent injunctions against the abuse of reason. It is within this context that claims to witnessing miracles were increasingly identified as the rants of "enthusiasts." Disassociated from the divine and demonic, enthusiasm was increasingly identified with a form of unreason that had no other reference beyond itself—the disturbed wanderings of an undisciplined imagination.[77] It was a subject most famously discussed by Hume who discounted the veracity of miracles, but the dangers of enthusiasm also elicited commentaries from Descartes, Hobbes, Swift and Locke.[78] Thus, portents and miracles came to be associated, by men of letters, not with the powers of God or machinations of the devil, but, to quote Lord Shaftesbury, with "all the common causes of deceit, *Superstition, melancholy, natural weakness of sight, softness of imagination.*"[79]

Such imaginative license whether intentional or not, sincere or mischievous, nevertheless carried with it the danger of destabilizing the political order. Meric Casaubon was not alone in suspecting that enthusiasm was being enlisted "for politick ends . . . the nature of the common people being such, that neither force, nor reason, nor any other means, or considerations whatsoever, have the power with them to make them plyable and obedient, as holy pretensions and interests, though grounded (to more discerning eyes) upon very little probability."[80]

Such political concerns were not confined to English Protestants. What was labeled enthusiasm in England was defined as superstition among the Catholic ecclesiastical authorities in France.[81] Chevalier de Jaucourt writing for the *Encyclopédie*, went so far as to suggest that atheism was less of a danger to political stability than enthusiasm because the former "is interested in public tranquility, out of love for his own peace and quiet; but fanatical superstition, born of troubled imagination, overturns empires."[82] It was such superstition that preoccupied French revolutionaries. Lynn Hunt for example, documents the revolutionary efforts to re-educate the masses. In one instance the revolutionary government was outraged to learn that the parading of a statue of the Black Virgin in Paris had resulted in a substantial collection for the Catholic Church. As one administrator stated in exasperation "at the end of an enlightened century, we have seen reproduced in our commune those miserable means of fanaticism which only owed their deadly success to the times of ignorance and superstition."[83] The statue was burnt.

Whether superstition or enthusiasm, be it in France or in England, by the late seventeenth century such expressions of religious devotion were effectively reduced to a malady that inflicted the imagination—an imagination that was particularly undisciplined among the vulgar populace.[84]

The case of Mary Toft took place against the backdrop of increasingly urgent injunctions against the unrestrained effects of the imagination. Consequently, it brought into stark relief the contradictory anxieties that beset Classical reasoning wherein the influence accorded the imagination within seventeenth-century and eighteenth-century thought sustained the possibility of monstrous births but at the same time it was this same imagination that was held responsible for the deception of educated men who, seduced by their imagination rather than governed by their reason, so readily believed the absurd stories of an illiterate, working-class woman.

Thus far I have argued, with reference to commentaries on the imagination, that the body in Classical thought was rendered peripheral once man presumed for himself the privileged status of subject, the exclusive bearer of knowledge, and the sole agent of conscious will. Such an exalted portrait presumed an understanding of human reason that was unencumbered by the fact of human bodies. Whether the body was responsive to the fancies of the imagination or passively oblivious and detached from the workings of the mind, these conflicting medical theories nevertheless shared an essential premise: that lacking agency or conscious will, the body neither curtailed nor enabled man's efforts to know and shape his world. Human corporeality was detached from Man's more exalted status as a knowing, reasoning, free-willed subject. Consequently, if a threat existed to the sovereignty of reason, such a threat emanated not from the body but from reason itself—in the volatile and unpredictable realm of the imagination. This is why the public agitation initiated by Mary Toft's body morphed into a more general anxiety pertaining to the human mind.

But if the Classical Age was preoccupied with the dangers posed to human knowledge when reason was compromised by the imagination, we must also remember that the source of such anxiety—the ontological privileging of man as the sole bearer of knowledge and free will—also promised a future of human perfectibility. When the sovereignty of reason was permitted to reign, the scope of human potential was seemingly infinite. There is no better example of the unlimited possibilities the Classical Age accorded to man than the energy expended on seeking to (re)fashion him—a fact made dramatically evident in the wake of a series of sensational stories concerning the capture of "wild children."

The pedagogical instructions of Locke, the cautions of Hume, and the efforts of the revolution all speak to the fact that, if the Classical period was alert to the dangers of a willful, undisciplined imagination, it was equally sustained by the promise of human perfectibility, by the possibility of fashioning subjects keenly attuned to the necessity of privileging reason, regulating thought, and subordinating the imagination to the higher faculties of the mind. What better figure to dramatize these possibilities than a wild child: a figure untamed by societies mores and uncorrupted by society's conceits?

It was only two years before the Toft incident, in 1724, that a young boy, who came to be known as Peter of Hanover, generated enormous interest after his capture.[85] (Indeed, that interest abated only after a fickle public turned from the spectacle of Peter to Toft's spectacular births.)[86] As with Toft, the significance of Peter was no longer couched in the reverential idiom of devotion or the fear of demonic sorcery. But unlike the Toft affair, Peter inspired not anxiety and condemnation but literary and political speculation on the essential nature of man.

An adolescent boy described as anywhere between eleven and fifteen years old was found wandering the woods of Hanover, Germany, naked and alone. When he was captured, Peter was sent to a House of Correction but was later removed to the House of Hanover, where he was presented to King George I. In the spring of 1726, Peter was sent to London and placed under the care of Dr. John Arbuthnot, a fellow of the Royal Society. Peter quickly became something of a public sensation, attracting the attention of the curious, the literary, and the court. Jonathan Swift, who was in London to oversee the publication of *Gulliver's Travels*, reported to a friend, "This night I saw the wild Boy, whose arrival here hath been the subject of half our Talk this fortnight. He is in the keeping of Dr. Arbuthnot, but the King and Court were so entertained with him that the Princess could not get him till now."[87]

The intellectual excitement surrounding Peter ("His arrival [in London] produced a number of pamphlets, a sermon, a book length satire by Daniel Defoe, and at least one poem")[88] resided not in his subversion of human corporeality or of the social and political order but in his very humanness, which had not relinquished the innocent simplicity that was said to distinguish natural man from his social counterpart. In *Mere Nature Delineated* (1726), the longest tract on Peter written at the time, Defoe offered the most devastating contrast:

> To act as a Man, and to have no Pride, no Ambition, no Avarice, no Rancour or Malice, no ungovern'd Passions, no unbounded Desires, how infinitely more happy is he than Thousands of his more inform'd and better-taught Fellow Brutes in human Shape, who are every Day raging with Envy, gnawing their own Flesh, that they are not rich, great, and cloath'd with Honours and Places and such-and-such, studying to supplant, suppress, remove, and displace those above them, and even to slander, accuse, murder, and destroy them to get into their Places? Had Nature been beneficent to him, in bestowing something more upon him other ways, and yet kept his Soul lock'd up as to these Things, how had he been the happiest of all the Race of Rationals in the World?[89]

The instructive appeal of Peter is significant, for if the wild boy of Hanover was called on to reveal to social man a nature he once possessed and had subsequently lost, then presumed in such a logic was the premise that man was, for good or bad, capable of change. In other words, Peter's capture inspired an outpouring of debate about the essential qualities of man's nature within an intellectual environment that presumed man's malleability. As I argued in chapter 2 with reference to Locke, the presumption that man did not come born possessed of innate qualities but was, rather, a blank slate (or, as Defoe would have it, man is a "Lump of soft Wax, which is always ready to receive any Impression")[90] licensed—indeed, necessitated—the feverish production of educational manuals, of which Locke's *Some Thoughts Concerning Education* and Rousseau's *Émile* are perhaps the two most notable examples. If man had a human nature, then this was nevertheless a nature that was malleable to social engineering. Citizen subjects could be fashioned through education, example, and experience. Thus, Peter was not permitted to return to the "pristine" innocence of his pre-social wanderings. Instead, he became the object of courtly efforts to educate him into language and social etiquette. That such efforts proved to little avail (Peter was eventually given a royal pension and handed over to the care of a farmer in Hertfordshire, no more capable of speech or social decorum than when he was first discovered) did not undermine the prevailing view that man was malleable to change.

Indeed, the case of Marie-Angélique Leblanc, the wild girl captured in 1731 near the village of Songi, France, illustrated how a brute, animalistic child could be transformed (after numerous years in a nunnery) into a woman educated into language, religion, and the gendered affectations of French society. In her later years Marie-Angélique reportedly entertained visitors regularly, and although she never married, she died relatively wealthy in 1775.[91]

Perhaps the most famous wild child is Victor of Aveyron.[92] Sighted in the forests and mountains near the district of Tarn, France, in 1798, Victor was finally captured in 1800 and sent to Aveyron on the grounds that his presence would be of "great interest for observers and naturalists."[93] Some months later, Victor was housed in the Institution Nationale des Sourds-Muets and placed under the guardianship of the physician Jean Itard. Against the advice of some of his mentors and following the educational philosophy of Condorcet, Itard took it upon himself to educate and transform this seemingly dumb, wild mute into a respectable social subject. Itard finally resigned himself to the cognitive limitations of his patient, but only after six years of patient effort to make nature receptive to social fashioning.

The capture and exhibition of Peter, Marie-Angélique, and Victor generated public curiosity and written commentary. Much of that commentary, while tempered with the cynicism of some, nevertheless saw in these children of the wild the reflection of man's original nature and the promise of his future possibilities. The fact that "Enlightenment writers conceptualized mankind as an infinitely malleable entity" suggested the potential for man's infinite improvement, that he could be fashioned and shaped through the medium of education and the models of a rational society.[94] Peter, Marie-Angélique, and Victor embodied such possibilities. This optimism was not subdued by concerns regarding the body.

As with Mary Toft, gender certainly informed the differential treatment accorded to Marie-Angélique and her male counterparts. After all, neither Peter nor Victor found himself in a nunnery. Yet while the nature of Marie-Angélique's education reflected gendered norms, the presumption that her wildness could be subdued and her character reformed was not in question. What is absent in the literatures and debates surrounding the wild children of the seventeenth century and eighteenth century is any deterministic correlation between their physiology and their capacity for improvement. This is not to say that their physical appearance went unnoted by their contemporaries: In addition to Marie-Angélique's sex, other, more general physical markers were recorded, such as their youth, their nudity or semi-nudity on discovery, their animal-like nails and teeth, their ability to endure cold weather, and their agility. Yet, as with the Toft case, whatever significance was accorded the body was secondary to the concern that most preoccupied Classical thought—namely, man's relationship to knowledge, his capacity to transform himself and the world around him.

Human knowledge promised infinite possibilities for human improvement. Our efforts to understand the sustained interest generated by the discovery of wild children in the Classical Age must begin with the epistemological premise that it is with man that knowledge and agency reside. Despite the numerous differences that distinguish the case studies of Mary, Peter, Marie-Angélique, and Victor, what is striking is the fact that none of these figures were read, as their predecessors often were, as possessing otherworldly powers, as a portent or prodigy of divine or demonic machinations.

As we have seen, in the medieval period and the Renaissance, monsters were located within a larger cosmology of nature wherein nature was attributed transformative and transgressive powers. This same potential was accorded to the body that was porous and fluid, volatile and unpredictable. Such possibilities were born of the fact that man was neither the exclusive bearer of knowledge nor the sole agent of volition. Indeed, God's presence, demonic sorcery, and the forces of nature that transpired to punish or undermine man's social order continually tempered his actions.

Classical knowledge no longer permitted such possibilities. Wild men were no longer a ubiquitous threat; monstrous births ceased to carry prodigal significance; and nature, the body included, was no longer accorded a volatile autonomy. The sanitized and (often) benign appropriation of wild-man figures in Classical thought worked to deny them the wonder and fear they once possessed.

But if Mary, Peter, Marie-Angélique, and Victor testify to the demise of Weber's enchanted world, what is equally significant, and in contrast to the nineteenth century, is that the commentaries their presence incited did not (even in the case of Mary Toft and Marie-Angélique) foreground their physiology as the explanatory site for their philosophical and literary significance. Such considerations were secondary when man's capacity to reason and thereby know, transform, and render his world meaningful were at issue.

Thus, within the context of the Classical episteme the significance of the body was essentially disavowed. As I have argued thus far, one reason for this lies in the fact that concerns about the body were often subsumed and eclipsed by larger questions pertaining to man's status as a knowing subject on whose shoulders rested the weight of truth, agency, and reason. Such an awesome responsibility had the dual effect of generating anxious commentaries concerning the fallibility of human reason (evident by the Toft controversy) but it also offered the promise of human perfectibility, of unlimited human potential (as eighteenth-century representations of wild children bear witness). In both instances, however, what we encounter in Classical thought is the privileging of pure, disembodied reason. It is this disembodied reason that constitutes the precondition for man as knowing subject, and it is this same reason that safeguards and enables the production of knowledge.

The body is rendered peripheral to Classical understandings of subjectivity and knowledge. But if the privileging of reason at the expense of corporeality goes some way in accounting for the relative lack of significance accorded the body in Classical thought, such marginalization cannot be reduced to this explanation alone. What is largely absent in my narrative thus far—not surprisingly, since I have sought to account for absence—is an exploration of how the body *was* represented in Classical thought. After all, the Classical period engaged in a feverish production of medical atlases, a compulsive compilation of physiological taxonomies, and a generous compendium of scientific treatises. What conclusions can be drawn of Classical renderings of the body in those instances in which the body was an object of, rather than incidental to, intellectual inquiry?

If a veritable obsession with natural history—which included physiology within its gambit—was one of the hallmarks of the Classical Age, such enthusiasm, I would argue, did not translate into a deterministic privileging of the natural world. Rather, nature, including the human body, was recognized as malleable and thus receptive to the ingenuity of human invention. Classical man embraced nature as a resource that bore witness to the unlimited potential of human reason to fashion the world around him.

When subordinated to the authority of human reason, human will could transform not only individuated subjects but also the social and material world. Centuries of experimentation with plant and animal breeding and cross-breeding demonstrated the extent to which "it was a plastic world, ready to be shaped and moulded."[95] Indeed, as one gardener put it in 1734, man now possessed the power "to govern the vegetable world to a much greater improvement, satisfaction and pleasure than ever was known in the former ages of the world."[96] But it was not simply the world of crops that were malleable to human ingenuity. The same could be said of animal breeding. As Keith Thomas notes, the breeding of horses had long been a favorite pastime of the British aristocracy, and by the eighteenth century, "cattle, sheep, foxhounds and even pigeons were being bred with comparable attention."[97] That the natural world could thus be transformed—indeed, engineered to human specifications—suggested to some the possibilities available for improving man himself. It was precisely such a vision of the future that Charles Vandermonde opened up to inquiry, for "since one has succeeded in perfecting the race of horses, dogs, cats, chickens, [and] canaries, why would one not try and improve the human species?"[98]

While Vandermonde envisioned a future of physiologically perfected citizens, more humble demonstrations of physical transgressions already existed. As documented in a growing body of contemporary scholarship on the subject (briefly engaged with earlier in this section), sexual transgression, racial and gender passing, ambiguous gender identities, and species confusion all suggest that in the Classical Age, man's potential to effect change did not end at the threshold of the body politic but extended to include the physiological body itself. If this is the case, then it raises questions about, and has implications for, Classical understandings of race.

I would suggest that the Classical privileging of man as the source of agency and bearer of knowledge impeded racialized representations of non-Western peoples in the seventeenth century and eighteenth century. This is to suggest not that discussions about race were altogether absent during the period in question but that "race" had an ambiguous and ambivalent status. It is undoubtedly true that the Classical Age, unlike the Renaissance, produced taxonomies that sought to classify and order human diversity in terms more familiar to us. Positing European man at the pinnacle of civilization, François Bernier's (1625–88) hierarchical ordering proceeded in descending order to include Europe, Africa Proper, Asia Proper, Lapps. In the eighteenth century, Carl Linnaeus (1707–78) produced an alternative model that included wild men—*Homo ferus, Europaeus albus, Americanus rubescus, Asiaticus luridus, Afer niger.* Count Buffon (1707–88), Linnaeus's contemporary and rival, mocked his fellow naturalist's list and promptly produced his own: Lapp Polar, Tartar, South Asian, European, Ethiopian, American.[99]

What is curious about these lists is that they at once elicit recognition from the modern reader while simultaneously resonating with a certain unfamiliarity. The reason for this dissonance, I would suggest, lies not only in Linnaeus's inclusion of wild men or Bernier's and Buffon's reference to Laplanders but also in what is omitted—a physiological language of race like the one that characterized the nineteenth century. Where we expect to find references to the Negroid, Caucasian, and Mongoloid we instead confront categories such as African, European, and Asian. What these lists share, in other words, is a distinct and marked privileging of geography.

But we should be wary of reading into these typologies either the absence of a more rigorous science or an immature precursor of nineteenth-century racial classifications. What is illuminating about Bernier's, Linnaeus's, and Buffon's efforts to classify human typology is the extent to which it reflects the epistemic conditions of Classical thought, which accorded the body a certain malleability. The prevailing theory at the time, witnessed in these classifications, was that skin color, and physiology more generally, were unreliable and unstable variants precisely because they were malleable to climate, geography, and food.[100]

Charles de Secondat Montesquieu is the most famous advocate for recognizing the influence of environmental conditions that affect not only physiology but also customs and political institutions. But Montesquieu was by no means alone in endorsing such theories. Count Buffon notoriously argued that the inferiority of the New World natives derived from the "wetness" and geological "newness" of the American continent.[101] But if particular geographies were detrimental to the human constitution, it logically followed that a changed environment had the potential to remedy the damage. Thus, Buffon also maintained that if you placed an African in Paris and fed him French food, his grandchildren or great-grandchildren would be blessed with white skin.[102]

No less than gender, "savage" physiology, as the typologies of Linnaeus and Buffon testify, was not immaterial to Classical thought, and yet its significance was again subsumed under the mantle of geography and the promises of human ingenuity. Ultimately, when we turn to Classical writings on non-Western peoples—Rousseau's elevation of the noble savage, Diderot's erotic fantasies of Tahitian sexual practices, Montesquieu's environmentalist explanations, Voltaire's enthusiasm for all things Chinese, or even Buffon's damning descriptions of Amerindians—what remains strikingly absent from all such accounts is the presumption of biological determinism, of an irreversible correlation between physiology and savage life.

Indeed, as Wahrman has argued by citing countless examples from the period, racial physiology in the Classical Age was infinitely negotiable: the skin color of the "Hottentots" or the American Indians was presumed to be the effect of the grease or paint they put on their skin; racial passing was a literary device that commonly found expression in novels and travel diaries; and, of course, the environment was often evoked to account for physical differences.[103] Even where we confront seemingly deterministic accounts of race (e.g., in Hume's disparaging footnote on "Negroes" or Edward Long's defense of slavery),[104] such determinism was still a subject of debate in the Classical period, and, indeed, the majority view continued to appeal to such explanatory factors as custom, religion, education, geography, and diet. Even defenders of cross-Atlantic slavery, as most contemporary scholars now argue, did not appeal exclusively or overwhelmingly in the seventeenth century and eighteenth century to racial justifications.[105] The defense of slavery, as Kenan Malik has suggested, was a defense of private property.[106]

Indeed, precisely in those spaces where one would expect to encounter the primacy of the body, the Classical body keeps eluding us. Its plasticity precedes and thus escapes the biological determinism that was to define nineteenth-century racial science.

What all these examples—Mary Toft, wild children, physiological malleability, the engineering of nature, and the education of man—testify to is the fact that the body in Classical thought was neither immutable nor overdetermined. My objective, however, has not been limited to documenting this fact by way of examples. I have also sought to account for why the body, in Classical thought, was recognized as a malleable and pliable entity. Again, as with my earlier discussion of the Renaissance, what is apparent is that any discussion of Classical representations of the body cannot be detached from Classical conceptions of knowledge and subjectivity. The foundational premise of Classical thought was that the very condition of knowledge presumed a knowing mind—it presumed conscious human agency. It presumed, in short, the centrality of human beings to shape and fashion the world.

The status man accorded to himself as the author of meaning, order, and volition produced, as one of its effects, a profound sense of urgency and anxiety concerning the fallibility of human reason. Hence, the injunctions, cautions, and pedagogical instructions offered through the course of the late seventeenth century and much of the eighteenth century against permitting the free rein of the imagination. Not only did it indulge the passions, but it risked collapsing the ontological distinction between the subject and the object world.

Yet if man's status as sovereign subject fueled an unsettling sense of apprehension, it also promised a future of possibilities wherein the full potential for human perfectibility would eventually be realized. Out of human nature could be crafted rational citizens. If an undisciplined imagination posed a threat to reason, reason, when properly trained, could subordinate the imagination. Ultimately, however, whether wrestling with a willful imagination or basking in the sovereignty of reason, the effect was the same: that the body carried little prestige or explanatory authority within Classical thought. It was not an obstacle to human agency but a site for demonstrating human ingenuity.

This sovereign subject, equipped with reason and possessed of unlimited potential, could extend his will to subdue, reform, and transform nature. But imagining such possibilities, in its turn, depended on a particular rendering of bodies and environments as malleable and responsive to human fashioning. Physiological man, no less than plants and animals, constituted a nature that was neither immutable nor intransigent. Indeed, some expressed hope that in the not too distant future, human progress would render the human body obsolete.

There is perhaps no better testimony of the hopes of the Classical Age than a work that in many ways marked its conclusion: William Godwin's *An Enquiry Concerning Political Justice* (1793). In his revelries on the future, Godwin imagined a time when corporeal nature would be all but irrelevant to the human condition. He envisioned a world where corporeal desires would be transcended and human life indefinitely extended. Human agency elevated by human knowledge would transcend the limitations of human corporeality. If race thinking existed in the Classical Age, it is only recognizable as such through the mist of nineteenth-century science.

## Bodies of/as Evidence

Ignorance and credulity have ever been companions, and have misled and enslaved mankind; philosophy has in all ages endeavoured to oppose their progress, and to loosen the shackles they had imposed; philosophers have on this account been called unbelievers; unbelievers of what? of the fictions of fancy, of witchcraft, hobgoblins, apparitions, vampires, fairies; of the influence of stars on human actions, miracles wrought by the bones of saints, the flights of ominous birds, the predictions from the bowels of dying animals, expounders of dreams, fortune tellers, conjurors, modern prophets, necromancy, cheiromancy, animal magnetism, metallic tractors, with endless variety of folly? These they have disbelieved and despised, but have ever bowed their hoary heads to Truth and Nature.[107]

Erasmus Darwin's unceremonious dismissal of witches, miracles, fairies, and the like appears to validate Weber's insistence that man entered the modern world equipped with the knowledge that meaning, truth, and order were of his making, but he did so at a cost—that of his own disenchantment. Yet we should not presume, from Darwin's summary rejection of "fictions of fancy," that monsters had been altogether erased from the world by the late eighteenth century. What is true is that the monstrous body that had once possessed the powers of transformation or came in hybrid form or was marked by anatomical excess or lack (two heads or no arms) was a body that by the nineteenth century was largely confined to circus freak shows and the pages of fiction. The Barnum and Bailey Circus is an example of the former; Frankenstein's monster the most famous example of the latter. But one of the most revealing late-eighteenth-century evocations of the monstrous comes not from the novel or the exhibition but from an unlikely, scholarly source. I refer to T. R. Malthus's *An Essay on the Principle of Population* (1797):

> In the famous Leicestershire breed of sheep, the object is to procure them with small heads and small legs. Proceeding upon these breeding maxims, it is evident that we might go on till the heads and legs were evanescent quantities; but this is so palpable an absurdity that we may be quite sure that the premises are not just, and that there really is a limit, though we cannot see it, or say exactly where it is. . . . I should not scruple to assert, that were the breeding to continue for ever, the heads and legs of these sheep would never be so small as the head and legs of a rat.[108]

The purpose of Malthus's evocation of the monstrous was to open to ridicule the infinite promises of human agency. Offering a sharp critique of utopian philosophies—most notably, those of Godwin and Condorcet—Malthus sought to challenge the prevailing thesis that nature, be it human, animal, or plant, was malleable to human correction and thus posed little impediment to social progress. Malthus, on the contrary, dismissed such "improbable and unfounded hypotheses," suggesting that while some genuine progress had been made by science, this had the effect of producing "the late rage for wide and unrestrained speculation," leaving men who were "elate and giddy with such successes" with the "illusion" that "everything . . . [was] within the grasp of human power" when in fact, "no real progress could be proved."[109] Such illusions had led to the dangerous presumption that human misery (and, by implication, human happiness) stemmed from human institutions. Malthus insisted that the reverse was true: "The truth is, that though human institutions appear to be the obvious and obtrusive causes of much mischief to mankind, they are, in reality, light and superficial in comparison with those deeper-seated causes of evil which result from the laws of nature."[110]

As is well known, the law of nature that most concerned Malthus was the human propensity to reproduce. Malthus identified a direct correlation between population growth and future scarcity, arguing, against the grain of prevailing theories, that large populations were not a sign of health in the civil body; rather, large populations promised a future of scarce resources, increased poverty, greater economic disparity, and social and political turmoil. Instead of gazing into a future of utopian possibilities, Malthus offered a grimmer prophecy of social decline. In short, the promises of human agency so dear to seventeenth-century and eighteenth-century thinkers confronted in Malthus biologically determined limitations.

The immediate purpose of Malthus's reference to the Leicester sheep was to ridicule utopian philosophy. Its larger significance lies in its value as a signpost marking a distinctive shift away from Classical understandings of the body. The monstrous body for Malthus was not one suffering from the consequences of the imagination but obligingly following the prescripts of nature. It is the body that, at the level of individuals, feels compelled to reproduce but in so doing produces potentially disastrous consequences for the population at large.

Residing at the core of Malthus's argument are two central contentions: that nature in general, and the human body in particular, are essentially untranscendable, immutable objects (their desires and demands cannot be neutralized by the agency of man); and this very intransigence and resistance to human malleability accords the body a pivotal role in shaping human institutions and social arrangements (as insurmountable, they must constantly be attended to). It is this dual logic that Catherine Gallagher identifies as the novel element of Malthus's work, because by "making the body absolutely problematic . . . [Malthus] helps place it in the very centre of social discourse."[111] It is precisely this paradox that finds expression in Malthus's work on population that Gallagher identifies as crucial to nineteenth-century discourses on the body more generally. The monstrous, in nineteenth-century thought, is not the unnatural, grotesque body but human corporeality as such—at once deeply problematic and, for that reason, completely valorized:

Completely untranscendable, the body is thus absolutely problematic. For a body that should and could be overcome would provide its own means of displacement from the centre of social discourse. Absolutely problematic, thus, relies on complete valorization. These, then, are the two fast interlocking elements of the nineteenth-century's discourse of the body that place it at the heart of so much Victorians social thought. They are the features that mark a definitive break with earlier European thought on the subject, even that of the Enlightenment.[112]

It was this intractable, immutable body that was both productive of and available for racial classification. What we witness in the nineteenth century (and what will be mapped out in the following discussion) are four interrelated presumptions that underwrote nineteenth-century discourses on the body. While thoroughly infused and inseparable in practice, these four premises can be identified briefly in the following terms. First, both the unstable and fluid body of the Renaissance and the pliable body of the Classical Age had ceased to have any resonance by the nineteenth century. What we witness in the nineteenth century is the emergence of the body as a fixed, immutable entity that, for that very reason, was classifiable within rigid typologies—most notably, gender, race, and sexuality. Second, implicit in representations of the body as intransigent and stable was the premise that the body as a gendered or racial entity was essentially immune to the forces of history. Third, and following from the second point, it was the very a-historicity of the body wherein lay its value as an object of nineteenth-century discourse. The a-historicity accorded the body was not produced out of ignorance or lack of historical sensibility but in full and profound recognition of man's immersion within history. Confronted with the historicity of language, customs, laws, and exchange—confronted, in other words, with the variability and inconstancy of the human condition over time—the body seemed to proffer a site resistant to the forces of temporality. The body promised what other objects of human knowledge could not: an absolute, measurable index to determine conclusively the nature of human difference. Fourth, and finally, this immutable, transparent, temporally resistant nineteenth-century body provided the conditions for assessing collective and individual identities. As I will argue in reference to police technologies in colonial India, the body became the privileged locus in the nineteenth century for establishing and grounding identity.

The body as an immutable, stable, and transparent object was to become the hegemonic representation of corporeality by the mid-nineteenth century. However, we can witness the emergence of this paradigmatic shift in representation as early as the late 1700s—most notably, in reference to gender distinctions. By the late eighteenth century, Laqueur argues, the one-sex model that for a millennium had constituted the foundational tenet of medical anatomy was increasingly coming under attack. The hierarchical system of the one-sex model, which had recognized in the female form a lesser version of the male body, gave way to an "anatomy and physiology of incommensurability."[113] Londa Schiebinger documents this shift by referring to late-eighteenth-century medical atlases. While earlier medical treatises had provided illustrations of only the male skeleton (presuming its universal applicability), by 1796 the German anatomist Samuel Thomas von Soemmerring was defending the urgency of diagramming female skeletons on the grounds that the female bone structure was radically different from that of her male counterpart.[114]

But while the body was increasingly accorded a deterministic authority in matters of gender, when it came to matters of race, a certain physiological malleability was still being defended. We have already noted, in reference to Bernier, Linnaeus, and Buffon, that typologies of human difference were organized around geography rather than physiognomic classifications.

In the third edition of On the Natural Variety of Mankind (1795), Johann Friedrich Blumenbach distinguished the races of men into a system more resonant with nineteenth-century scholarship: Caucasian, Mongolian, Ethiopian, American, and Malay.[115] Blumenbach is also credited as the first European to collect human skulls for the precise purpose of systematically measuring cranial sizes to extract a statistically and scientifically authorized basis for his racial taxonomy. Even here we need to be cautious in discerning in Blumenbach's work the history to come, for Blumenbach, like Bernier, Linnaeus, Buffon (indeed, most natural philosophers before the nineteenth century), was a firm defender of monogenesis—that is, of man's common origins.[116] In light of this fact, and again like Bernier, Linnaeus, and Buffon, Blumenbach accounted for differences in human physiognomy through reference to geography, climate, and time. The body, in other words, was susceptible to change. In the area of racial differences, therefore, the body was yet to become an absolute barometer for innate, irreversible, and immutable differences.

By the 1820s, the racial body had become the site of an increasingly acrimonious and heated debate most dramatically witnessed in the first half of the nineteenth century in the polemics between the monogenists and polygenists. Whereas the monogenists insisted on the essential unity of human origins that ultimately could be traced back to Adam and Eve, the polygenists maintained that the existence of different races was evidence that no such unity had existed—that different races corresponded to separate origins.

On the side of the British monogenists loomed the philologist and ethnologist James Cowles Prichard (1786–1848). Following in the wake of late-eighteenth-century Orientalist scholarship—defined most particularly by William Jones's philological work on Sanskrit—Prichard maintained that the striking linguistic similarities between seemingly disparate racial and national groupings suggested that contemporary languages were a derivative of, because they diverged from, a shared, original tongue. The conclusion to be drawn in matters pertaining to human diversity was therefore significant, for, as Prichard argued in his Anniversary Address to the Ethnological Society of London, we cannot assume "diversity of origins on the mere ground of physical difference"; rather, "we must begin by establishing the historical fact of relationship or consanguinity between tribes or people, before we venture to refer them to one race, or to assert their diversity of origin."[117]

It was against such efforts to entangle humanity in a dense, opaque web of linguistic migration that polygenists such as Josiah Nott, George Gliddon, and John Crawfurd sought to posit the "transparency" of racialized bodies as the essential point of departure for the ethnological study of man. In their famous publication *Types of Mankind*, Nott and Gliddon quoted with approval the definition of ethnology as provided by Luke Burke, the editor of *London Ethnology*: "as a science which investigates the mental and physical differences of mankind."[118] Against the Prichardian view of ethnology as the history of man, Burke's definition, they argued, allowed a "far more comprehensive grasp—to include the whole mental and physical history of the various Types of Mankind, as well as their social relations and adaptations," thereby making ethnology relevant to "the philanthropist, the naturalist and the statesman."[119]

For the polygenists, race was not a feature of God's will or a consequence of environmental conditions, diet, or customs. Rather, it was an irreversible, biologically fixed, and scientifically measurable expression of human diversity. From the mid-1800s on, racial classification became the obsession of many an ethnologist.

One such figure, John Crawfurd (an ethnologist, polygenist, and prolific writer), defended the need to classify racial differences on the basis of complexion, hair, eyes, face, stature, skeleton, skull, brain, and intellectual capacity. Proceeding in this way meant not only that the different races of men were systematically classified, but that the intellectual and moral capacities (and limitations) of the various racial groupings could be extracted from these classificatory lists. The results of such scientific investigation, Crawfurd argued, invariably revealed "a very wide disparity" between racial types.[120]

The debate between the monogenists and polygenists reveals that, regardless of whether "race" existed before the 1800s, by the middle of the nineteenth century defending the biological immutability of race was no longer a maverick or marginal thesis within ethnological or scientific circles. Indeed, the gradual legitimacy accorded to racial theories and the increasing rigidity attributed to racial categories has been recognized as an outgrowth of these early-nineteenth-century polemics. Moreover, the enormous influence of polygenism well into the late 1800s attests to the merits of Gallagher's thesis that, having been marginal to Classical thought, the body in the nineteenth century had acquired an overarching and deterministic authority.[121] The construction of the racialized body and the consequent privileging of its essentialist nature contributed to its transformation as an object of scientific investigation, a reservoir of "evidence" for the innate differences between the people of Europe and those of the colonies.

We can extrapolate from Gallagher's thesis and argue that the very intransigence accorded the nineteenth-century body is what enabled the cementing of racial classification and racial thinking more generally. This observation in itself, however, does not allow us to account for why, when medieval, Renaissance, and Classical thinkers accorded the body varying degrees of plasticity, we encounter in the nineteenth century, a body impervious to change—impermeable, unalterable, and inescapably fixed.

It is again in the debate between the monogenists and polygenists that something of an explanation can be discerned. We must look for it, however, not in the polemical differences that polarized these two schools of thought, but in the crucial and fundamental premise that they shared—namely, a nineteenth-century consciousness of history.

In the case of Prichard's work, the appeal of history is clearly apparent. It was in the history of language, after all, that Prichard rested his defense of monogenism. In his anniversary address, Prichard distinguished the natural sciences from ethnology on the basis of the presence and absence of history. Ethnology, he argued,

> is distinct from natural history in as much as the object of its investigations is not *what is* but *what has been*. Natural History is an account of the phenomena which Nature at present displays. It relates to processes ever going on, and to effects repeated and to be repeated so long as the powers of Nature . . . remain unchanged. Ethnology refers to the Past. It traces the history of human families from the most remote times that are within reach of investigation.[122]

In contrast to Prichard's work, the polygenetic thesis appears to be—and, I would argue, is—fundamentally ahistorical. As we have seen, it was precisely the trans-historicity of the racialized body that lent authority to the polygenetic thesis. Indeed, it was primarily the polygenetic defense of the raced body as historically immutable that in 1863 led to the split of the Ethnological Society (formed in 1843) and the subsequent formation of a second organization self-titled the Anthropological Society of London.[123] The fault line between the two institutions largely mirrored the ongoing, and increasingly explosive, disagreement regarding the unity of human origins.[124] The Anthropological Society of London, which housed the adherents of polygenetic theory, was less concerned with the history of man's origins than with the racial distinctions that appeared, at least to its members, to radically distinguish and separate humanity. The principle presumption uniting this learned body of men was that the body constituted a biologically fixed and temporally resistant entity.

What is significant to note, however, is that while Prichard was to embrace history in his defense of common origins, the polygenists' rejection of the historicity of the body was articulated in defiance of, and in contrast to, the historical malleability of all other indices of human difference, including custom, language, and religion. In other words, the trans-historical positioning of the body in the works of polygenetic theorists should not be confused with the much maligned a-historicism of the Classical Age. When defenders of polygenism disavowed the historicity of the body, they did so not from a lack of historical modern consciousness, but in profound recognition of the historicity of everything else. Herein lies the distinctive difference between Classical and nineteenth-century reasoning.

As I argued in the previous section, in denuding the world of signs, the Classical Age rendered knowledge the product of representation. In other words, it privileged Man as the bearer of knowledge. Knowledge was no longer there to be discovered, as it had been for the Renaissance. Instead, if man were to arrive at truth, he would do so through his own volition, his own ability to represent the world to himself. Or, to put it somewhat differently, for the Classical Age the only impediment to human knowledge and human perfectibility lay at the altar of human agency.

The nineteenth century distinguished itself from the Classical Age not because it reverted authority back to God as the author of truth—man continued to be privileged as the source of knowledge, order, and meaning—but because man's authority was now profoundly qualified by an overwhelming consciousness of humanity's immersion within history. In the nineteenth century, man is not simply the bearer of knowledge distinct from the objects he experiences and senses but an object constituted by knowledge. He is simultaneously the agent who produces meaning and is produced by it.[125] It is precisely for this reason, as I argued in the previous chapter, that so many Romantic thinkers and nineteenth-century historians were suspicious of Classical appeals to universality and human reason: They failed to recognize the productive force of history in shaping human diversity. But if historicity became a means by which to assert human diversity rather than universality, its scientific authority was nevertheless muted precisely because history presumed malleability. The problem with history, whether one gained access to it through philology, custom, or religion, was its tendency toward contingency, its disconcerting openness to the possibility that time brings about change. It was precisely this logic that made historical evidence appealing to monogenists: Even the racial body was malleable to the effects of time. By the same token, however, it was the recognized transience and contingency of all other aspects of human existence that led to the polygenists' privileging of the human body. Unlike customs, religion, and language, polygenists argued, physiological man remained immutable. This was why the body was such a precious commodity: It promised constancy and temporal immutability.

One might object that the presumed trans-historicity of the body, while perhaps true for the first half of the nineteenth century, ceased to be true with the publication of Charles Darwin's *The Origin of Species* in 1859. It was not lost on opponents and advocates that Darwin's oblique reference to man in the concluding chapter of *Origin* ("In the distant future I see open fields for far more important researches. . . . Light will be thrown on the origin of man and his history")[126] gestured at the inclusion of man within his evolutionary history. Appeasing neither side, Darwin's thesis (elaborated in *The Descent of Man* [1861]) defended the unity of human origins but did so through reference to natural selection rather than heavenly creation.

But if Darwin's theory seemed to offer a direct challenge to polygenism with its assertion that man as such owed his lineage to a common source and, consequently, that not only social but biological man was born of history, this did not result in the demise of the body as an authoritative and privileged object of inquiry. Indeed, the body continued to be valued for its historical intransigence. This was so not only because of the appropriation of Darwin's theories by social Darwinists,[127] but because fossil and geological discoveries expanded the history of man well beyond the six thousand years accorded him in the Bible. The co-author of the theory of natural selection, Alfred Russell Wallace, was not alone in his insistence that, while man shared a common origin, the moment of origin was so far back in history that it was not unreasonable to treat the present race of men *as if* they did stem from different stock.[128] Even Darwin appeared to reassure the polygenetically inclined by arguing that "at the most ancient period, of which we have as yet obtained any record, the races of man had already come to differ nearly or quite as much as they do at the present day."[129] Appealing to this logic is how Nott resigned himself to Darwin's theory, for he accepted that while different races of men did not in fact represent "distinct species," they nevertheless constituted *"permanent varieties,"* because any further evolutionary development "requires *millions of years* to carry out the changes by infinitesimal steps of progression."[130] In other words, whereas for the polygenist the authority of the body resided in its trans-historicity, for the Darwinist the very historicity attributed to the body worked, for all intents and purposes, to make such history obsolete.

But the authority of the body lay not only in its negative appeal as an object steadfastly resistant to the distortions and permutations inflicted by time. Integral to this logic was also the recognition that as a "body of evidence," the body was the most precious form of evidence. In its very fixity, it divulged information that was more reliable than the confused and contested records offered by man's political and social history.

The fusion of a racial science that presumed the intransigence and immutability of the body within a Darwinian paradigm finds expression in the shifting emphasis of colonial policy within late-nineteenth-century India.

India had first attracted the attention of the philologist rather than the phrenologist. By the second half of the nineteenth century, however, this emphasis had changed. As I argued in chapter 3, what we confront in the colonial scholarship is a shift from the primacy of texts to the authority of anthropological data. "Unlike the traditional orientalists," Gyan Prakash argues, "anthropologists studied people instead of texts and observed culture in action rather than studying its textual remnants."[131]

Mapped onto the methodological transition from the textual to the empirical was a classificatory shift from linguistic distinctions to an increasing emphasis on caste variations. In his study of British colonial narratives on caste, Nicholas Dirks points to the fact that, while remarkably little attention was paid to caste by colonial administrators in the early 1800s, by the time the first All-India Census was taken in 1871, "There was general agreement among most of the administrators of the census . . . that caste should be the basic category used to organize population accounts."[132]

The plethora of statistical information, myriad ethnological descriptions, and interminable tables detailing castes, sub-castes, tribes, and regional variations were inspired by, and contributed to, different aspects of colonial knowledge. Infused through the discourse on caste was the assumption of race.

The significance Thomas Trautmann attributes to India as a privileged site in the growth of racial science appears to be validated when one reads the proposal for the ethnological survey of India written by the secretary to the Indian government:[133] "It has often been observed that anthropometry yields particularly good results in India by reason of the caste system, which prevails among Hindus, and of the divisions, often closely resembling castes, which are recognised by Muhammadans."[134]

The fact that such strict sanctions existed against inter-caste and inter-religious marriage, the secretary explains, ensured that "the difference of physical type, which measurement is intended to establish are more marked and more persistent than anywhere else in the world."[135]

H. H. Risley, director of ethnology and census commissioner in colonial India (1901), is the most commonly cited representative of the thesis that collapses caste membership with racial identity.[136] In *The Tribes and Castes of Bengal* (1892), Risley offered three main conclusions emanating from his anthropometrically inspired ethnology.[137]

First, he argued that *caste stratification in India was in fact premised on race* and had been since the Aryans first drifted south to India. Referring to the Brahmans, Risley argued that the "Aryan type" is "preserved . . . in comparative purity throughout North India because unlike their European counterparts they confronted a black race." The presence of, and antipathy toward, a black alien race fostered "an elaborate system of taboo for the prevention of inter-caste marriage." The caste system, then, was established in an effort to maintain Aryan purity.[138]

Second, the success in preserving this purity was discernible not by linguistic evidence or ethnological data on custom and beliefs (all of which have suffered the ravages and confused modifications of time), but by *statistical data derived from, and ordered along, physical racial types*. However minute verbal descriptions may be, Risley informs us, they will always "fall short of the numerical analysis" provided by anthropometrical measurements, from which a "mass of figures" attained from a "specimen population," once reduced to averages, can ultimately "bring out a uniform trial type to which all individuals tend to conform."[139]

Finally, while customs, language, and religion can change, and while many previous tribes have since embraced the Brahmanical caste system, *the fixity of, and distinctions between, physical types* (often "only discernible by scientific methods") nevertheless "renders it possible, within certain limits, to make a fair guess of a man's caste from his personal appearance."[140]

In short, Risley proceeded by ascertaining the recognized castes within India (including the so-called criminal castes),[141] classifying each caste as a distinctive racial type and then tracing its lineage back, with little variation, to the "Aryan invasion." Risley's contention was that the stability of racialized-caste bodies permitted statistical measurement whose mathematical precision (or so it was assumed) offered evidential authority that temporally inflected indices such as customs or religion could not boast.

What is notable about Risley's thesis—and it reflects a more general trend in the late nineteenth century—is the dual presumption that its logic carries. Integral to Risley's argument is that *because* the racialized body is resistant to the vagaries of time, it can be offered as—indeed, it constitutes the central locus for—establishing identity. Whereas for the Renaissance and the Classical Age identity was notoriously ambiguous, precarious, and contingent, the immutable, intransigent body of nineteenth-century thought harbored the promise that, if anchored in physiology, identity itself could be rendered stable and fixed.

Risley was by no means alone in drawing this correlation between fixed bodies and stable identities. Indeed, it is important to note that, while the history of anthropometry has most commonly been associated with nineteenth-century efforts to establish collective identities (specifically, the production of racial and gendered typologies), this same science of measurement was equally conducive to the identification of individual subjects. In other words, the presumed immutability of the body also lent itself to inextricably tying the individual body to individual identity. Thus, anthropometry, the science of statistically measuring particular body parts, was appealed to not only by Cesare Lombroso in Italy (to identify prostitutes as a physical type) or by Risley in India (to establish racial classifications) but by Alphonse Bertillon in France, who sought, through anthropometrical means, to identify individual criminals.[142]

In the late 1870s, Bertillon devised an elaborate, complex, and highly regulated system that would enable authorities to identify recurring criminals. The Bertillon system, as it came to be known, involved recording the anthropometrical data of each new convict who entered the prison system in Paris. This required the measurement and recording of eleven distinct body parts, in addition to details regarding the convict's eye color (of which there were numerous gradations), hair, and so forth. More significantly (for this ensured the success and quick appropriation of the Bertillon system in other parts of the world), Bertillon devised a system whereby the details about an individual could be quickly retrieved if he was a repeat offender. A convict might try to escape recognition through various disguises, but he could not elude the anatomical immutability of the length of his nose or shape of his ear. As Simon Cole elaborates:

No longer a name or a position in society, the individual became biological, defined simply, crudely, as a unique body, distinguishable, in the eyes of science, from all others. No name change, no change in personality could elude Bertillon's classification system, which ensnared the body in a textual net made of its own naked corporeality. The individual, perhaps for the first time, began and ended at its skin and bones. In short, Bertillon created a definition of the individual that the body could not escape.[143]

The meticulous and detailed system of measurement employed by Bertillon received the praise of the criminal anthropologist Lombroso, who referred to Bertillon's systematization of anthropometrical data as an "ark of salvation."[144] Yet the Bertillon system distinguished itself from that of Lombroso, Risley, and other physical anthropologists because by emphasizing the identity of the individual rather than the group, criminal-identification techniques were coming to visualize the body in terms that did not neatly correlate with those of their anthropological colleagues. As Cole explains, "The authorities did not read criminality in the body itself, but rather used the body as an index to a written criminal record."[145] In this context, anthropological measurements simply established identity, not character. The logic behind criminal identification was not to establish group affinity (be that racial or criminal) but quite the reverse: to assert the stark, measurable permanence of corporeal individuality, and thus the in-transigence of individual identity. As one Belgian prosecutor put it, "To fix the human personality, to give to each human being an identity, a positive, lasting and invariable individuality always recognizable and easily demon-strable, such seems to be the broadest aim of this new method."[146]

Despite the differences that distinguished the work of Bertillon from that of physical anthropologists, the underlying premise was the same: that the body was an immutable, stable, measurable entity. Moreover, the intran-sigence attributed to the body—be it for group identification or individual detection—was comprehensible only in reference to temporality. As with the polygenist and post-Darwinists, the question of temporality—or, more specifically, a-temporality—was the defining logic behind criminal identi-fication. The anatomical parts chosen for anthropometrical measurement by Bertillon were selected precisely because they were not malleable to change over a person's lifetime. It was this reduction of individual identity to the presumed fixity of body parts that set the stage for contemporary methods of criminal identification—most notably, that of fingerprinting.

India's place in the history of criminal identification is significant for two reasons.[147] First, we witness in India a fusion of racial-caste classification (such as that which we encountered in Risley's work) with colonial efforts at criminal identification and policing. Hysteria was emerging among the bourgeoisie in European capitals around what they perceived as increasing crime rates and the interminable problem of the recidivist (the habitual or professional criminal).[148] In British India, the repeat offender had become nothing short of a colonial obsession. The problem the colonial authorities identified was not with the incorrigible individual addicted to crime but with entire populations collectively recognized as criminal castes or tribes.[149] Criminality, in other words, was identified with ethnic or racial groups whose cultural and hereditary orientation predisposed them to criminal behavior. The seemingly ubiquitous presence of criminal castes came into colonial view shortly after British authorities suffered their first major trauma with what has gone down in official colonial history as the Indian Mutiny of 1857.

It is against this background, confronted with an increasingly hostile, ungrateful, and unruly native population, that the Criminal Tribes Act of 1871 was introduced for the "registration, surveillance and control of certain criminal tribes."[150] When the Bertillion system was introduced in India in 1892, it represented a mere extension of the now familiar science of anthropometry to include individual criminals in addition to racial groups and castes.

However (and this speaks to the second reason that India occupies an important place in the history of criminal identification), it was the very same colonial context that offered the conditions for testing a new system of criminal identification—one that was more efficient and less complicated and that required less intricate measuring techniques to identify repeat offenders. The Bertillon system, it was increasingly argued, was time-consuming, demanded expensive measuring equipment, and, most important in the colonial context, was hampered by its reliance on a skilled and honest police force that was, almost by definition, not to be found in a force overwhelmingly made up of natives.[151]

Francis Galton (associated most infamously with the eugenics movement) had already begun researching the possibility of employing fingerprint technology to identify criminals.[152] Galton's research was aided in large part by data collected by William Herschel, the chief administrative officer of the Hooghly district in Bengal. After some twenty years of experience in India, Herschel had assembled a collection of fingerprints (which included the fingerprints of the same individuals over an extended period of time) that demonstrated that the prints on one's hands remain constant throughout a person's lifetime. In other words, the immutability of finger-prints was no longer in question.[153]

Herschel's experience in colonial India was crucial to establishing the reliability of fingerprints in determining identity. It was the work of an-other colonial official, E. R. Henry, the superintendent of police in colonial Bengal, however, that resulted in the practical application of fingerprinting by the police. With help from native assistants, Henry devised a classifi-cation system that removed the final advantage boasted by the Bertillon method: a method of organizing criminal records so that, without much skill or education, an arresting officer could quickly retrieve information on repeat offenders.[154] On June 12, 1897, India became the first place in the world to completely dismantle the Bertillon system of anthropometrical measurements and substitute a system of criminal identification based on fingerprinting.

Despite the much publicized differences and advantages accorded to fin-gerprinting, the fact remains that the principle that underscored both meth-ods of criminal identification were the same: Fingerprinting, like anthro-pometry, derived its authority from the presumed immutability and fixity of the individual body. Particular anatomical parts were recognized to be resistant to the ravages of time and, for this reason, were deemed to be a more reliable source of information than history, customs, or languages.

Yet what is curious about the history of fingerprinting is that a system born out of colonial race relations ultimately reduced the body to whorls, loops, and arches (the broad descriptive classification of human prints) that were seemingly gender- and race-neutral. As Galton himself was to con-cede, all efforts, including his own, to derive collective markers of moral, intellectual, and racial significance from fingerprints had resolutely failed. By the early twentieth century, fingerprinting was largely identified with policing methods and held little significance beyond that of individual criminal identification. Indeed, police authorities berated the occasional appropriation of fingerprinting by physical anthropologists precisely on the grounds that their efforts to read collective identities undermined police efforts to have fingerprints recognized as authoritative in identifying sus-pected offenders. In 1925, T. G. Cook, the head of a fingerprinting school in Chicago, complained that efforts to read hereditary characteristics in fingerprinting "smack[ed] too much of phrenology, character reading, and all such black arts to be taken seriously. . . . It is not to the finger-print expert's advantage to be accorded in the minds of the public with fortune tellers and palm readers. The science of finger print identification is a real science and should not be dragged to the level of pseudo-science."[155] Phrenology, a close cousin of anthropometry, had been reduced to a "black art" no different from palm reading and other such "pseudo-sciences."

The history of fingerprinting is instructive for scholars studying nineteenth-century discourses on race. I recognize that such a claim may seem at odds with contemporary usages of fingerprints as a form of identification. After all, the continued appeal of fingerprinting today relies largely on the presumption of its objectivity, irrespective of what its colonial origins may have been. It is a form of identification that, in appealing to universality (the knowledge that all human beings have prints on the surface of their fingers), it asserts its cultural, racial, and gendered neutrality.

This, however, is precisely why any history of race thinking has to be situated within the larger context of historically shifting representations of the body. It suggests that any study of race has to take into account a particular historical and cultural rendering of the body as a reliable (because stable and immutable) index of identity. Like the Classical Age before it, the nineteenth century posited man as the subject of knowledge; where it distinguished itself was in the recognition that this transcendental, knowing subject was also a figure mired in history: Man was the subject who produced knowledge but was also produced by it. It was man and not God who was the source of history, customs, religion, and language, and yet it was the very same history, customs, religion, and language that shaped and constituted man. It is from within this specific positioning of man as both subject and object that the body came to occupy a privileged space in nineteenth-century thought.

The body—its racial, gendered, criminal, and individuated being—promised itself as the last bastion of absolute truth. For all of the important differences that distinguish the sciences of polygenesis, physical ethnology, Darwinism, criminal anthropometry, and fingerprinting, what they share is a faith that the body, in its object(ive) parts, stands defiantly resistant to the infinite variables and contingencies inflicted by the passage of time. For this reason, what is distinctive about the nineteenth century is not necessarily the invention of racial discourse but the essential premise on which this discourse relied for its enunciation—namely, that the body was an object that, unlike all other indices of diversity and difference, defied temporality, thereby allowing identities to be definitively and biologically fixed.

## Conclusion

Bertillon once bemoaned the fact that, "while there have existed from time immemorial, under the name of *Hippology*, special marks for the precise description of the shape and color of the horse, there has never existed until the present time, so far as we know, a methodical treatise on human description."[156] While Bertillon regarded the absence of such a treatise as "astonishing," the necessity of such a work appeared self-evident—and possible—only with the close of the eighteenth century. What had first to be presumed was a particular rendering of the body as mute, immutable, measurable, and, thus, valuable—available as an object passively receptive to the investigations of a knowing subject. If, as I argued in the previous chapter, historicity revealed the fact of human diversity, the presumed trans-historicity of the body permitted such diversity to be measured and defined once and for all. In the face of history's colonization of cultures, language, religion, politics, and society, the body came to be privileged in nineteenth-century discourse as the sole remaining bastion of permanence, stability, and measurability and, thus, as a privileged marker of intrinsic human difference. It was the very recognition of the historicity of everything else that made the body—that of women, criminals, prostitutes, and races—so significant.

While it is true, as the history of fingerprinting suggests, that mapping identities onto bodies will not ipso facto produce racial discourses, the fact that the body was, and continues to be, regarded as a passive, transparent, mute, trans-historical object ensures that race (and gender) will continue to shape the contours of modern representations of difference and identity.

# Epilogue

SOME FIFTEEN YEARS after three Muslim girls were suspended for wearing headscarves in a French public school in the town of Creil, the incident that had provoked sustained controversy, and public comment came to a dramatic conclusion with the passage of a law in 2004 banning all "ostentatious" religious symbols from French public schools.[1] Two years later, this time in Britain, a similar issue flared up. Public schools were again the site of controversy, but in this instance the protagonist was a Muslim schoolteacher who was suspended from teaching by a school board in Yorkshire on the grounds that the *niqab* (full veil) she wore was hindering students' ability to comprehend her lessons. Prime Minister Tony Blair described the veil as a "mark of separation," while an opinion poll found that 57 percent of Britons surveyed believed that British Muslims had not done enough to integrate. Only 22 percent believed they had.[2]

In January 2005, an article on the "Science and Technology" page of the *Guardian Weekly* began as follows: "If you want to understand human evolution, it may be worth starting with Johannes Daak from the remote village of Akel in the heavily forested centre of the Indonesian island of Flores." A team of physical anthropologists in Indonesia claimed to have discovered in a remote Indonesian village on the island of Flores a "species" of man who may be descendants of early human sapiens—the *homo floresiensis*, a.k.a. Hobbits. The hypothesis that an earlier ancestor of man long considered to be extinct may in fact have living descendants is being defended on the grounds that members of the Manggarai ethnic group are short in stature (approximately one meter tall) and live in close proximity to the fossil remains of a 13,000-year-old skeleton discovered in 2004. The skeleton, nicknamed the "little lady of Flores," is a one-meter-tall hominid with a brain that is one-third the size of that of modern man.[3]

"In a tradition-bound swath of India where the younger generation is nudging for change," the *New York Times* reports (in an article titled "Is Public Romance a Right? The Karma Sutra Doesn't Say"), a public backlash has ensued against overly zealous police officers who have been beating and arresting young, unmarried couples for engaging in public displays of affection. The controversy was first ignited when, in the middle of the day and undeterred by the presence of television cameras, police officers in Meerut beat and arrested young couples charged with sitting in "objectionable poses" in a public space, Gandhi Park. The small-town incident became a national spectacle that led to the suspension, pending an official inquiry, of the city's police superintendent and three other police officers involved in the raid.[4]

In October 2007, the French government proposed an amendment to an already sweeping immigration bill that would include voluntary DNA testing to ensure that prospective immigrants petitioning for entry into France on the grounds of family reunion shared the bloodline of their alleged family.[5] Fingerprinting and photographing are the method of choice employed by the U.S. government as part of a screening process of all visitors entering the country since 2004. The policy was introduced selectively, targeting visitors from predominately Muslim countries. It has since been expanded to apply to all visitors in an effort to counter threats of terrorism since the attacks on the World Trade Centers on September 11, 2001.[6]

The question of how one engages with and represents difference is not a question we can relegate to history textbooks. "Religion," "integration," "tradition," "culture," racially tinged evolutionary theories, ethnically encoded policing practices—so much of the discourse of the nineteenth century, ranging from benign and amusing to offensive and inhuman, continues to find expression in the newspapers, political pronouncements, public controversy, and legislative decisions that frame contemporary debates within Western nations and contemporary representations of non-Western societies.

But alongside continuity we can also discern marked shifts in the constitution and articulation of truth. "The modern times that W. E. B Du Bois once identified as the century of the color line have now passed."[7] The issue is not whether we agree with the beginning sentence of Paul Gilroy's controversial book *Against Race*, but that at the close of the twentieth century such a claim can be made at all. It marks the culmination of more than fifty years of debate over the scientific legitimacy of racial classification. By the year 2000, the publication date of Gilroy's book, race had ceased to be an incontestable biological "fact"; it had joined the ranks of other embarrassing relics of the past that constitute the treasure trove of social and historical constructionists.

The realignment of race with culture is revealing. While racial science is no longer a site of knowledge production and "race" is now firmly entrenched within scare quotes, its demise has corresponded with a new vocabulary organized around "culture." While contemporary anthropologists are increasingly wary of the "culture concept,"[8] it is in fact culture (an amorphous entity that consumes religion, tradition, history, ethnicity, and much else) that has become the discursive site on which difference is being contested. But even here we witness formulations that would have been unfamiliar to the late nineteenth century and early twentieth century. Most notably, cultural difference is no longer that which is "out there," the exotic spaces populated by anthropologists in quest of cannibals and headhunters. Rather, difference now inhabits the domestic space of post–Second World War Western nations populated by "foreigners" engaged in cultural practices (such as wearing the *hijab*) that seem no less controversial (if public hysteria is anything to go by) than widow burning. With cultural difference finding expression closer to home, we encounter new political and philosophical vocabularies. Intertwined with the Classical privileging of individuality is the language of multiculturalism, enmeshed with nineteenth-century understandings of tradition, are appeals to integration; embedded within color-coded racism is cultural racism, and alongside Western converts to Islam are Muslim defenders of public secularism.

Moreover, representing difference, whether through the language of tradition, race, culture, religious identity, or liberal secularism, is no longer a right reserved for the colonizer. While some Muslims denounced Danish cartoons of the Prophet Muhammad in the name of religious tradition, others, such as one Muslim Labor legislator in Britain, defended the secularism of British schools when opposing the wearing of the *hijab* by Muslim teachers.[9] Indeed, efforts to rescind the law prohibiting the wearing of the veil in Turkish universities has, at the time of writing, been defeated by the Turkish courts.

Whether we choose to emphasize continuity with the past or its moments of rupture, the fact remains that controversies surrounding European representations of postcolonial difference have not dissipated in the face of colonialism's demise. The imperative to write *Europe's Indians* was born out of a profound sense (one could call it distress or dismay) that the modern West is no closer to resolving the question of how to engage with cultural difference outside of liberal frameworks of "tolerance"—frameworks that, for all of their variation, nevertheless presume a liberal subject. Invariably, the "solutions" lie in presupposing a subject who recognizes and practices her difference (couched in the sociological terms of "religion" or "culture") within a private realm (family, cultural communities, places of worship) while upholding a secular, individualized persona in the public sphere.[10]

Whether one turns to global politics of war since September 11 or the intricacies of national politics focused on domestic concerns—such as prohibitions on the veil, policies that curtail immigration, and sanctions against particular cultural practices (such as clitoridectomy)—what is diagnosed as a "problem" is how one deals with "minorities" (in the West) who refuse to "integrate," or "majorities" (in the non-West) who fail to recognize the moral superiority of Western political and cultural norms. Yet as debates continue to rage between relativism and moral absolutism, between allowing for cultural difference and demanding homogeneity, between a moderate Islam and its fundamentalist alternative, between freedom of speech and cultural sensitivity, between the norms of a majority and the exceptionalism of minorities, the question that is constantly elided is the very question that urgently needs to be addressed: Why are the terms of the debate couched in the polarized language of self and otherness? Is it the case that contemporary debates are echoes of a long history of European imperialism, in which, as Edward Said famously argued, the West has historically constituted itself through the production of a non-Western other?[11]

Certainly, a quick survey of much intellectual scholarship since the 1980s (often from those who would characterize their position as politically "progressive") seems to legitimate such a conclusion. Indeed, so pervasive has the mantra of self–other become in any works concerned with European representations of the non-West that this oppositional binary has come to acquire the status of a truism—a "fact" that can be evoked in passing, without need for elaboration.

To do so, however, is deeply problematic. It is so not only because of the disabling implications it holds for imagining better futures, but also in its appeals to a history whose accuracy is more than a little dubious. Unseating this truism, revealing the self–other binary as born of a particular historical moment and reflecting a particular way to render the unfamiliar commensurable, is one of the concerns that has framed this work. If the language of self–other envelops much of the contemporary debate about cultural difference, it is crucial to recognize in such polemics a very modern way to conceive difference. Such recognition, however, requires not simply describing the content of Renaissance, seventeenth-century and eighteenth-century (Classical Age), or nineteenth-century representations of the non-West but also excavating the epistemic conditions that enabled the *thinking* of difference at different historical junctures. In pursuing this concern, my intention has been not only to encourage a rethinking of our historical narratives on European representations of the non-West, but also to offer a "diagnosis of the present." History writing, Foucault argued, "does not consist in simply characterizing what we are, but in following the lines of fragility of the present. . . . And it is in this sense that the description should always be made according to that kind of virtual rupture that opens a space of freedom, understood as a space of concrete freedom, that is to say, of possible transformation."[12]

Foucault goes on to argue that the function of studying history is not to reveal the irrationality of past conceptions of reason but, rather, to recover the networks of contingencies through which reason found expression. A history that seeks "to show that that which exists didn't always exist . . . that it is always at the confluence of encounters, of accidents," is a history that recognizes in the presumed obviousness of our thoughts and practices the "fragile, precarious history" that bore them. It is a history that allows for the possibility that, "since . . . things have been made, they can, provided that one knows how they were made, be unmade."[13]

I have sought in this work to trace the historically located nature of European representations of difference. From a Renaissance world of resemblances and Classical efforts to subsume difference under the matrix of identity, this work concludes with the nineteenth-century privileging of cultures and races as radically distinct. What should now be evident is that the oppositional logic of self–other has a history—a very recent history. Tracing how this history was made is, I hope, a step toward its unmaking. Historicizing European representations of difference is an effort to open the present to other possibilities.

## Introduction

1  I thank Michael Dutton for directing my attention to the racially ambiguous representation of the Chinese at Potsdam.

2  Bengal Police, from Henry, *Criminal Identification by Means of Anthropometry*, 1.

3  Ibid., 61–62.

4  Ibid., 61.

5  Florescano, *Memory, Myth, and Time in Mexico*, esp. 65–99; Mignolo, *The Darker Side of the Renaissance*.

6  Kuhn, *The Structure of Scientific Revolutions*; Hacking, "Language, Truth and Reason," and, "Making Up People," 222–36; Davidson, *The Emergence of Sexuality*, 93–124.

7  Kuhn, *The Structure of Scientific Revolutions*, 2.

8  Foucault, quoted in Davidson, *The Emergence of Sexuality*, 201.

9  Ibid., 129.

10  Ibid., 67, 141.

11  McClintock, *Imperial Leather*.

12  Stoler, *Race and the Education of Desire*.

13  Florescano, *Memory, Myth, and Time in Mexico*, 65–99.

14  On "culture," see, e.g., Young, *Colonial Desire*, esp. 53–54; Dirks, "Introduction: Colonialism and Culture," and, *Colonialism and Culture*, 1–26; Rosaldo, *Culture and Truth*. For discussion of the colonial lineage of "tradition," see, e.g., Mani, "Contentious Traditions"; Chakrabarty, "Afterword."

15 Florescano, *Memory, Myth and Time in Mexico*; Gruzinski, *The Conquest of Mexico*, and *The Mestizo Mind*.

16 Nandy, "History's Forgotten Doubles"; Chakrabarty, *Provincializing Europe*.

17 Seth, *Subject Lessons*.

18 Foucault, *The Order of Things*, 17–45.

19 E.g., Davis, "Boundaries and the Sense of Self in Sixteenth-Century France"; Greenblatt, "Psychoanalysis and Renaissance Culture"; Taylor, *Sources of the Self*; Martin, "Inventing Sincerity, Refashioning Prudence."

## 1 Self and Similitude

1 Said, "Introduction," in *Orientalism*. In so doing, Said acknowledges his debt to Michel Foucault's reconceptualization of power as intricately tied to, and implicated in, knowledge production.

2 Said, *Orientalism*, 57.

3 Hartog, *The Mirror of Herodotus*.

4 Greenblatt, *Marvelous Possessions*, 122.

5 Certeau, *Heterologies*, 68.

6 Herodotus, *Histories*, 321.

7 Mary Louise Pratt discusses this form of appropriation through the concept of "transculturation." See Pratt, *Imperial Eyes*, esp. 1–11.

8 Take, for example, criminal castes. Sanjay Nigam, in a lengthy two-part essay, points to the fact that in the late nineteenth century British colonial officials identified particular castes in India as criminal—that is, the defining feature of these castes was the fact that they earned their livelihood through theft and other illegal activities. Having thus identified particular socio-economic groups as inherently criminal, the social marginality of these castes was ensured, as too was their routine harassment by police. Not surprisingly, the implications that followed from the identification of criminal castes, was that the label, which preceded them, was followed by the very criminal acts that defined them. What the example of criminal castes shows us is that the Self does not merely represent the Other for its own consumption—it actually brings the Other into being: see Nigam, "Disciplining and Policing the 'Criminals by Birth,' Part 1," and "Disciplining and Policing the 'Criminals by Birth,' Part 2."

9 Quoted in Burke, "Did Europe Exist before 1700?" 23.

10 Quoted ibid.

11 Quoted in Mikkeli, *Europe as an Idea and an Entity*, 40; quoted in Hale, *The Civilization of Europe in the Renaissance*, 5.

12 Quoted ibid., 3; quoted in Thompson, "Ideas of Europe during the French Revolution and Napoleonic Wars," 44.

13 Quoted in Hay, *Europe*, 123; quoted in Thompson, "Ideas of Europe during the French Revolution and Napoleonic Wars," 39.

14 Delanty, *Inventing Europe*, 3.

15 Burke, "Did Europe Exist before 1700?" 23.

16 Ibid.

17 Hay, *Europe*, 96.

18 Ibid.

19 Ibid., 115.

20 Delanty, *Inventing Europe*, 38.

21 Ibid., 30.

22 Columbus, "The Letter of Columbus (1493)," 15.

23 Yapp, "Europe in the Turkish Mirror," 138.

24 Delanty, *Inventing Europe*, 11; Hale, *The Civilization of Europe in the Renaissance*, 38–39.

25 Yapp, "Europe in the Turkish Mirror," 138.

26 Greenblatt, *Renaissance Self-Fashioning*, 71.

27 For an interesting account of the decline of spoken Latin, see Hale, "The Renaissance Idea of Europe," 56–60.

28 Following common usage, I will continue to use the term "discovery," although I do so in full knowledge of the relative nature of this term—that the America's were a "discovery" only in reference to the Old World.

29 Burke, "Did Europe Exist before 1700?" 25.

30 Hale, *The Civilization of Europe in the Renaissance*, 11.

31 Hay, *Europe*, 117.

32 Heller, "Europe," 12; Delanty, *Inventing Europe*, 6.

33 Burke, "Did Europe Exist before 1700?" 26.

34 Ibid.

35 Heller, "Europe," 14; Delanty, *Inventing Europe*, 80–81.

36 Heller, "Europe," 14, 12; emphasis added.

37 I evoke here an extensive contemporary literature on the subject of race which is increasingly arguing that race as an organizing category for ordering and classifying difference is a product of modernity, a feature of nineteenth (or at the earliest, late eighteenth century) thought. Two works that are reflective of this scholarship are Hannaford, *Race*, and Malik, *The Meaning of Race*. I will be returning to this debate in chapter 4. This thesis has, of course, been contested. Of particular relevance is Greer et al., *Re-reading the Black Legend*, which emphasizes the racial logic that underwrote Spanish conquest of the Americas since first contact. For a fuller discussion of race and the Renaissance, see chapter 4 of the present work.

38 Columbus, "The Letter of Columbus (1493)," 15.

39 Heller, "Europe," 13.

40 Seed, *Ceremonies of Possession*. 3–4. As I am citing this text extensively, all further references, in this section, will appear as page numbers in the body text.

41 Bucher, *Icon and Conquest*, 6–9.

42 Hale, *The Civilization of Europe in the Renaissance*, 40–41.

43 Vitoria, "On the American Indians." 258–64.

44 Elliot, *The Old World and the New, 1492–1650*, 100.

45 Hodgen, *Early Anthropology in the Sixteenth and Seventeenth Centuries*, 12–13; Arciniegas, *America in Europe*, 104–5; Bucher, *Icon and Conquest*, 1–6.

46 Pagden, *The Fall of Natural Man*, 58.

47 Hodgen, *Early Anthropology in the Sixteenth and Seventeenth Centuries*, 113.

48 Sale, *The Conquest of Paradise*, 11–12.

49 Traboulay, *Columbus and Las Casas*, 192; Greenblatt, *Marvelous Possessions*, 104.

50 Vespucci, *Mundus Novus*.

51 Hodgen, *Early Anthropology in the Sixteenth and Seventeenth Centuries*, 113.

52 Elliot, *The Old World and the New, 1492–1650*, 12–13.

53 Bucher, *Icon and Conquest*, 4; Arciniegas, *America in Europe*, 9.

54 Bucher, *Icon and Conquest*, 4; Elliot, *The Old World and the New, 1492–1650*, 14.

55 Ibid., 8.

56 Grafton, *New Worlds, Ancient Texts*, 16.

57 Ryan, "Assimilating New Worlds in the Sixteenth and Seventeenth Centuries," 523.

58 Columbus, "The Letter of Columbus (1493)," 14.

59 Quoted in Elliot, *The Old World and the New, 1492–1650*, 43.

60 Hodgen, *Early Anthropology in the Sixteenth and Seventeenth Centuries*; Barta, *Wild Men in the Looking Glass*, esp. 178–202; Bernheimer, *Wild Men in the Middle Ages*.

61 Sale, *The Conquest of Paradise*, 15fn. For a more detailed account of the literary influences on Columbus, see Flint, *The Imaginative Landscape of Christopher Columbus*.

62 Arciniegas, *America in Europe*, 31. Also see Pagden, *European Encounters with the New World*, esp. 1–15.

63 Greenblatt, *Marvelous Possessions*, 14–21.

64 Columbus, *The Four Voyages of Christopher Columbus*.

65 Greenblatt, *Marvelous Possessions*, 12–20.

66 Foucault, *Discipline and Punish*.

67 Said, *Orientalism*; Kabbani, *Imperial Fictions*.

68 Schmitt, *The Concept of the Political*, 26. I thank Michael Dutton for bringing this text to my attention.

69 Dutton, "The Gift of the Political," 2.

70 Ibid.

71 Braudel, *The Perspective of the World*, 393.

72 Las Casas, *The Devastation of the Indies*; Vitoria, "On the American Indians," 238; Díaz, *The Conquest of New Spain*, 353–413; Oveido, quoted in Sale, *The Conquest of Paradise*, 158.

73 Vitoria, "On the Law of War," 314–27.

74 Theodore Daübler (via Schmitt), quoted in Meier, *The Lesson of Carl Schmitt*, 4. Heinrich Meier's commentary on this quote is: "In epigrammatic sharpness this poetic phrase seems to give expression to the insight that the political serves self-knowledge and arises from self-knowledge," ibid., 44.

75 Quoted in Elliott, *The Old World and the New, 1492–1650*, 33.

76 The most extensive commentary on the Valladolid Debate remains Hanke, *Aristotle and the Indians*.

77 Hanke, *The Spanish Struggle for Justice in the Americas*, 20.

78 Hanke, *Aristotle and the Indians*, esp. chaps. 5–6.

79 Grafton, *New Worlds, Ancient Texts*, 35.

80 Serge Gruzinski describes the extent to which Ovid in particular was enthusiastically taken up in the Americas: see Gruzinski, *The Mestizo Mind*, 91–106.

81 See, e.g., Todorov, *The Conquest of America*, 14–33; Grafton, *New Worlds, Ancient Texts*, 11–58; Greenblatt, *Marvelous Possessions*, 86–91.

82 Ryan, "Assimilating New Worlds in the Sixteenth and Seventeenth Centuries," 525.

83 Foucault, *The Order of Things*, 18. As I will be citing this text extensively, all future references in this section will appear as page numbers in parentheses in the text.

84 Hanke, *Aristotle and the Indians*, 9; Todorov, *The Conquest of America*, 170–71.

85 Greenblatt, *Marvelous Possessions*, 87.

86 Sale, *The Conquest of Paradise*, 59.

87 Todorov, *The Conquest of America*, 17. See also Pagden, *European Encounters with the New World*, esp. 89–99.

88 Greenblatt, *Marvelous Possessions*, 88.

89 Ibid., 86.

90 Columbus, "The Letter of Columbus (1493)," 14.

91 Ibid., 14–15.

92 Lucien Febvre argues that the word "civilization" first appears in French. He dates its first appearance to 1766: Febvre, "*Civilisation*," 221; White, "The Forms of Wildness"; Robe, "Wild Men and Spain's Brave New World."

93 Quoted in Arciniegas, *America in Europe*, 69.

94 Quoted in Hodgen, *Early Anthropology in the Sixteenth and Seventeenth Centuries*, 371.

95 Montaigne, "On Cannibals," 110.

96 Sale, *The Conquest of Paradise*, 46. For an account of the social, economic, and political character of the late Middle Ages, see the classic text by Huizinga, *The Waning of the Middle Ages*, esp. chap. 1.

97 Quoted in Hodgen, *Early Anthropology in the Sixteenth and Seventeenth Centuries*, 371.

98 Vespucci, *Mundus Novus*, 7.

99    Columbus, *The Four Voyages of Christopher Columbus*; Vespucci, *Mundus Novus*, 7; Montaigne, "On Cannibals," 119.

100   Hodgen, *Early Anthropology in the Sixteenth and Seventeenth Centuries*, 114–16. For an overview of the history of curiosity cabinets and collections during the Renaissance, see Impey and Macgregor, *The Origins of Museums*.

101   Quoted in Hanke, *Aristotle and the Indians*, 47.

102   Hulme, *Colonial Encounters*.

103   Vespucci, *Mundus Novus*, 6; Chanca, "The Letter Written by Dr. Chanca to the City of Seville," 36.

104   Hulme, *Colonial Encounters*, 15.

105   Chanca, "The Letter Written by Dr. Chanca to the City of Seville," 136–37.

106   Hulme, *Colonial Encounters*, 20–21.

107   Peter Hulme makes the point that "burning the flesh off the bones of dead bodies was common mortuary practice throughout the native Caribbean": ibid., 69.

108   Vespucci, "Third Voyage of Amerigo Vespucci," 38.

109   Vespucci, *Mundus Novus*, 37–38.

110   Chanca, "The Letter Written by Dr. Chanca to the City of Seville," 137; Hulme, *Colonial Encounters*, 69.

111   Vitoria, "On the American Indians," 250; Díaz, *The Conquest of New Spain*, 133.

112   "Not only did they howl, but also, leaping violently into the air, they made their breasts shake and they foamed at the mouth—in fact, some, like those who have falling-sickness here, fell in a dead faint; I can only believe that the Devil entered their body and that they fell into a fit of madness": quoted in Greenblatt, *Marvelous Possessions*, 14–15.

113   Ryan, "Assimilating New Worlds in the Sixteenth and Seventeenth Centuries," 530.

114   Pagden, *The Fall of Natural Man*, 122; Elliot, *The Old World and the New, 1492–1650*, 48.

115   Montaigne, "On Cannibals," 118; Grafton, *New Worlds, Ancient Texts*, 116.

116   Bucher, *Icon and Conquest*, 6.

117   Ryan, "Assimilating New Worlds in the Sixteenth and Seventeenth Centuries," 527.

118   Ibid., 528.

119   Ibid., 528.

120   Hodgen, *Early Anthropology in the Sixteenth and Seventeenth Centuries*, 468; Popkin, "Pre-Adamism in Nineteenth Century American Thought."

121   Hodgen, *Early Anthropology in the Sixteenth and Seventeenth Centuries*, 313; Grafton, *New Worlds, Ancient Texts*, 149, 151.

122   Grafton, *New Worlds, Ancient Texts*, 210; Rubiés, "Hugo Grotius's Dissertation on the Origin of the American Peoples and the Use of Comparative Method."

123 Ryan, "Assimilating New Worlds in the Sixteenth and Seventeenth Centuries," 533.

124 Ibid.

125 Vitoria, "On the American Indians," 250; Montaigne, "On Cannibals," 108.

126 Grafton, *New Worlds, Ancient Texts*, 19, 100.

127 Gruzinski, *The Mestizo Mind*, 35–36.

128 Darwin, *The Descent of Man and Selection in Relation to Sex*, 796.

## 2 "Constructing" Individuals

1 Geertz, *The Interpretation of Cultures*. It is a theme that runs throughout Foucault's work. The texts that inform this chapter are *Archaeology of Knowledge*; *Discipline and Punish*; *History of Sexuality*; *Madness and Civilization*; *The Order of Things*. For interviews and critical engagements with, and essays by, Foucault, see Martin et al., *Technologies of the Self*; Rabinow, *The Foucault Reader*; Kritzman, *Politics, Philosophy and Culture*.

The breadth of this literature is vast. Indeed, the success of this intellectual enterprise can be measured by the publication of a journal (*Representations*) indebted to the field, as well as by a number of edited works on New Historicism: see e.g., Veeser, *The New Historicism*. Of Greenblatt's works, see esp. "Fiction and Friction"; *Learning to Curse*; "Psychoanalysis and Renaissance Culture"; and *Renaissance Self-Fashioning*.

2 For an excellent overview of Jacob Bzurkhardt's *The Civilisation of the Renaissance in Italy*, see Martin, "Inventing Sincerity, Refashioning Prudence," esp. 1309–11.

3 Martin, "Inventing Sincerity, Refashioning Prudence," 1313–20. The works by Greenblatt that are most pertinent to the subject of self-fashioning the individual are "Fiction and Friction," 30–52; *Learning to Curse*; "Psychoanalysis and Renaissance Culture"; and *Renaissance Self-Fashioning*.

4 It is important to recognize that while the new historicists have largely ignored the work of the contractarians in their studies on individual subjectivity, a growing literature nevertheless exists that has interrogated this relationship: see Taylor, *Sources of the Self*; Porter, *Rewriting the Self*; Gutman, "Rousseau's Confessions."

5 Clifford, "On Ethnographic Self-Fashioning."

6 While the other elements listed can be found in varying degrees in the work of Martin and Greenblatt, it is Natalie Zemon Davis who has sought to interrogate gender relations in the construction of individual identity: see Davis, "Boundaries and the Sense of Self in Sixteenth-Century France," "On the Lame," and *The Return of Martin Guerre*. For a critique of Davis's historical interpretation in *The Return of Martin Guerre*, of which "On the Lame" is the response, see Finlay, "The Refashioning of Martin Guerre."

7 This definition of history is indebted to Dipesh Chakrabarty's introductory chapters in *Provincializing Europe*, esp. 72–74.

8 Wolin, *Politics and Vision*, 246.

9 Hobbes, *Leviathan*, 186.

10 Hobbes, *Man and Citizen (De Homine and De Cive,)*. Henceforth, all references to this text will be specified as "De Homine" or "De Cive." Laird, "Hobbes on Aristotle's *Politics*," 6–7.

11 Aristotle, *Politics*, 59–60.

12 Rousseau, *A Discourse on Inequality*, 78, 166. Also see Pateman, *The Problem of Political Obligation*, 39.

13 Hobbes, "De Cive," 222.

14 Hobbes, *Leviathan*, 185.

15 This, in fact, is argued by Hobbes to be "the first, and Fundamentall Law of Nature": ibid., 190 (see also 223).

16 For an excellent commentary on this sensibility see Kolb, *The Critique of Pure Modernity*, 1–17.

17 Hobbes, *Leviathan*, 122–23, 125–26.

18 Ibid., 82.

19 Ibid., 217.

20 Greenblatt, "Psychoanalysis and Renaissance Culture," 221–23.

21 Ibid., 222.

22 Pateman, *The Problem of Political Obligation*, 18; Greenleaf, "Hobbes," 18.

23 Greenblatt, "Psychoanalysis and Renaissance Culture," 222–23. For other works by Greenblatt that address the question of Renaissance constructions of identity, see "Fiction and Friction"; *Learning to Curse*; *Renaissance Self-Fashioning*.

24 Oestreich, *Neostoicism and the Early Modern State*, 135–54.

25 Ibid. While Gerhard Oestreich looked specifically at the idea of the covenant of grace, the classic work on the history from status to contract is, of course, Maine, *Ancient Law*. For an excellent discussion on the natural laws and political obedience see Olafson, "Thomas Hobbes and the Modern Theory of Natural Law," 15–30. For additional information, see Bobbio, *Thomas Hobbes and the Natural Law Tradition*.

26 Hobbes, "De Cive," 97.

27 Hobbes, quoted in Laird, "Hobbes on Aristotle's *Politics*," 5.

28 Martin, "Inventing Sincerity, Refashioning Prudence," 1329–33. See also Hill, *The World Turned Upside Down*, 87–106.

29 Wolin, *Politics and Vision*, 274–75.

30 Hobbes, *Leviathan*, 188. Similarly, in "De Homine" (43), Hobbes writes, "For before covenants and laws were drawn up, neither justice nor injustice, neither public good nor public evil, was natural among men any more than it was among beasts."

31 We cannot "accuse man's nature," Hobbes argued, for "Desires and other Passions of Man are in themselves no Sin. No more are the Actions, that proceed from those Passions" until such time as laws (external authority) prohibit them. Hobbes, *Leviathan*, 187 (see also 185).

32 Mehta, *The Anxiety of Freedom*. The second part of this chapter addresses Mehta's work more extensively.

33 Wolin, *Politics and Vision*, 264–65.

34 Ibid., 265.

35 Chakrabarty, *Provincializing Europe*, esp. 73–74.

36 Hobbes, *Leviathan*, 186; emphasis added.

37 Ibid., 254.

38 As Joel Kidder points out, when speaking of the "savages," Hobbes's accounts for their "inferior" intelligence not through reference to any innate causes, but because knowledge of the sciences had not been imparted to them: Kidder, "Acknowledgements of Equals," 145.

39 Hobbes, *Leviathan*, 216.

40 Hobbes, "De Cive," 118.

41 Hobbes, *Leviathan*, 187.

42 See, e.g., Raynal, *A Philosophical and Political History of the Settlements of Trade in the East and West Indies*, 3.8, 4.13, 5.17; Robertson, *The History of America*. For a secondary source that offers a comprehensive study of eighteenth-century representations of indigenous Americans, see Gerbi, *The Dispute of the New World*.

43 Hobbes, *Leviathan*, 227.

44 Ibid., 301.

45 Ibid., 255–56.

46 Ibid., 252.

47 Ibid., 255. For an informative commentary on Hobbes's discussion of slavery see Kidder, "Acknowledgements of Equals."

48 Cited in Kidder, "Acknowledgements of Equals," 145.

49 Hobbes, *Leviathan*, 266, and "De Cive," 103.

50 Gary Fuller, Robert Stecker, and John P. Wright, "Introduction," 28. See also Taylor, *Sources of the Self*. For an interesting critical review of Taylor's work, see Skinner, "Who Are 'We'?"

51 Locke, *An Essay Concerning Human Understanding*, 26.27.189. All references to this work include, respectively, the section number, chapter number, and page number.

52 Locke, *A Letter Concerning Toleration*, 32, 47.

53 Locke, "Second Treatise" in *Two Treatises of Government*, 6.271; emphasis added. This chapter is mainly concerned with the *Second Treatise of Government* (hereafter, *Second Treatise*). All future references to the *Second Treatise* in this chapter will appear in the text and will include section and page numbers. All

references to the *First Treatise of Government* (hereafter, *First Treatise*) will be cited in the endnotes.

54  Mehta, *The Anxiety of Freedom*.

55  Ibid., 127.

56  Macpherson, *The Political Theory of Possessive Individualism*, 232.

57  Pateman, *The Sexual Contract*.

58  Tully, *An Approach to Political Philosophy: Locke in Contexts*. James Tully makes the important point that, while Locke's defense of the slave trade has often been understood to refer to Africa, the trading in Indian slaves was equally relevant to the economy of Carolina. Locke's temporary law forbidding Amerindian slavery (to force agricultural settlement) did little to stop a burgeoning trade. "By 1680 the fur trade and the sale of Indian slaves to the West Indies were the staples of a Carolina's economy": ibid. 144. Other works on Locke and the slave trade include Bracken, "Essence, Accident and Race"; Drescher, "On James Farr's 'So Vile and Miserable an Estate'"; Farr, "Slaves Bought with Money," and "So Vile and Miserable an Estate"; Glausser, "Three Approaches to Locke and the Slave Trade"; Squadrito, "Locke's View of Essence and Its Relation to Racism."

59  Lebovics, "The Uses of America in Locke's *Second Treatise of Government*," 567.

60  Details of Locke's various official capacities with the colonies is described in Glausser, "Three Approaches to Locke and the Slave Trade," 203. Wayne Glausser argues that, while the extent of Locke's involvement in the drafting of the Carolina Constitution is a source of debate, recent scholarship seems to point to his co-authorship with Ashley.

61  Batz, "The Historical Anthropology of John Locke."

62  Lebovics, "The Uses of America in Locke's *Second Treatise of Government*," 575. For detailed information on Locke's engagement with the New World theoretically, politically, and economically, see Arneil, *John Locke and the Defense of English Colonialism*.

63  Arneil, *John Locke and the Defense of English Colonialism*, 2–3.

64  A. John Simmons offers a useful and detailed account of the differences that mark Hobbes's and Locke's depictions of the state of nature: Simmons, "Locke's State of Nature."

65  Pateman, *The Sexual Contract*, chap. 4.

66  Similarly, in the following section Locke writes, "Thus the natural fathers of families; by an insensible change, became the political monarchs of them too": Locke, *Second Treatise*, 76.318.

67  William Batz, for example, lists three stages in Locke's state of nature: nomadic, hunter-and gatherer-existence; the introduction of money and landed property; and, finally, a state of increasing disputes and conflicts: Batz, "The Historical Anthropology of John Locke," 248.

68 Mauss, *The Gift*. Mauss's study also considers gift relations among Melanesians and the Australian aborigines.

69 Also relevant in this context is an essay by Mayfair Mei-Hui Yang on gift relations in China: Yang, "The Gift Economy and State Power in China."

70 Oestreich, *Neostoicism and the Early Modern State*, 140. In a similar vein, F. J. West describes the complexity of feudal relations wherein obedience, obligation, services, and status mediated between personal relationships and the possession of property: West, "On the Ruins of Feudalism—Capitalism?"

71 Arneil, *John Locke and the Defense of English Colonialism*, 62. See also Tully, *A Discourse on Property*, 116–28.

72 Macpherson, *The Political Theory of Possessive Individualism*, 209–10.

73 Gordley, *The Philosophical Origins of Modern Contract Doctrine*, 117–20.

74 Ibid., chap. 1; Cheshire and Fifoot, *The Law of Contract*.

75 Quoted in Pocock, "Early Modern Capitalism," 80.

76 Mehta, *The Anxiety of Freedom*, 7. See also Hirshman, *The Passions and the Interests*.

77 Dunn, *Political Thought of John Locke*, 97: "The state of nature . . . is not an asocial condition but an ahistorical condition. It is that state in which men are set by God. The state of nature is a topic for theological reflection, not for anthropological research."

78 Pocock, "Early Modern Capitalism," 67.

79 Brenner, *Merchants and Revolution*, 106.

80 Ibid., 95.

81 Ibid., 94.

82 Ibid., 114.

83 Arneil, *John Locke and the Defense of English Colonialism*, 124–25.

84 From a 1670 memorandum written by Locke, quoted ibid.

85 Locke, *First Treatise*, 130.255.

86 Chakrabarty, *Provincializing Europe*, 245.

87 Locke, *An Essay Concerning Human Understanding*, 26.189.

88 The title of this section derives from a signature concluding a letter falsely ascribed to Jean-Jacques Rousseau quoted in Frayling and Wokler, "From the Orang-outan to the Vampire," 113. Rousseau's conjecture that the orangutan may well be human received much notoriety and was ridiculed by many of his contemporaries. I will be addressing what can safely be described as the "orangutan debate" later in this chapter.

89 Gutman, "Rousseau's Confessions," 107.

90 Rousseau, *Reveries of the Solitary Walker*.

91 Rousseau, *Confessions*, 17.

92 As Genevieve Lloyd rightly argues, one of the distinctive features of the autobiographical genre is that the subject is transformed into the object of study: Lloyd, "The Self as Fiction," 170. A large and growing literature exists on the

subject of Rousseau and the construction of the individual self. The most relevant to the present work are Ferrara, *Modernity and Authenticity*; Gauthier, *"Le Promeneur Solitaire"*; O'Hagan, *Jean-Jacques Rousseau and the Sources of the Self*; Swain, *"La Neuvième Rêverie"*; Wokler, "A Reply to Charvet." Rousseau, *A Discourse on Inequality*. Rousseau's *A Discourse on Inequality* is also known by the title *Second Discourse*. As my discussion on Rousseau is primarily concerned with this text, page references will appear in parentheses in the text. References to all other works by Rousseau will be cited in the endnotes.

93  Noble, "Freedom and Sentiment in Rousseau's Philosophical Anthropology." See also Horowitz, "Laws and Customs Thrust Us Back into Infancy."

94  Symcox, "The Wild Man's Return," 225.

95  Dudley and Novak *The Wild Man Within*.

96  Bernheimer, *Wild Men in the Middle Ages*, 8: "The status of the wild man was . . . reached not by a gradual ascent from the brute, but by a descent."

97  A fact immediately evident from the sources he evokes in his *Second Discourse*.

98  Wokler, "Deconstructing the Self on the Wild Side," 112.

99  Jahoda, *Images of Savages*, 49–50.

100  Moran, "Between Primates and Primitives," 39.

101  Roger, *Buffon*, 85.

102  Ibid., 312.

103  Jahoda, *Images of Savages*, 41.

104  Ibid. Also see Bynum, "The Great Chain of Being after Forty Years," 21; Roger, *Buffon*, 288–89.

105  Lovejoy, *The Great Chain of Being*, 228–29.

106  Wokler, "Deconstructing the Self," 113; Frayling and Wokler, "From the Orang-outan to the Vampire."

107  Foucault, *The Order of Things*, 150.

108  Moran, "Between Primates and Primitives," 38–39.

109  Quoted in Roger, *Buffon*, 289. Jacques Roger suggests that while initially espousing a theory of vertical gradation (i.e., the chain of being), Buffon increasingly appealed to a horizontal metaphor of networks and relationships: ibid., 290–91. While there may be some truth in the argument that Buffon's theoretical vision was more nuanced than the chain metaphor allows, he nevertheless equally relied on a language (e.g., gradations and gaps) that remained within the chain-of-being tradition. Arthur Lovejoy makes the point that so vague and amorphous was the principle of the chain that it was open to adaptability—thus making it a durable framework until the early nineteenth century: Lovejoy, *The Great Chain of Being*, 288.

110  Roger, *Buffon*, 289.

111  Bynum, "The Great Chain of Being after Forty Years," 21.

112  Ibid., 20.

113  Hodgen, *Early Anthropology in the Sixteenth and Seventeenth Centuries*, 434.

114 Lovejoy, *The Great Chain of Being*, chap. 9.

115 Melzer, *The Natural Goodness of Man*, 49.

116 It is precisely this interpretation that Lovejoy famously critiqued: Lovejoy, "The Supposed Primitivism of Rousseau's *Discourse on Inequality*."

117 White, "The Forms of Wildness," 25–26.

118 Rousseau, *The Social Contract and Discourses*, 195–96.

119 Ibid., 98–99.

120 "Beyond the range of thought and feeling of the brutish men of the earliest times, and no longer within the grasp of the 'enlightened' men of later periods, the happy life of the Golden Age could never really have existed for the human race. When men could have enjoyed it they were unaware of it; and when they could have understood it they had already lost it": Rousseau, "The General Society of the Human Race," 170–71.

121 Rousseau, *Émile*, 7.

122 Rousseau's work has often been regarded as a forerunner to Romanticism: see, e.g., Barnard, "National Culture and Political Legitimacy"; Gutman, "Rousseau's Confessions," 99–120 (esp. 101). Isaiah Berlin, on the contrary, challenges this oft-quoted relationship between Rousseau and Romanticism: see Berlin, *The Roots of Romanticism*, 52–62.

## 3   Traditions of History

1 Raynal, *A Philosophical and Political History of the Settlements of Trade of the Europeans in the East and West Indies*, 1:39, 2:341.

2 Ibid.

3 Robertson, *The History of America*. For a critical commentary on Robertson's *History of America*, see Womersley, "The Historical Writings of William Robertson."

4 Robertson, *An Historical Disquisition Concerning Ancient India*, 183–84.

5 Burke, "Speech on Fox's India Bill."

6 Ibid.

7 Chakrabarty, *Provincializing Europe*; Inden, *Imaging India*; Nandy, "History's Forgotten Doubles," 44–66; Prakash, "Writing Post-Orientalist Histories of the Third World."

8 Robertson, *An Historical Disquisition Concerning Ancient India*, 197 (appendix); Raynal, *A Philosophical and Political History of the Settlements of Trade of the Europeans in the East and West Indies*, 2:84.

9 Voltaire, *Fragments on India*, 20, 34.

10 Quoted in Halbfass, *India and Europe*, 75.

11 Quoted ibid., 70; quoted in Bearce, *British Attitudes towards India, 1784–1858*, 17.

12 Hegel, *The Philosophy of History*, 221.

13 William Jones, "Third Discourse," in Jones, *Discourses and Essays*, 9.

14 Schwab, *Oriental Renaissance*.

15   Schlegel, *On the Language and Wisdom of the Indians*, 523.

16   Hastings, "Warren Hastings," 185–86.

17   William Jones, "On the Hindus," in Jones, *Discourses and Essays*, 15.

18   Kejariwal, *The Asiatic Society of Bengal and the Discovery of India's Past*, 61.

19   Robert Orme, the East India Company's official historian, for example, criticized Indians on all fronts, from the effeminacy of the men to the despotism of the native government: see Orme, *Historical Fragments of the Mogul Empire*.

20   Grant, "Observations on the State of Society among the Asiatic Subjects of Great Britain," 33.

21   There exists a rich critical literature that has mapped the historicity of history. Some of the works that have informed this chapter include: Ankersmit "Historicism: An Attempt at Synthesis" 143–161; Becker, *The Heavenly City of the Eighteenth-Century Philosophers*; Chakrabarty, *Provincializing Europe*; Certeau, *The Writing of History*; Chandler, *England in 1819*; Collingwood, *The Idea of History*; Fabian, *Time and the Other*; Fasolt, *The Limits of History*; Finley, "Myth, Memory and History" 281–302; Iggers, *The German Conception of History*; Iggers, "Historicism"; Majeed, *Ungoverned Imaginings*; Pocock, *Politics, Language and Time*; Seth, "Reason or Reasoning"; White, *Metahistory*; Wolf, *Europe and People Without History*.

22   Foucault, *The Order of Things*.

23   Grafton, "Chronology and Its Discontents in Renaissance Europe," 141.

24   Grafton, *Cardano's Cosmos*, esp chap. 1.

25   Foucault, *The Order of Things*, 58–76, 131–32.

26   Quoted in Thomas, *Man and the Natural World*, 67.

27   Ibid., 66; Foucault, *The Order of Things*, 134–35, 141.

28   One need only look at the chapter headings to immediately appreciate the classificatory order Montesquieu imposes on his study of different cultures: Montesquieu, *The Spirit of the Laws*.

29   Jahoda, *Images of the Savages*, 41–42; Roger, *Buffon*, 309–12; Hannaford, *Race*, 203–4; Gillespie, *Science and Polity in France at the End of the Old Regime*, 337.

30   Becker, *The Heavenly City of the Eighteenth-Century Philosophers*, 101.

31   Bowler, *Evolution*, 65; Foucault, *The Order of Things*, 130–41; Roger, *Buffon*, 288–92.

32   This principle informs much of Rousseau's work, from the indignant proclamation that launches *The Social Contract* ("Man was born free, and he is everywhere in chains") to his introductory remarks in the *Second Discourse*. "Human society . . . appears at first to display only the violence of powerful men and the oppression of the weak . . . of poverty or riches [and thus] human institutions seem at first sight to be founded on piles of shifting sand. It is only . . . after clearing away the sand and dust which surrounds the edifice that one sees the solid base on which it is built, and learns to respect its foundations. For without the serious study of man, of man's natural faculties and their

successive developments, one will never succeed in analysing these distinctions, and separating, . . . that which the Divine Will has contrived from that which human artifice claims as its own": Rousseau, *A Discourse on Inequality*, 71.

33  From a different context, and with specific reference to philosophy, Carl Becker arrives at the same conclusion, namely that the philosophers of the eighteenth century felt compelled to "describe the qualities that were common to all men in order to determine what ideas and customs and institutions in their own time were out of harmony with the universal order": Becker, *The Heavenly City of the Eighteenth-Century Philosophers*, 87–88.

34  Roger, *Buffon*, 65–71.

35  Becker, *The Heavenly City of the Eighteenth-Century Philosophers*, 95.

36  Sakmann, "The Problems of Historical Method and of Philosophy of History in Voltaire," 31, 44. For Voltaire's own listings of what should and should not constitute history, see Voltaire, "On History." We can, of course, evoke a number of other proper names. For example, as late as 1792 Condorcet was arguing that there was no need to study the ancients, as they had not been governed by the principles of truth and reason: Hunt, *Politics, Culture, and Class in the French Revolution*, 31.

37  Hunt, *Politics, Culture, and Class in the French Revolution*, 70–71.

38  Becker, *The Heavenly City of the Eighteenth-Century Philosophers*, 92–93.

39  Iggers, *The German Conception of History*, 30.

40  Quoted in Oldroyd, "Historicism and the Rise of Historical Geology, Part 1" 192. Also see Oldroyd, "Historicism and the Rise of Historical Geology, Part 2," 227–257.

41  Quoted ibid., 195.

42  Sakmann, "The Problems of Historical Method and of Philosophy of History in Voltaire," 24.

43  Becker, *The Heavenly City of the Eighteenth-Century Philosophers*, 71–118.

44  Sakmann, "The Problems of Historical Method and of Philosophy of History in Voltaire," 25–59; Stern, *The Varieties of History*.

45  It is essentially this tension that Becker's work explores.

46  Becker, *The Heavenly City of the Eighteenth-Century Philosophers*, 71–118; Williams, *Problems in Materialism and Culture*, 68.

47  Popkin, "Hume's Racism"; quoted in Becker, *The Heavenly City of the Eighteenth-Century Philosophers*, 95.

48  Still, *"La Nouvelle Héloïse"*; Sakmann, "The Problems of Historical Method and of Philosophy of History in Voltaire," 30; Popkin, "Hume's Racism," 217.

49  Gerbi, *The Dispute of the New World*, 3–32.

50  Moran, "Between Primates and Primitives," 37–58.

51  Gerbi, *The Dispute of the New World*, 3–4.

52  Even Rousseau, who offered the novel and radical possibility that early man

possessed no speech, nevertheless argued that speech was inherent in man. It simply required social necessity for that peculiarly human attribute to be realized: Rousseau, *A Discourse on Inequality*, 111–12.

53 Daston and Galison, "The Image of Objectivity."

54 Ibid., 87.

55 Ibid., 91.

56 Ibid., 89–91.

57 Ibid., 91, 98–117, although, as Lorraine Daston and Peter Galison describe, the promises of scientific objectivity that photographic and X-ray technology appeared to offer were not as forthcoming as many scientists had hoped.

58 Lukács, *The Historical Novel*, 19.

59 Todorov, *Theories of the Symbol*, 288.

60 Sahlins, "'Sentimental Pessimism' and Ethnographic Experience," 160.

61 Koselleck, *Futures Past*, 23.

62 Certeau, *The Writing of History*, 2.

63 As Constantin Fasolt argues, "The distinction between the past and present also furnishes historians with their most basic principle of method. The principle consists of one command: thou shalt place everything in the context of its time. This keeps historians from committing anachronism": Fasolt, *The Limits of History*, 6.

64 Quoted in Chandler, *England in 1819*, 109.

65 Taylor, *Hegel*, 22; for a more complete discussion, see 3–126; Iggers, "Historicism."

66 Taylor, *Hegel*, 22.

67 Herder, *Outlines of a Philosophy of the History of Man*, 314.

68 Hegel, *The Philosophy of History*, 79.

69 Hobsbawm and Ranger, *The Invention of Tradition*, 182.

70 Hobsbawm, "Introduction," 1, 8. For a critique of Eric Hobsbawm's work and a further engagement with the concept of tradition, see Chakrabarty, "Afterword," 1–9.

71 Ibid., 12.

72 Shils, *Tradition*; Gross, *The Past in Ruins*.

73 Davidson, *The Emergence of Sexuality*, 30–65.

74 Eagleton, *Idea of Culture*; Williams, *Keywords*, 87–93.

75 Burke, *Reflections on the Revolution in France*; Herder, *Outlines of a Philosophy of the History of Man*, 458.

76 For example, Bentham argued that "to idolize, under the name of the wisdom of our ancestors, the wisdom of untaught, inexperienced generations" was to incorrectly elevate the past over the present when in fact, the present era was unquestionably superior to what preceded it: quoted in Gross, *The Past in Ruins*, 41.

77 Shils, *Tradition*, 6.

78 Locke, *An Essay Concerning Human Understanding*, 392.

79  d'Alembert, "Term of Architecture," 637.

80  Becker, *The Heavenly City of the Eighteenth-Century Philosophers*, 98–99.

81  Gross, *The Past in Ruins*, 26–27.

82  Marx, *The Eighteenth Brumaire of Louis Bonaparte*, 13.

83  Herder, *Outlines of a Philosophy of the History of Man*, 227.

84  Gross, *The Past in Ruins*, 41.

85  Zastoupil, *John Stuart Mill and India*; Stokes, *The English Utilitarians*; James Mill, *History of British India*, vol. 1. Also see Marshall, *The British Discovery of Hinduism in the Eighteenth Century*.

86  Zastoupil, *John Stuart Mill and India*.

87  William Jones, "L," in Jones, *The Works of Sir William Jones*, 2:140–41.

88  Malcolm, *A Memoir of Central India*, 2:433.

89  Guha, *An Indian Historiography of India*, 1–26. Also see Guha, *A Rule of Property for Bengal*; Lorenzen, "Imperialism and the Historiography of India."

90  For example see Dalrymple *White Mughals*; Gandhi, *Affective Communities*; Parsons, "Another India"; Spence *The Question of Hu*.

91  William Jones, "Letter to Cornwallis," in *The Works of Sir William Jones*, vol. 2, 141. Also see Mukherjee, *Sir William Jones*.

92  Even a cursory glance at *Reflections on the Revolution in France* reveals that Burke's thesis was not a *study in* tradition, but an *evocation of* it. The implicit presumption underwriting Burke's work is that the traditions he seeks to defend are recognizable *as* traditions in the minds of his readership. It is noteworthy, for example, that Burke's main adversary, Thomas Paine, objected not to whether Burke was right to identify the constitutional monarchy born of the Revolution of 1688 as an example of English political tradition but, rather, to whether it was a tradition worth defending and committing to posterity. In other words, the issue of contention was not which British practices and institutions constituted British traditions but whether the fact of tradition— Burke's appeal to antiquity, custom, experience, duration—merited the respect, awe, deference, defense, and continuance Burke took as self-evident: Paine, *The Thomas Paine Reader*.

93  Guha, *An Indian Historiography of India*, 12.

94  Mani, "Contentious Traditions," 88–126. There is an extensive literature on *sati*. For further reading, see Nandy, "*Sati*"; Spivak, "Can the Subaltern Speak?"

95  Pestonjee, "Minutes of Evidence," 21.

96  Hegel, *The Philosophy of History*, 141–42.

97  Ranke, "The Ideal of Universal History," 57. Stephen Bann offers an interesting and novel deconstruction of Ranke's famous definition: see Bann, *The Clothing of Clio*, 8–14.

98  Quoted in Iggers, *Historiography in the Twentieth Century*, 30.

99  Iggers, *The German Conception of History*, 30.

100  Ibid., 8.

101 Berlin, *The Roots of Romanticism*, 64–65.

102 Koselleck, *Futures Past*, 103.

103 Ibid., 92.

104 Ibid., 103.

105 Ibid.

106 Herder, *Outlines of a Philosophy of the History of Man*, 392.

107 Ibid., 270.

108 Ibid., 352.

109 Heidegger, *Questions Concerning Technology and Other Essays*, 115–54. I engage with Heidegger's thesis more extensively in the next chapter.

110 Mill, "On Liberty," in *Utilitarianism, Liberty and Representative Government*, 128.

111 Hobsbawm, "Mass-Producing Traditions."

112 Iggers, *The German Conception of History*, 5.

113 "Legends, Ballad stories, Traditions, must be excluded from such original history. These are but dim and hazy forms of historical apprehension, and therefore belong to nations whose intelligence is but half awakened": Hegel, *The Philosophy of History*, 2.

114 Thomas B. Macaulay, "Minute on Indian Education (1835)," in Macaulay, *Speeches by Lord Macaulay*, 350–51. Also see Viswanathan, *Masks of Conquest*.

115 Wilson, "Minutes of Evidence," *British Parliamentary Papers* (16) 1852–53, 290.

116 Ibid., 281.

117 Macaulay, "Minute on Indian Education," 357.

118 Ibid., 359.

119 Hegel, *The Philosophy of History*, 60.

120 Bann offers an interesting and novel deconstruction of Ranke's famous definition: Bann, *The Clothing of Clio*, 8–14.

121 Iggers, *Historiography in the Twentieth Century*, 25.

122 Quoted in Iggers, "Historicism," 146.

123 Ibid., 133.

124 Quoted in Iggers, *Historiography in the Twentieth Century*, 30.

125 Mignolo, *The Darker Side of the Renaissance*, esp. chaps. 1–3.

126 Yates "The Nalodaya or History of King Nala," 12.

127 Elliott, *The History of British India as Told by Its Historians*, xix.

128 Müller, *Chips from a German Workshop*, 1:5.

129 Prakash, "Writing Post-Orientalist Histories of the Third World," 386.

130 Dirks, "History as a Sign of the Modern," 27.

131 Müller, *India—What Can It Teach Us?*, 111.

132 Ibid., 14–15.

133 Ibid., 29.

134 Ibid., 89, 109; Müller, *Chips from a German Workshop*, 1:4, 1:26, 2:7, 2:74, 2:341.

135 Dumont, "The 'Village Community,' from Munro to Maine."

136 Maine, "The Effects of Observation of India on Modern European Thought," in *Village Communities in the East and West*, 224.

137 Maine, "The East and the Study of Jurisprudence," in Maine, *Village Communities in the East and West*, 10.

138 Maine, "The Sources of Indian Law," in Maine, *Village Communities in the East and West*, 62.

139 Of course, Hegel had already asserted, as early as 1818, that the idea of individuality (and its accoutrements—freedom, reason, equality) only found expression within the history of Europe. However, the transcendental nebulousness of the Hegelian Spirit did not, by the late nineteenth century, accord well with Ranke's prescription that history is about "what happened."

140 Maine, "The Effects of Observation of India on Modern European Thought," 224, and "The East and the Study of Jurisprudence," 12–13, both in *Village Communities in the East and West*.

141 Fabian, *Time and the Other*, 31.

142 Kolb, *The Critique of Pure Modernity*, 4.

## 4   Of Monsters and Man

1 Gossett, *Race*; Todorov, *On Human Diversity*.

2 Isaac, *The Invention of Racism in Classical Antiquity*.

3 Hannaford, *Race*, 4–5. See also Belmessous, "Assimilation and Racialism in Seventeenth- and Eighteenth-Century French Colonial Policy," 4–5.

4 Bartlett, "Medieval and Modern Concepts of Race and Ethnicity," 39–56. This is a special issue on race and racism in Medieval thought. It should be noted that Bartlett, unlike the other contributors in this volume, is critical of recent efforts to trace racial thinking back to the Middle Ages. See also Nirenberg, "Race and the Middle."

5 Goldberg, *Racist Culture*. For a collection of essays on race, the Renaissance, and the New World, see Greer et al., *Re-Reading the Black Legend*.

6 Mosse, *Toward the Final Solution*; Malik, *The Meaning of Race*; Seth, "Difference with a Difference."

7 Arendt, *Origins of Totalitarianism*; Hudson "From 'Nation' to 'Race'"; Stocking, *Victorian Anthropology*.

8 Arciniegas, *America in Europe*, 42–43.

9 Wittkower, "Marvels of the East," 162.

10 Bernheimer, *Wild Men in the Middle Ages*, 20; Barta, *Wild Men in the Looking Glass*, 10, 14fn12; White, "The Forms of Wildness."

11 Barta, *Wild Men in the Looking Glass*, 63–84.

12 Bernheimer, *Wild Men in the Middle Ages*, 33–35.

13 Daston and Park, *Wonders and the Order of Nature*.

14 Ibid., 38, 52.

15 Ibid., 51.

16 Veyne, *Did the Greeks Believe in Their Myths?*

17 Davidson, *The Emergence of Sexuality*, 93–124.

18  Daston, "The Nature of Nature in Early Modern Europe," 154–58.

19  Daston and Park, *Wonders and the Order of Nature*, 50.

20  Daston, "The Nature of Nature in Early Modern Europe," 155.

21  Ibid., 158.

22  Davidson, *The Emergence of Sexuality*, 100.

23  Daston and Park, *Wonders and the Order of Nature*, 52.

24  Quoted ibid., 183.

25  Quoted ibid.

26  Paré, *Of Monsters and Marvels*.

27  Ibid, 3–4; see also Davidson, *The Emergence of Sexuality*, 101.

28  Paré, *Of Monsters and Marvels*, 38.

29  Bynum, *Jesus as Mother*. Unless noted otherwise, page numbers from this work are cited in parentheses in the text.

30  Laqueur, "Orgasm, Generation and the Politics of Reproductive Biology," 2.

31  Quoted ibid., 5.

32  Laqueur, *Making Sex*, 4.

33  E.g., Daston and Park, "The Hermaphrodite and the Orders of Nature"; Foucault, *Herculin Barbin*; Greenblatt, "Fiction and Friction," 30–52.

34  Quoted in Laqueur, "Orgasm, Generation and the Politics of Reproductive Biology," 13. See Paré, *Of Monsters and Marvels*, 31–33, for other such stories.

35  Quoted in Laqueur, "Orgasm, Generation and the Politics of Reproductive Biology," 13.

36  Greenblatt, "Psychoanalysis and Renaissance Culture," 210–24.

37  Ibid., 215.

38  Ibid., 216.

39  Seth, "Difference with a Difference," 75–87.

40  Certeau *The Writing of History*, 141.

41  Ibid., 138.

42  Weber, *From Max Weber*. See esp. Weber's essays "Science as Vocation" and "Politics as Vocation." See also Konto " 'The World Disenchanted' and the Return of Gods and Demons."

43  "The world picture does not change from an earlier one, but rather, the fact that the world becomes picture at all is what distinguishes the essence of the modern": Heidegger, *Questions Concerning Technology and Other Essays*, 130.

44  Ibid., 129–30.

45  Ibid., 128.

46  My reading of Weber and Heidegger is indebted to my conversations with Sanjay Seth, as well as to his work on the subject: Seth, *Subject Lessons*.

47  Shakespeare, *Othello*, 23.

48  The following account of Mary Toft's monstrous birth is from Todd, *Imagining Monsters*, chap. 1, 1–37.

49  Quoted ibid., 1.

50  Ibid.

51  See Huet, *Monstrous Imaginations*, esp. 36–78.

52  Boucé, "Imagination, Pregnant Women, and Monsters in Eighteenth-Century England and France."

53  Rousseau and Porter, *Sexual Underworlds of the Enlightenment.*

54  Lynn Hunt, "Pornography and the French Revolution," in Hunt, *The Invention of Pornography*, 301–39; Douthwaite, *The Wild Girl, Natural Man and the Monster.*

55  Wahrman, *The Making of the Modern Self.*

56  Castle, "The Culture of Travesty: Sexuality and the Masquerade in Eighteenth-Century England," 158.

57  Rousseau, *Émile*, esp. book 5.

58  Todd, *Imagining Monsters*, 64–139.

59  For a detailed discussion of seventeenth-century and eighteenth-century medical thought, see Porter, *Flesh in the Age of Reason*, 44–61. See also Porter, "Medical Science and Human Science in the Enlightenment," 53–87; Figlio, "The Historiography of Scientific Medicine," 262–86; Todd, *Imagining Monsters*, 106–39.

60  Quoted in Porter, *Flesh in the Age of Reason*, 53.

61  Silvia Federici, for example, emphasizes the significance of mechanical philosophy to the newly emerging relations of capitalist production and the needs of a disciplined labor force in "The Great Caliban," in Federici, *Caliban and the Witch*, 133–62.

62  Todd, *Imagining Monsters*, esp. 106–16.

63  Porter, "Medical Science and Human Science in the Enlightenment," 58.

64  Todd, *Imagining Monsters*, 106–39.

65  Ibid., 95.

66  "In the sixteenth century, signs were thought to have been placed upon things so that men might be able to uncover their secrets . . . but they did not need to be known in order to exist: even if they remained silent, even if no one were to perceive them, they were just as much *there*. It was not knowledge that gave them their signifying function, but the very language of things": Foucault, *The Order of Things*, 59.

67  Gutting, *Michel Foucault's Archaeology of Scientific Reason*, 149.

68  Foucault, *The Order of Thing*, 59.

69  Quoted in Daston, "The Nature of Nature in Early Modern Europe," 166.

70  Ibid., 166.

71  Quoted in Smith, "The Language of Human Nature," 58.

72  Quoted in Foucault, *Madness and Civilization*, 94; Todd, *Imagining Monsters*, 95.

73  Mehta, *The Anxiety of Freedom*. See chapter 3 for a more detailed discussion of Mehta's work.

74  Quoted ibid., 21.

75  Quoted ibid., 80.

76  Quoted in Foucault, *Madness and Civilization*, 211–12.

77  Daston, "Marvelous Facts and Miraculous Evidence in Early Modern Europe," 93–124. As Daston notes, "Increasingly in the last quarter of the seventeenth century, the enemy was the enthusiast rather than the devil": ibid., 117. See also Todd, *Imagining Monsters*, 64–105.

78  For a detailed study of eighteenth-century debates on miracles, see Burns, *The Great Debate on Miracles*.

79  Quoted in Daston, "Marvelous Facts and Miraculous Evidence in Early Modern Europe," 118.

80  Quoted in Daston and Park, *Wonders and the Order of Nature*, 334.

81  Ibid., 337.

82  Quoted ibid., 338.

83  Quoted in Hunt, *Politics, Culture, and Class in the French Revolution*, 66.

84  Federici argues further that efforts to eradicate magic were motivated not only so as to discipline a potentially rebellious proletariat but were equally necessary as a precondition for capitalist transformation—a transformation that demanded the rationality and transparency of profit over the anarchical, opaque dangers of popular magic and superstition: Federici, "The Great Caliban."

85  For discussion on Peter of Hanover, see Douthwaite, *The Wild Girl, Natural Man and the Monster*, 21–28; Nash, *Wild Enlightenment*, esp. 45–50, 57–65; Novak, "The Wild Man Comes to Tea."

86  Nash, *Wild Enlightenment*, 69.

87  Quoted ibid., 43.

88  Novak, "The Wild Man Comes to Tea," 185.

89  Quoted ibid., 197–98.

90  Quoted ibid., 197.

91  For an account of Marie-Angélique Leblanc, see Douthwaite, *The Wild Girl, Natural Man and the Monster*, 29–52.

92  For discussions on Victor of Averyon, see Candland, *Feral Children and Clever Animals*, 17–37; Douthwaite, *The Wild Girl, Natural Man and the Monster*, 53–69; Itard, *Wild Boy of Aveyron*.

93  Commissioner of the département, quoted in Douthwaite, *The Wild Girl, Natural Man and the Monster*, 53.

94  Ibid., 10.

95  Thomas, *Man and the Natural World*, 28.

96  Quoted ibid., 28.

97  Ibid., 60.

98  Quoted in Douthwaite, *The Wild Girl, Natural Man and the Monster*, 7.

99  Hannaford, *Race*, 203–4.

100  See Wahrman, *The Making of the Modern Self*, 83–126, for a detailed discussion of the subject.

101 Debates about the "newness" of the American continent and Buffon's thesis are described extensively in Gerbi, *The Dispute of the New World*.

102 "If one transported Negroes to a northern province, their descendants in the eighth, tenth, or twelfth generation would be much less black than their ancestors, and perhaps as white as the original peoples of the cold climate where they would live": Buffon, quoted in Roger, *Buffon*, 179.

103 "Whites who become indistinguishable from Indians, 'savages' and Europeans differentiated through dress but not necessarily through their bodies, 'racial passing,' understandings of complexion and skin color predicated on climate, or culture, or civilization: these are the kinds of conceivable configurations reflecting eighteenth-century notions of race": Wahrman, *The Making of the Modern Self*, 86 (see also 83–126).

104 Popkin, "Hume's Racism"; Jahoda, *Images of Savages*, 55–57.

105 See for example, Barker, *The African Link*, 61–64, 162–66; Drescher, *Capitalism and Antislavery*, 19–20; Fredrickson, *Racism*, 54–55; Malik, *The Meaning of Race*, 61–68; Blackburn, *The Making of New World Slavery*; Bush, ed., *Serfdom and Slavery*; Phillips "Continuity and Change in Western Slavery," 71–88; Temperley, "New World Slavery, Old World Slavery," 144–57.

106 Malik, *The Meaning of Race*, 61–68.

107 Quoted in Porter, *Flesh in the Age of Reason*, 389.

108 Malthus, *An Essay on the Principle of Population*, 52.

109 Ibid., 55.

110 Ibid., 57.

111 Gallagher, "The Body versus the Social Body in the Works of Thomas Malthus and Henry Mayhew," 85.

112 Ibid., 90.

113 Laqueur, "Orgasm, Generation and the Politics of Reproductive Biology," 3.

114 Schiebinger, "Skeletons in the Closet."

115 Hannaford, *Race*, 207–208.

116 Ibid., 205–13.

117 Prichard, "On the Relations of Ethnology to Other Branches of Knowledge," 329.

118 Nott and Gliddon, *Types of Mankind*, 49.

119 Prichard, "On the Relations of Ethnology to Other Branches of Knowledge," 302; Nott and Gliddon, *Types of Mankind*, 45.

120 Crawfurd, "On the Classification of the Races of Man," 365. Crawfurd's other writings on the subject include "On Language as Test of the Races of Man," 1–9, and "On the Aryan or Indo-Germanic Theory," 268–86.

121 Stocking, *Race, Culture and Evolution*, 42–68.

122 Prichard, "On the Relations of Ethnology to Other Branches of Knowledge," 302.

123 The two organizations were to reunite in 1871 as the Anthropological Institute of Great Britain and Ireland: see Bolt, "Race and the Victorians," 129.

124 Ibid.

125 Foucault, *The Order of Things*, 368–69; Gutting, *Michel Foucault's Archaeology of Scientific Reason*, 199, 225.

126 Darwin, *The Origin of Species*, 458.

127 Hawkins, *Social Darwinism in European and American Thought*; Jones, *Social Darwinism and English Thought*; Young, "Darwinism is Social," 609–38.

128 Stocking, *Race, Culture and Evolution*, 46. The argument was echoed by Thomas Huxley: see Haller, "The Species Problem," 1326.

129 Quoted in Stocking, *Race, Culture and Evolution*, 46.

130 Haller, "The Species Problem," 1324.

131 Prakash, "Writing Post-Orientalist Histories of the Third World," 392.

132 Dirks, "Caste of Mind," 68.

133 Trautmann, *Aryans and British India*, 199.

134 Quoted in Dirks, "Caste of Mind," 69.

135 Quoted ibid.

136 It is important to note however, that he was not the first to argue that differences in caste appeared to correspond with biological differences. In what one hopes was not too expensive a study, Charles R. Havelock, captain of the Bengali Medical Centre and professor of anatomy in Lahore, concluded his measurement of different castes by observing, among other things equally profound, that "the lower the caste the greater will be the differences between the *skull* and *head* nasal index." He failed to elaborate on the significance of this finding: Havelock, "The Nasal Index Compared with the Skull," 6.

137 Risley, *The Tribes and Castes of Bengal*. It should be noted that Risley was also an advocate of Darwinism: see Risley, "Notes on Anthropology," 95–99.

138 Risley, *The Tribes and Castes of Bengal*, xxxviii.

139 Ibid., xxx.

140 Ibid., xix.

141 On criminal castes, see Henry, *Criminal Identification by Means of Anthropometry*; Nigam, "Disciplining and Policing the 'Criminals by Birth,' Part 1"; "Disciplining and Policing the 'Criminals by Birth,' Part 2."

142 My information regarding the Bertillon system is largely derived from Cole, *Suspect Identities*.

143 Ibid., 35.

144 Quoted ibid., 57.

145 Ibid., 58.

146 Quoted ibid., 53.

147 On the history of anthropometry and fingerprinting in India, see Sengoopta, *Imprint of the Raj*. See also Cole, *Suspect Identities*, 60–96. For an interesting discussion of the history of fingerprinting in Argentina, where it was introduced

into policing techniques soon after its success in India, see Rodriguez, "South Atlantic Crossings."

148 Cole, *Suspect Identities*, 33.

149 See n. 141. Brown, "Ethnology and Colonial Administration in Nineteenth-Century British India," 201–19.

150 Quoted in Sengoopta, *Imprint of the Raj*, 126.

151 The case was put most forcefully by E. R. Henry, superintendent of police in colonial Bengal: Henry, *Classification and Uses of Finger Prints*.

152 Sengoopta, *Imprint of the Raj*, 93–107.

153 Ibid., 102–106.

154 The credit for devising such a system, as Chandak Sengoopta suggests, goes to Henry's native 'aides' (Azizul Haque and Hem Chandra Bose), who in fact had to spend some time explaining the system to their superior: ibid., 141–45.

155 Quoted in Cole, *Suspect Identities*, 112–13.

156 Quoted ibid., 37.

## Epilogue

1 For a detailed account of this controversy, see Scott, *The Politics of the Veil*.

2 Alan Cowell, "For Multiculturalist Britain, Uncomfortable New Clothes," *New York Times*, October 22, 2006, 3.

3 John Vidal, "Bones of Contention," *Guardian Weekly*, January 21–27, 2005, 21.

4 Somini Sengupta, "Is Public Romance a Right? The Karma Sutra Doesn't Say," *New York Times*, January 4, 2006, 7.

5 Elaine Sciolino, "Plan to Test DNA of Some Immigrants Divides France," *New York Times*, October 11, 2007.

6 "U.S. Fingerprints 'Allied' Visitors," BBC News, available online at http://bbc.co.uk/go/pr/fr/-2/hi/americas/3595221.stm (accessed June 2007).

7 Gilroy, *Against Race*, 1.

8 For a brief overview of this debate, see Sahlins, "'Sentimental Pessimism' and Ethnographic Experience."

9 Joel Brinkley and Ian Fisher, "U.S. Says It Also Finds Cartoons of Muhammad Offensive," *New York Times*, February 4, 2006, 3; Cowell, "Multiculturalist Britain, Uncomfortable New Clothes," 3.

10 This position was well captured by a commentator for the left-leaning British newspaper *Independent*, in which the columnist Yasmin Alibhai-Brown argued against the practice of wearing the *niqab* (the full veil worn by some Muslim women) at work. "What any of us does in our own lives is a private matter—a precious inalienable right. But once we enter the job market or national and local authority domains, or tread into places where there is interaction with difference citizens, privacy and individual choice become contested—quite rightly, for there is such a thing as British society" quoted in Cowell, "For

Multiculturalist Britain, Uncomfortable New Clothes," 3. For a critique of liberal conceptions of multiculturalism, see Seth, "Liberalism and the Politics of (Multi)Culture."

11  Said, *Orientalism*.

12  Quoted in Davidson, *The Emergence of Sexuality*, 189.

13  Quoted ibid.

BIBLIOGRAPHY

Ankersmit, F. R. "Historicism: An Attempt at Synthesis." *History and Theory* 34, no. 3 (1995): 143–61.

Arciniegas, Germán. *America in Europe: History of the New World in Reverse.* Trans. Gabriela Arciniega and R. Victoria Arana. San Diego, Calif.: Harcourt Brace Jovanovich, 1986.

Arendt, Hannah. *Origins of Totalitarianism.* London: George Allen and Unwin, 1967.

Aristotle. *Politics.* London: Penguin Classics, 1992.

Arneil, Barbara. *John Locke and the Defence of English Colonialism.* Oxford: Clarendon Press, 1996.

Bann, Stephen. *The Clothing of Clio: A Study of the Representation of History in Nineteenth-Century Britain and France.* Cambridge: Cambridge University Press, 1984.

Barker, Anthony J. *The African Link: British Attitudes to the Negro in the Era of the Atlantic Slave Trade, 1550–1807.* London: Frank Cass, 1978.

Barnard, F. M. "National Culture and Political Legitimacy: Herder and Rousseau." *Journal of the History of Ideas* 44 (1983): 231–54.

Barta, Roger. *Wild Men in the Looking Glass: The Mythic Origins of European Otherness.* Trans. Carl T. Berrisford. Ann Arbor: University of Michigan Press, 1994.

Bartlett, Robert. "Medieval and Modern Concepts of Race and Ethnicity." *Journal of Medieval and Early Modern Studies* 31, no. 1 (2001): 39–56.

Batz, William G. "The Historical Anthropology of John Locke." *Journal of the History of Ideas* 35, no. 4 (1991): 663–70.

Bearce, George. *British Attitudes towards India, 1784–1858*. Oxford: Oxford University Press, 1961.

Becker, Carl L. *The Heavenly City of the Eighteenth-Century Philosophers*. New Haven, Conn.: Yale University Press, 1932.

Belmessous, Saliha. "Assimilation and Racialism in Seventeenth- and Eighteenth-Century French Colonial Policy." *American Historical Review* 110, no. 2 (2005): 1–27.

Bengal Police. From E. R. Henry, *Criminal Identification by Means of Anthropometry*, 2nd ed. Calcutta, 1894.

Berlin, Isaiah. *The Roots of Romanticism*, ed. Henry Hardy. Princeton: Princeton University Press: n. p., 1999.

Bernheimer, Richard. *Wild Men in the Middle Ages*. Cambridge, Mass.: Harvard University Press, 1952.

Blackburn, Robin. *The Making of New World Slavery*. London: Verso, 1998.

Bobbio, Norberto. *Thomas Hobbes and the Natural Law Tradition*. Trans. Daniela Gobetti. Chicago: University of Chicago Press, 1993.

Bolt, Christine. "Race and the Victorians." In *British Imperialism in the Nineteenth Century*, ed. C. C. Eldridge, 126–47. London: Macmillan, 1984.

Boucé, Paul-Gabriel. "Imagination, Pregnant Women, and Monsters in Eighteenth-Century England and France." In *Sexual Underworlds of the Enlightenment*, eds. G. S. Rousseau and Roy Porter, 86–100. Manchester: Manchester University Press, 1987.

Bowler, Peter J. *Evolution: The History of an Idea*. Berkeley: University of California Press, 1989.

Bracken, H. M. "Essence, Accident and Race." *Hermathena* (Winter 1973): 81–96.

Braudel, Fernand. *The Perspective of the World*. Berkeley: University of California Press, 1992.

Brenner, Robert. *Merchants and Revolution: Commerical Change, Political Conflict, and London's Overseas Traders, 1550–1653*. Princeton: Princeton University Press, 1993.

Brown, Mark. "Ethnology and Colonial Administration in Nineteenth-Century British India: The Question of Native Crime and Criminality." *British Journal of History and Science* 36, no. 2 (2003): 201–19.

Bucher, Bernadette. *Icon and Conquest: A Structural Analysis of de Bry's Great Voyages*. Trans. Basia Muller Gulati. Chicago: University of Chicago Press, 1981.

Burke, Edmund. *Reflections on the Revolution in France*. Middlesex: Penguin, 1984.

———. "Speech on Fox's India Bill." In *The Writings and Speeches of Edmund Burke*, vol. 4, ed. P. J. Marshall, 389–90. Oxford: Clarendon Press, 1981.

Burke, Peter. "Did Europe Exist before 1700?" *History of European Ideas* 1 (1980): 21–29.

Burns, R. M. *The Great Debate on Miracles: From Joseph Granville to David Hume.* Lewisburg, Pa.: Bucknell University Press, 1981.

Bush, M. L, ed. *Serfdom and Slavery: Studies in Legal Bondage.* London: Longman, 1996.

Bynum, Caroline Walker. *Jesus as Mother.* Berkeley: University of California Press, 1982.

Bynum, William F. "The Great Chain of Being after Forty Years: An Appraisal." *History of Science* 13 (1975): 1–28.

Candland, Douglas Keith. *Feral Children and Clever Animals.* New York: Oxford University Press, 1993.

Castle, Terry. "The Culture of Travesty: Sexuality and Masquerade in Eighteenth-Century England," in *Sexual Underworlds of the Enlightenment*, eds. G. S. Rousseau and Roy Porter, 156–180. Manchester: Manchester University Press, 1987.

Chakrabarty, Dipesh. "Afterword: Revisiting the Tradition/Modernity Binary," In *Mirror of Modernity: Invented Traditions of Modern Japan*, ed. Stephen Vlastos, 1–9. Berkeley: University of California Press, 1998.

———. *Provincializing Europe.* Princeton: Princeton University Press, 2000.

Chanca, Deigo Alvarez. "The Letter Written By Dr. Chanca to the City of Seville." In *The Four Voyages of Christopher Columbus*, ed. and trans. J. M. Cohen, 129–157. Middlesex: Penguin, 1969.

Chandler, James. *England in 1819: The Politics of Literary Culture and the Case of Romantic Historicism.* Chicago: Chicago University Press, 1999.

Clifford, James. "On Ethnographic Self-Fashioning: Conrad and Malinowski." In *Reconstructing Individualism: Anatomy, Individuality, and the Self in Western Thought*, eds. Thomas C. Heller, Morton Sosne, and David E. Wellbery, 140–62. Stanford, Calif.: Stanford University Press, 1986.

Cole, Simon A. *Suspect Identities.* Cambridge, Mass.: Harvard University Press, 2002.

Collingwood, R. C. *The Idea of History.* Oxford: Oxford University Press, 1993.

Columbus, Christopher. *The Four Voyages of Christopher Columbus.* Trans. and ed. J. M. Cohen. Middlesex: Penguin Classics, 1969.

———. "The Letter of Columbus (1493)." In *Wild Majesty: Encounters with Caribs from Columbus to the Present Day, an Anthology*, trans. and eds. Peter Hulme and Neil L. Whitehead, 9–15. Oxford: Clarendon Press, 1992.

Crawfurd, John. "On Language as a Test of the Races of Man." *Transactions of the Ethnological Society of London* 3 (1865): 1–9.

———. "On the Aryan or Indo Germanic Theory." *Transactions of the Ethnological Society* 1 (1861): 268–86.

———. "On the Classification of the Races of Man." *Transactions of the Ethnological Society* 1 (1861): 354–78.

d'Alembert, Jean Le Rond. "Term of Architecture." In *Encyclopedia*. Diderot, d'Alembert, and others. Trans. Nelly S. Hoyt and Thomas Cassirer. 634–41. Indianapolis: Bobbs and Merrill, 1965.

Dalrymple, William. *White Mughals*. London: HarperCollins, 2002.

Darwin, Charles. *Descent of Man and Selection in Relation to Sex*, 2nd. ed., 2 vols. New York: P. F. Collier and Son, 1905.

———. *The Origin of Species* (1859). Ed. J. W. Burrow. Middlesex: Penguin, 1979.

Daston, Lorraine. "Marvelous Facts and Miraculous Evidence in Early Modern Europe." *Critical Inquiry* 18 (1991): 93–124.

———. "The Nature of Nature in Early Modern Europe." *Configurations* 16 (1988): 149–72.

Daston, Lorraine, and Peter Galison. "The Image of Objectivity." *Representations* 40 (Fall 1992): 81–128.

Daston, Lorraine, and Katharine Park. "The Hermaphrodite and the Orders of Nature." In *Premodern Sexualities*, eds. L. Fradenburg and C. Freccero, 117–36. New York: Routledge, 1996.

———. *Wonders and the Order of Nature, 1150–1750*. New York: Zone Books, 1998.

Davidson, Arnold I. *The Emergence of Sexuality*. Cambridge, Mass.: Harvard University Press, 2001.

Davis, Natalie Zemon. "Boundaries and the Sense of Self in Sixteenth-Century France." In *Reconstructing Individualism: Anatomy, Individuality, and the Self in Western Thought*, eds. Thomas C. Heller, Morton Sosne, and David E. Wellbery, 53–63. Stanford, Calif.: Stanford University Press, 1986.

———. "On the Lame." *American Historical Review* 93, no. 3 (1988): 572–603.

———. *The Return of Martin Guerre*. Cambridge, Mass.: Harvard University Press, 1983.

de Certeau, Michel. *Heterologies: Discourse on the Other*. Trans. Brian Massumi. Minneapolis: University of Minnesota Press, 1985.

———. *The Writing of History*. Trans. Tom Conley. New York: Columbia University Press, 1988.

Delanty, Gerard. *Inventing Europe: Idea, Identity, Reality*. London: Macmillan, 1995.

Díaz, Bernal. *The Conquest of New Spain*. Trans. I. M. Cohen. Middlesex: Penguin Classics, 1976.

Dirks, Nicholas B. "Caste of Mind." *Representations* 37 (Winter 1992): 56–78.

———. "History as a Sign of the Modern." *Public Culture* 2, no. 2 (Spring 1990): 25–31.

———. "Introduction: Colonialism and Culture." In *Colonialism and Culture*, ed. Nicholas Dirks, 1–25. Ann Arbor: University of Michigan Press, 1992.

Douthwaite, Julia V. *The Wild Girl, Natural Man, and the Monster*. Chicago: University of Chicago Press, 2002.

Drescher, Seymour. *Capitalism and Antislavery*. New York: Oxford University Press, 1987.

————. "On James Farr's 'So Vile and Miserable an Estate.'" *Political Theory* 16, no. 2 (1988): 502–503.

Dudley, Edward and Maximillian E. Novak., eds. *The Wild Man Within: An Image in Western Thought from the Renaissance to Romanticism*. Pittsburgh: University of Pittsburgh Press, 1972.

Dumont, Louis. "The 'Village Community,' from Munro to Maine." *Contributions to Indian Sociology* 9 (December 1966): 67–81.

Dunn, John. *Political Thought of John Locke*. Cambridge: Cambridge University Press, 1969.

Dutton, Michael. "The Gift of the Political." Paper presented at the Problems of Comparability / Possibilities for Comparative Studies Conference, New York University, March 1–4, 2002.

————. "Lead Us Not Into Translation: Notes towards a Theoretical Foundation for Asian Studies." *Nepantla* 3, no. 3 (November 2002): 459–537.

Eagleton, Terry. *Idea of Culture*. Oxford: Blackwell, 2000.

Elliot, J. H. *The Old World and the New, 1492–1650*. Cambridge: Cambridge University Press, 1992.

Elliott, Henry. *The History of British India as Told by Its Historians*, ed. John Dowson. Allahabad: Kutab Mahal, 1898.

Fabian, Johannes. *Time and the Other: How Anthropology Makes Its Object*. New York: Columbia University Press, 1983.

Farr, James. "'Slaves Bought with Money': A Reply to Drescher." *Political Theory* 17, no. 3 (1989): 471–74.

————. "'So Vile and Miserable an Estate': The Problem of Slavery in Locke's Political Thought." *Political Theory* 14, no. 2 (1986): 263–89.

Fasolt, Constantin. *The Limits of History*. Chicago: University of Chicago Press, 2004.

Febvre, Lucien. "*Civilisation*: Evolution of a Word and a Group of Ideas." In *A New Kind of History and Other Essays*, ed. Peter Burke, trans. K. Folca, 219–57. London: Routledge and Kegan Paul.

Federici, Silvia. *Caliban and the Witch: Women, the Body, and Primitive Accumulation*. New York: Autonomedia, 2004.

Ferrara, Alessandro. *Modernity and Authenticity: A Study in the Social and Ethical Thought of Jean-Jacques Rousseau*. New York: State University of New York Press, 1993.

Figlio, Karl. "The Historiography of Scientific Medicine: An Invitation to the Human Sciences," *Comparative Studies in Society and History*, 19 no. 3 (1977): 262–82.

Finlay, Robert. "The Refashioning of Martin Guerre." *American Historical Review* 93, no. 3 (1988): 553–71.

Finley, M. I. "Myth, Memory and History." *History and Theory* 4, no. 5 (1965): 281–302.

Flint, Valerie I. J. *The Imaginative Landscape of Christopher Columbus*. Princeton: Princeton University Press, 1992.

Florescano, Enrique. *Memory, Myth, and Time in Mexico: From Aztecs to Independence*. Trans. Albert G. Bork. Austin: University of Texas Press, 1994.

Foucault, Michel. *Archaeology of Knowledge and the Discourse on Language*. Trans. Alan Sheridan Smith. New York: Pantheon, 1972.

———. *Discipline and Punish: The Birth of the Prison*. Trans. Alan Sheridan. New York: Vintage, 1979.

———. *Herculin Barbin, Being the Recently Discovered Memoirs of a Nineteenth-Century French Hermaphrodite*. Trans. Richard McDougall. New York: Pantheon, 1980.

———. *History of Sexuality*, vol. 1. Trans. Robert Hurley. London: Penguin, 1990.

———. *Madness and Civilization: A History of Insanity in the Age of Reason*. Trans. Richard Howard. London: Tavistock, 1985.

———. *The Order of Things: An Archaeology of the Human Sciences*. New York: Vintage, 1973.

Frayling, Christopher, and Robert Wokler. "From the Orang-outan to the Vampire: Towards an Anthropology of Rousseau." In *Rousseau after Two Hundred Years: Proceedings of the Bicentennial Colloquium*, ed. R. A. Leigh, 109–24. Cambridge: Cambridge University Press, 1982.

Fredrickson, George M. *Racism: A Short History*. Princeton: Princeton University Press, 2002.

Fuller, Gary, Robert Stecker, and John P. Wright. "Introduction" In *John Locke—An Essay Concerning Human Understanding, in Focus*, eds. Gary Fuller, Robert Stecker, and John P. Wright: 1–44. London: Routledge, 2000.

Furmston, M. P., G. C. Cheshire, and C. H. S. Fifoot. *Cheshire, Fifoot and Furmston's Law of Contract*. Oxford: Oxford University Press, 2007.

Gallagher, Catherine. "The Body versus the Social Body in the Works of Thomas Malthus and Henry Mayhew." In *The Making of the Modern Body*, ed. Catherine Gallagher and Thomas Laqueur, 83–106. Berkeley: University of California Press, 1987.

Gandhi, Leela. *Affective Communities: Anti-colonial Thought, Fin-de-Siècle Radicalism, and the Politics of Friendship*. Durham: Duke University Press, 2006.

Gauthier, David. "*Le Promeneur Solitaire*: Rousseau and the Emergence of the Post-Social Self." *Social Philosophy and Policy* 8, no. 1 (1990): 35–58.

Geertz, Clifford. *The Interpretation of Cultures*. New York: Basic Books, 1973.

Gerbi, Antonelle. *The Dispute of the New World: The History of a Polemic, 1750–1900*. Trans. Jeremy Moyle. Pittsburgh: University of Pittsburgh Press, 1973.

Gillespie, Charles Coulston. *Science and Polity in France at the End of the Old Regime*. Princeton: Princeton University Press, 1980.

Gilroy, Paul. *Against Race*. Cambridge, Mass.: Harvard University Press, 2004.

Glausser, Wayne. "Three Approaches to Locke and the Slave Trade." *Journal of the History of Ideas* 51, no. 2 (1990): 199–216.

Goldberg, David T. *Racist Culture: Philosophy and the Politics of Meaning*. Oxford: Blackwell, 1993.

Gordley, James. *The Philosophical Origins of Modern Contract Doctrine*. Oxford: Clarendon Press, 1991.

Gossett, Thomas. *Race: The History of an Idea in America*. Dallas: Southern Methodist University Press, 1963.

Grafton, Anthony. *Cardano's Cosmos: The Worlds and Words of a Renaissance Astrologer*. Cambridge, Mass.: Harvard University Press, 1999.

———. "Chronology and Its Discontents in Renaissance Europe." In *Time, Histories, and Ethnologies*, eds. Diane Owen Hughes and Thomas Trautmann, 139–66. Ann Arbor: University of Michigan Press, 1995.

———. *New Worlds, Ancient Texts: The Power of Tradition and the Shock of Discovery*. Cambridge, Mass.: Harvard University Press, 1992.

Grant, Charles. "Observations on the State of Society among the Asiatic Subjects of Great Britain, Particularly with Respect to Morals; and on the Means of Improving It." In *British Parliamentary Papers*, vol. 5 (1831–32), 3–92. Shannon: Irish University Press, 1970.

Greenblatt, Stephen. "Fiction and Friction." In *Reconstructing Individualism: Anatomy, Individuality, and the Self in Western Thought*, eds. Thomas C. Heller, Morton Sosne, and David E. Wellbery, 30–52. Stanford, Calif.: Stanford University Press, 1986.

———. *Learning to Curse: Essays on Early Modern Culture*. New York: Routledge, 1990.

———. *Marvelous Possessions*. Chicago: University of Chicago Press, 1991.

———. "Psychoanalysis and Renaissance Culture." In *Literary Theory/Renaissance Texts*, ed. Patricia Parker and Davis Quint, 120–224. Baltimore: John Hopkins University Press, 1986.

———. *Renaissance Self-Fashioning: From More to Shakespeare*. Chicago: University of Chicago Press, 1985.

Greenleaf, W. H. "Hobbes: The Problem of Interpretation." In *Hobbes and Rousseau*, eds. Maurice Cranston and Richard S. Peters, 16–30. Garden City, N.Y.: Anchor Books, 1972.

Greer, Margaret, Walter Mignolo, and Maureen Quilligan, eds. *Re-reading the Black Legend: The Discourses of Religious and Racial Difference in the Renaissance Empires*. Chicago: University of Chicago Press, 2007.

Gross, David. *The Past in Ruins: Tradition and the Critique of Modernity*. Amherst: University of Massachusetts Press, 1992.

Gruzinski, Serge. *The Conquest of Mexico*. Trans. Eileen Corrigan. Cambridge: Polity Press, 1993.

———. *The Mestizo Mind*. Trans. Deke Dusinberre. New York: Routledge, 2002.

Guha, Ranajit. *A Rule of Property for Bengal: An Essay on the Idea of Permanent Settlement*. New Delhi: Orient Longman, 1981.

————. *An Indian Historiography of India: A Nineteenth-Century Agenda and Its Implications*. Calcutta: Centre for Studies in Social Sciences, 1987.

Gutman, Huck. "Rousseau's Confessions: A Technology of the Self." In *Technologies of the Self: A Seminar with Michel Foucault*, eds. Luther H. Martin, Huck Gutman, and Patrick H. Hutton, 99–120. Amherst: University of Massachusetts Press, 1988.

Gutting, Mark. *Michel Foucault's Archaeology of Scientific Reason*. Cambridge: Cambridge University Press, 1989.

Hacking, Ian. "Language, Truth, and Reason." In *Rationality and Relativism*, eds. Martin Hollis and Steven Lukes, 48–66. Cambridge, Mass.: MIT Press, 1982.

————. "Making Up People." In *Reconstructing Individualism: Autonomy, Individuality, and Self in Western Thought*, eds. Thomas Heller, Morton Sosna, and David E. Wellbury, 222–36. Stanford, Calif.: Stanford University Press, 1986.

Halbfass, Wilhelm. *India and Europe*. New Delhi: Motilal Banarsidass, 1990.

Hale, John. *The Civilization of Europe in the Renaissance*. London: HarperCollins, 1993.

————. "The Renaissance Idea of Europe." In *European Identity and the Search for Legitimacy*, ed. Soledad Garcia, 46–63. London: Punter Publishers, 1993.

Haller, John S., Jr. "The Species Problem: Nineteenth-Century Concept of Racial Inferiority in the Origin of Man Controversy." *American Anthropologies* 70, no. 6 (1970): 1319–29.

Hanke, Lewis. *Aristotle and the Indians*. London: Hollis and Carter, 1959.

————. *The Spanish Struggle for Justice in the Americas*. Boston: Little, Brown, 1965.

Hannaford, Ivan. *Race: The History of an Idea in the West*. Baltimore: John Hopkins University Press, 1996.

Hartog, François. *The Mirror of Herodotus: The Representation of the Other in the Writing of History*. Trans. Janet Lloyd. Berkeley: University of California Press, 1988.

Hastings, Warren. "Warren Hastings, 'Letter to Nathaniel Smith,' from *The Bhagvat-Geeta*." In *The British Discovery of Hinduism in the Eighteenth Century*, ed. P. J. Marshall, 184–91. Cambridge: Cambridge University Press, 1970.

Havelock, Charles R. "The Nasal Index Compared with the Skull, with Notes upon the Nasal Bones and the Anterior Nasal Aperture." *Journal of Asiatic Society of Bengal* 63, no. 1, pt. 3 (1894): 1–10.

Hawkins, Mike. *Social Darwinism in European and American Thought*. Cambridge: Cambridge University Press, 1997.

Hay, Denys. *Europe: The Emergence of an Idea*. Edinburgh: Edinburgh University Press, 1968.

Hegel, Georg Wilhelm Friedrich. *The Philosophy of History*. Trans. J. Sibree. New York: Dover Publications, 1956.

Heidegger, Martin. *Questions Concerning Technology and Other Essays*. Trans. William Lovitt. New York: Harper, 1977.

Heller, Agnes. "Europe: An Epilogue?" In *The Idea of Europe: Problems of National and Transnational Identity*, eds. Brian Nelson, David Roberts, and Walter Veit, 12–25. New York: Berg Publishers, 1992.

Henry, E. R. *Classification and Uses of Finger Prints*. London: Routledge and Sons, 1900.

Herder, Johann Gottfried von. *Outlines of a Philosophy of the History of Man* (1784). Trans. T. Churchill. New York: Bergman, 1800.

Herodotus. *Histories*, trans. George Rawlinson. London: Wordsworth, 1996.

Hill, Christopher. *The World Turned Upside Down: Radical Ideas during the English Revolution*. London: Penguin, 1975.

Hirshman, Albert O. *The Passions and the Interests*. Princeton: Princeton University Press, 1977.

Hobbes, Thomas. *Leviathan*, ed. C. B Macpherson. Middlesex: Penguin, 1980.

———. *Man and Citizen (De Homine and De Cive)*, ed. Bernard Gert. Indianapolis: Hackett, 1991.

Hobsbawm, Eric. "Introduction: Inventing Traditions." In *The Invention of Tradition*, eds. Eric Hobsbawm and Terence Ranger, 1–14. Cambridge: Cambridge University Press, 1997.

———. "Mass-Producing Traditions: Europe, 1870–1914." In *The Invention of Tradition*, eds. Eric Hobsbawm and Terence Ranger, 263–308. Cambridge: Cambridge University Press, 1997.

Hobsbawm, Eric, and Terence Ranger., eds. *The Invention of Tradition*. Cambridge: Cambridge University Press, 1997.

Hodgen, Margaret T. *Early Anthropology in the Sixteenth and Seventeenth Centuries*. Philadelphia: University of Pennsylvania Press, 1964.

Horowitz, Asher. "'Laws and Customs Thrust Us Back into Infancy': Rousseau's Historical Anthropology." *Review of Politics* 52, no. 2 (1990): 215–42.

Hudson, Nicholas. "From 'Nation' to 'Race': The Origin of Racial Classification in Eighteenth Century Thought." *Eighteenth-Century Studies* 29, no. 3 (1996): 247–64.

Huet, Marie-Hélène. *Monstrous Imaginations*. Cambridge, Mass.: Harvard University Press, 1993.

Huizinga, J. *The Waning of the Middle Ages*. Trans. F. Hopman. Middlesex: Penguin, 1972.

Hulme, Peter. *Colonial Encounters*. London: Methuen, 1986.

Hunt, Lynn, ed. *The Invention of Pornography: Obscenity and the Origins of Modernity, 1500–1800*. New York: Zone Books, 1983.

———. *Politics, Culture, and Class in the French Revolution*. Berkeley: University of California Press, 1984.

Iggers, Georg G. *The German Conception of History: The National Tradition of Historical Thought from Herder to the Present*. Middletown, Conn.: Wesleyan University Press, 1983.

———. "Historicism: The History and Meaning of the Term." *Journal of the History of Ideas* 56, no. 2 (1995): 129–52.

———. *Historiography in the Twentieth Century*. Hanover, N.H.: Wesleyan University Press/University Press of New England, 1997.

Impey, Oliver, and Arthur Macgregor, eds. *The Origins of Museums: The Cabinet of Curiosities in Sixteenth and Seventeenth Century Europe*. North Yorkshire: House of Stratus, 2001.

Inden, Ronald. *Imaging India*. Cambridge: Blackwell Publishers, 1992.

Isaac, Benjamin. *The Invention of Racism in Classical Antiquity*. Princeton: Princeton University Press, 2004.

Itard, Jean Marc. *Wild Boy of Aveyron*. Trans. George Humphrey and Muriel Humphrey. New York: Appleton Century-Crofts, 1962.

Jahoda, Gustav. *Images of Savages: Ancient Roots to Modern Prejudices*. London: Routledge, 1999.

Jones, Greta. *Social Darwinism and English Thought*. Sussex: Harvester Press, 1980.

Jones, William. *Discourses and Essays*. Ed. Moni Bagchee. New Delhi: Peoples Publishing House, 1984.

———. *The Works of Sir William Jones*, vol. 2. New Delhi: Agam Prakashan, 1976.

Kabbani, Rana. *Imperial Fictions. Europe's Myths of the Orient*. London: Pandora, 1988.

Kejariwal, O. P. *The Asiatic Society of Bengal and the Discovery of India's Past*. New Delhi: Oxford University Press, 1988.

Kidder, Joel. "Acknowledgments of Equals: Hobbes's Ninth Law of Nature." *Philosophical Quarterly* 33, no. 131 (1993): 133–46.

Kolb, David. *The Critique of Pure Modernity: Hegel, Heidegger, and After*. Chicago: University of Chicago Press, 1986.

Konto, Alkis. " 'The World Disenchanted' and the Return of Gods and Demons." In *The Barbarism of Reason: Max Weber and the Twilight of the Enlightenment*, eds. Asher Horowitz and Terry Maley, 223–47. Toronto: University of Toronto Press, 1994.

Koselleck, Reinhart. *Futures Past: On the Semantics of Historical Time*. Trans. Keith Tribe. Cambridge, Mass.: MIT Press, 1985.

Kritzman, Lawrence D., ed. *Politics, Philosophy, and Culture: Interviews and Other Writings, 1977–1984*. New York: Routledge, 1990.

Kuhn, Thomas. *The Structure of Scientific Revolutions*. Chicago: University of Chicago Press, 1970.

Laird, J. "Hobbes on Aristotle's *Politics*." *Proceedings of the Aristotelian Society* 43 (1943): 1–20.

Laqueur, Thomas. *Making Sex*. Cambridge, Mass.: Cambridge University Press, 1990.

———. "Orgasm, Generation and the Politics of Reproductive Biology." In *The Making of the Modern Body*, eds. Catherine Gallagher and Thomas Laqueur, 1–41. Berkeley: University of California Press, 1987.

Las Casas, Bartolomé de. *The Devastation of the Indies: A Brief Account.* Trans. Herma Briffault. Baltimore: John Hopkins University Press, 1992.

Lebovics, Herman. "The Uses of America in Locke's *Second Treatise of Government.*" *Journal of the History of Ideas* 47, no. 4 (1986): 567–81.

Lloyd, Genevieve. "The Self as Fiction: Philosophy and Autobiography." *Philosophy and History* 10 (1986): 168–85.

Locke, John. *A Letter Concerning Toleration*, eds. John Horton and Susan Mendus. London York: Routledge, 1991.

———. *An Essay Concerning Human Understanding*, ed. John W. Yolton. London: Everyman, 1996.

———. *Two Treatises of Government*, ed. Peter Laslett. Cambridge: Cambridge University Press, 2002.

Lorenzen, D. "Imperialism and the Historiography of India." In *India: History and Thought*, ed. S. N. Mukherjee, 84–102. Calcutta: Subarnarekha, 1982.

Lovejoy, Arthur O. *The Great Chain of Being.* Cambridge, Mass.: Harvard University Press, 1964.

———. "The Supposed Primitivism of Rousseau's *Discourse on Inequality.*" In *Essays in the History of Ideas*, 15–37. Baltimore: Johns Hopkins University Press, 1948.

Lukács, Georg. *The Historical Novel* (1962). Trans. Hannah and Stanley Mitchell. Lincoln: University of Nebraska Press, 1983.

Macaulay, Thomas B. *Speeches by Lord Macaulay*, ed. G. M. Young. London: Oxford University Press, 1935.

Macpherson, C. B. *The Political Theory of Possessive Individualism: Hobbes to Locke.* Oxford: Oxford University Press, 1962.

Maine, Henry Sumner. *Ancient Law; Its Connections with the Early History of Society and its Relation to Modern ideas* (1861), 16th ed. London: John Murray, 1897.

———. *Village Communities in the East and West: Six Lectures Delivered at Oxford.* London: John Murray, 1876.

Majeed, Javed. *Ungoverned Imaginings: James Mill and the History of British India and Orientalism.* Oxford: Clarendon Press, 1992.

Malcolm, John. *A Memoir of Central India* (1826), vol. 2 New Delhi: Sagar Publications, 1970.

Malik, Kenan. *The Meaning of Race: Race, History, and Culture in Western Society.* New York: New York University Press, 1996.

Malthus, Thomas. R. *An Essay on the Principle of Population* (1797). Cambridge: Cambridge University Press, 1992.

Mani, Lata. "Contentious Traditions: The Debate on *Sati* in Colonial India." In *Recasting Women*, eds. Kumkum Sangari and Sudesh Vaid, 88–126. New Delhi: Kali Press, 1989.

Marshall, P. J., ed. *The British Discovery of Hinduism in the Eighteenth Century.* Cambridge: Cambridge University Press, 1970.

Martin, John. "Inventing Sincerity, Refashioning Prudence: The Discovery of the Individual in Renaissance Europe." *American Historical Review* 102, no. 5 (1997): 1309–42.

Martin, Luther H., Huck Gutman, Patrick H. Hutton, eds. *Technologies of the Self: A Seminar with Michel Foucault.* Amherst: University of Massachusetts Press, 1988.

Marx, Karl. *The Eighteenth Brumaire of Louis Bonaparte* (1852), ed. C. P. Dutt. New York: International Publishers, n.d.

Mauss, Marcel. *The Gift: The Form and Reason for Exchange in Archaic Societies.* London: Routledge, 1990.

McClintock, Anne. *Imperial Leather.* London: Routledge, 1995.

Mehta, Uday Singh. *The Anxiety of Freedom: Imagination and Individuality in Locke's Political Thought.* Ithaca, N.Y.: Cornell University Press, 1992.

Meier, Heinrich. *The Lesson of Carl Schmitt: Four Chapters on the Distinction between Political Theology and Political Philosophy.* Trans. Marcus Brainard. Chicago: University of Chicago Press, 1998.

Melzer, Arthur M. *The Natural Goodness of Man: On the System of Rousseau's Thought.* Chicago: University of Chicago Press, 1990.

Mignolo, Walter D. *The Darker Side of the Renaissance: Literacy, Territoriality, and Colonization.* Ann Arbor: University of Michigan Press, 1995.

Mikkeli, Heikki. *Europe as an Idea and an Entity.* Houndsmill: Macmillan, 1998.

Mill, James. *The History of British India,* vol. 1. New York: Chelsea House, 1968.

Mill, John Stuart. "On Liberty." In *Utilitarianism, Liberty, Representative Government,* 65–170. London: Dent (Everyman), 1964.

Montaigne, Michel de. "On Cannibals." In *Essays,* ed. J. M Cohen, 105–119. Middlesex: Penguin Classics, 1958.

Montesquieu, Charles de Secondat. *The Spirit of the Laws.* Trans. Anne M. Cohler, Basia C. Miller, and Harold Stone. Cambridge: Cambridge University Press, 1989.

Moran, Francis, III. "Between Primates and Primitives: Natural Man as the Missing Link in Rousseau's *Second Discourse.*" *Journal of the History of Ideas* 54, no. 1 (1993): 37–58.

Mosse, George L. *Toward the Final Solution: A History of European Racism.* Madison: University of Wisconsin Press, 1985.

Mukherjee, S. N. *Sir William Jones: A Study in Eighteenth Century British Attitudes to India.* London: Cambridge University Press, 1968.

Müller, Max. *Chips from a German Workshop.* London: Longmans, Green, 1867.

———. *India—What Can It Teach Us?* London: Longmans, Green, 1883.

Nandy, Ashis. "History's Forgotten Doubles." *History and Theory* 34 (1995): 44–66.

———. "*Sati*: A Nineteenth Century Tale of Women, Violence and Protest." In *At the Edge of Psychology: Essays In Politics and Culture,* 1–31. New Delhi: Oxford University Press, 1980.

Nash, Richard. *Wild Enlightenment*. Charlottesville: University of Virginia Press, 2003.

Nigam, Sanjay. "Disciplining and Policing the 'Criminals by Birth,' Part 1: The Making of a Colonial Stereotype—The Criminal Tribes and Castes of North India." *Indian Economic and Social History Review* 27, no. 2: 131–64.

———. "Disciplining and Policing the 'Criminals by Birth,' Part 2: The Development of a Disciplinary System, 1871–1900." *Indian Economic and Social History Review* 27, no. 3 (1990): 257–87.

Nirenberg, David. "Race and the Middle Ages: The Case of Spain and Its Jews." In *Re-reading the Black Legend: The Discourses of Religious and Racial Difference in the Renaissance Empires*, eds. Margaret Greer, Walter Mignolo, and Maureen Quilligan, 71–87. Chicago: University of Chicago Press, 2007.

Noble, Richard. "Freedom and Sentiment in Rousseau's Philosophical Anthropology." *History of Political Thought* 9, no. 2 (1988): 263–81.

Nott, J. C., and G. R. Gliddon. *Types of Mankind*. London: Trubner, 1854.

Novak, Maximillian. "The Wild Man Comes to Tea." *The Wild Man Within: An Image in Western Thought from the Renaissance to Romanticism*, eds. Edward Dudley and Maximillian E. Novak, 183–222. London: University of Pittsburgh Press.

O'Hagan, Timothy, ed. *Jean-Jacques Rousseau and the Sources of the Self*. Avebury: Aldershot, 1997.

Oestreich, Gerhard. *Neostoicism and the Early Modern State*, eds. Brigitta Oestreich and H. G. Keonigsberger. Cambridge: Cambridge University Press, 1982.

Olafson, Frederick A. "Thomas Hobbes and the Modern Theory of Natural Law." *Journal of the History of Philosophy* 4 (1966): 15–30.

Oldroyd, D. R. "Historicism and the Rise of Historical Geology, Part 1." *History of Science* 17, no. 38 (1979): 191–213.

———. "Historicism and the Rise of Historical Geology, Part 2." *History of Science* 17, no. 38 (1979): 227–257.

Olender, Maurice. *The Languages of Paradise: Race, Religion, and Philology in the Nineteenth Century*. Trans. Arthur Goldhammer. Cambridge, Mass.: Harvard University Press, 1992.

Orme, Robert. *Historical Fragments of the Mogul Empire* (1782). New Delhi: Associated Publishing House, 1974.

Pagden, Anthony. *European Encounters with the New World*. New Haven, Conn.: Yale University Press, 1993.

———. *The Fall of Natural Man*. Cambridge: Cambridge University Press, 1982.

Paine, Thomas. *The Thomas Paine Reader*. London: Penguin, 1987.

Paré, Ambroise. *Of Monsters and Marvels* (1573). Trans. Janis L. Pallister. Chicago: University of Chicago Press, 1982.

Parsons, Grant. "Another India: Imagining Escape from the Masculine Self." In *At the Edge of International Relations*, ed. Phillip Darby, 166–96. London: Cassells, 1997.

Pateman, Carole. *The Problem of Political Obligation: A Critical Analysis of Liberal Theory*. Chichester: John Wiley and Sons, 1979.

———. *The Sexual Contract*. Cambridge: Polity Press, 1988.

Pestonjee, Jerangee. "Minutes of Evidence." In *British Parliamentary Papers*, vol. 14 (1852–53), 17–22. Shannon: Irish University Press, 1970.

Phillips, William D., Jr. "Continuity and Change in Western Slavery: Ancient to Modern Times." In *Serfdom and Slavery: Studies in Legal Bondage*, ed. M. L. Bush, 71–88. London: Longman, 1996.

Pocock, J. G. A. "Early Modern Capitalism: the Augustan Perception." In *Feudalism, Capitalism and Beyond*, eds. Eugene Kamenka and R. S. Neale, 62–83. Canberra: Australian National University Press, 1975.

———. *Politics, Language, and Time: Essays on Political Thought and History*. New York: Atheneum, 1973.

Popkin, Richard H. "Hume's Racism." *Philosophical Forum Quarterly* 9 (Winter–Spring 1977–78): 211–26.

———. "Pre-Adamism in Nineteenth Century American Thought: 'Speculative Biology' and Racism." *Philosophia* (Israel) 8, nos. 2–3 (1978): 207–12.

Porter, Roy. *Flesh in the Age of Reason*. New York: W. W. Norton, 2003.

———. "Medical Science and Human Science in the Enlightenment." In *Inventing Human Science: Eighteenth-Century Domains*, eds. Christopher Fox, Roy Porter and Robert Wokler, 53–87. Berkeley: University of California Press, 1995.

Porter, Roy, ed. *Rewriting the Self: Histories from the Renaissance to the Present*. London: Routledge, 1997.

Prakash, Gyan. "Writing Post-Orientalist Histories of the Third World: Perspectives from Indian Historiography." *Comparative Studies in Society and History* 32, no. 2 (April 1990): 383–408.

Pratt, Mary Louise. *Imperial Eyes: Travel Writing and Transculturation*. London: Routledge, 1992.

Prichard, J. C. "On the Relations of Ethnology to Other Branches of Knowledge." *Journal of the Ethnological Society of London* 1 (1848): 301–29.

Rabinow, Paul, ed. *The Foucault Reader*. New York: Pantheon, 1984.

Ranke, Leopold von. "The Ideal of Universal History: Ranke." *The Varieties of History, From Voltaire to the Present*, ed. Fritz Stern. London: Macmillian, 1970: 54–62.

Raynal, Abbé. *A Philosophical and Political History of the Settlements of Trade of the Europeans in the East and West Indies*, 5 vols. Trans. J. Justamond. London: T. Cadell, 1777.

Risley, H. H. "Notes on Anthropology." *Journal of the Asiatic Society of Bengal* 63, no. 3 (1893): 95–99.

———. *The Tribes and Castes of Bengal*. Calcutta: Secretariat Press, 1892.

Robe, Stanley L. "Wild Men and Spain's Brave New World." In *The Wild Man Within: An Image in Western Thought from the Renaissance to Romanticism*, eds.

Edward Dudley and Maximillian E. Novak, 39–54. London: University of Pittsburgh Press, 1972.

Robertson, William. *An Historical Disquisition Concerning Ancient India* (1818). New Delhi: Rare Prints, 1981.

———. *The History of America*, 12th ed., 3 vols. London: n.p., 1812.

Rodriguez, Julia. "South Atlantic Crossings: Fingerprints, Science and the State in Turn-of-the-Century Argentina." *American Historical Review* 109, no. 2 (April 2004): 387–416.

Roger, Jacques. *Buffon.* Trans. Sarah Lucille Bonnefoi. Ithaca, N.Y.: Cornell University Press, 1997.

Rosaldo, Renato. *Culture and Truth.* London: Routledge, 1993.

Rousseau, G. S., and Roy Porter. *Sexual Underworlds of the Enlightenment.* Manchester: Manchester University Press, 1987.

Rousseau, Jean-Jacques. *Confessions.* Trans. J. M Cohen. Middlesex: Penguin, 1967.

———. *A Discourse on Inequality.* Trans and ed. Maurice Cranston. London: Penguin Classics, 1984.

———. *Émile.* Trans. Barbara Foxley. London: Everyman, 1993.

———. "The General Society of the Human Race." In *The Social Contract and Discourses*, 169–77. Trans. G. D. H. Cole. London: Everyman, 1990.

———. *Reveries of the Solitary Walker.* Trans. Peter France. London: Penguin, 1979.

———. *The Social Contract and Discourses* Trans. G. D. H. Cole. London: Everyman, 1990.

Rubiés, Joan-Pau. "Hugo Grotius's Dissertation on the Origin of the American Peoples and the Use of Comparative Method." *Journal of the History of Ideas* 52, no. 2 (April–June 1991): 221–24.

Ryan, Michael T. "Assimilating New Worlds in the Sixteenth and Seventeenth Centuries." *Comparative Studies in Society and History* 23 (1981): 518–38.

Sahlins, Marshall. "'Sentimental Pessimism' and Ethnographic Experience; or, Why Culture Is Not a Disappearing 'Object.'" In *Biographies of Scientific Objects*, ed. Lorraine Daston, 158–202. Chicago: University of Chicago Press, 2000.

Said, Edward. *Orientalism.* London: Penguin, 1978.

Sakmann, Paul. "The Problems of Historical Method and of Philosophy of History in Voltaire." *History and Theory* 11, no. 10 (1971): 24–57.

Sale, Kirkpatrick. *The Conquest of Paradise.* New York: Alfred A. Knopf, 1990.

Schiebinger, Londa. "Skeletons in the Closet: The First Illustrations of the Female Skeleton in Eighteenth Century Anatomy." In *Making of the Modern Body*, eds. Catherine Gallagher and Thomas Laqueur, 42–82. Berkeley: University of California Press, 1987.

Schlegel, Carl Wilhelm Friedrich von. *On the Language and Wisdom of the Indians* (1849). London: Ganesha, 2001.

Schmitt, Carl. *The Concept of the Political.* Chicago: University of Chicago Press, 1988.

Schwab, Raymond. *Oriental Renaissance*. Trans. Gene Patterslon-Black and Victory Reinking. New York: Columbia University Press, 1984.

Scott, Joan. *Politics of the Veil*. Princeton: Princeton University Press, 2007.

Seed, Patricia. *Ceremonies of Possession: Europe's Conquest of the New World, 1492–1640*. Cambridge: Cambridge University Press, 1995.

Sengoopta, Chandak. *Imprint of the Raj*. London: Macmillan, 2003.

Seth, Sanjay. "Liberalism and the Politics of (Multi)Culture: Or, Plurality Is Not Difference." *Postcolonial Studies* 14, no. 1 (2001): 65–77.

———. "Reason or Reasoning? Clio or Siva?" *Social Text* 22, no. 1 (2004): 85–101.

———. *Subject Lessons: The Western Education of India*. Durham: Duke University Press, 2007.

Seth, Vanita. "Difference with a Difference: Wild Men, Gods and Other Protagonists." *Parallax* 29 (2003): 75–87.

Shakespeare, William. *Othello*, eds. Alice Walker and John Dover Wilson. London: Cambridge University Press, 1971.

Shils, Edward. *Tradition*. Chicago: University of Chicago Press, 1981.

Simmons, A. John. "Locke's State of Nature." *Political Theory* 17, no. 3 (1989): 449–70.

Skinner, Quentin "Who Are 'We'? Ambiguities of the Modern Self." *Inquiry* 34 (1991): 133–53.

Smith, Roger. "The Language of Human Nature." In *Inventing Human Science*, eds. Christopher Fox, Roy Porter, and Robert Wokler, 88–111. Berkeley: University of California Press, 1996.

Spence, Jonathan S. *The Question of Hu*. New York: Vintage Books, 1989.

Spivak, Gayatri Chakravorty. "Can the Subaltern Speak?" In *Marxism and the Interpretation of Cultures*, eds. Cary Nelson and Lawrence Grossberg, 271–324. Urbana: University of Illinois Press, 1988.

Squadrito, Kathy. "Locke's View of Essence and Its Relation to Racism: A Reply to Professor Bracken." *Locke Newsletter* 6 (Summer 1975): 41–54.

Stern, Fritz. ed. and trans. *The Varieties of History: From Voltaire to the Present*. London: Macmillan, 1970.

Still, Judith. "*La Nouvelle Héloise*; Passion, Reserve, and the Gift." *The Modern Language Review* 91 (January 1996): 40–52.

Stocking, George W., Jr. *Race, Culture, and Evolution: Essays in the History of Anthropology*. New York: Free Press, 1968.

———. *Victorian Anthropology*. New York: Free Press, 1987.

Stokes, Eric. *The English Utilitarians and India*. Oxford: Oxford University Press, 1989.

Stoler, Ann Laura. *Race and the Education of Desire*. Durham: Duke University Press, 1999.

Swain, Virginia E. "*La Neuvième Rêverie*: On Reading a 'Man's' Autobiography." *Studies in Romanticism* 26 (1987): 573–90.

Symcox, Geoffrey. "The Wild Man's Return: The Enclosed Vision of Rousseau's *Discourses*." In *The Wild Man Within: An Image in Western Thought from the Renaissance to Romanticism*, eds. Edward Dudley and Maximillian E. Novak, 223–47. Pittsburgh: University of Pittsburgh Press, 1972.

Taylor, Charles. *Hegel*. Cambridge: Cambridge University Press, 1975.

———. *Sources of the Self: The Making of the Modern Identity*. Cambridge, Mass.: Harvard University Press, 1989.

Temperley, Howard. "New World Slavery, Old World Slavery." In *Serfdom and Slavery: Studies in Legal Bondage*, ed. M. L. Bush, 144–57. London: Longman, 1996.

Thomas, Keith. *Man and the Natural World*. Middlesex: Penguin, 1984.

Thompson, Martyn P. "Ideas of Europe during the French Revolution and Napoleonic Wars." *Journal of the History of Ideas* 55, no. 1 (1994): 37–58.

Todd, Denis, *Imagining Monsters*. London: University of Chicago Press, 1995.

Todorov, Tzvetan. *The Conquest of America*. Trans. Richard Howard. New York: Harper Perennial, 1982.

———. *On Human Diversity*. Trans. Catherine Porter. Cambridge and London: Harvard University Press, 1994.

———. *Theories of the Symbol*. Trans. Catherine Porter. Ithaca, N.Y.: Cornell University Press, 1982.

Traboulay, David M. *Columbus and Las Casas*. Lanham, Md.: University Press of America, 1994.

Trautmann, Thomas R. *Aryans and British India*. Berkeley: University of California Press, 1997.

———. "The Revolution in Ethnological Time." *Man* 27 (1991): 379–97.

Tully, James. *A Discourse on Property: John Locke and His Adversaries*. Cambridge: Cambridge University Press, 1982.

———. *An Approach to Political Philosophy: Locke in Contexts*. Cambridge: Cambridge University Press, 1993.

Veeser, H. Aram, ed. *The New Historicism*. New York: Routledge, 1989.

Vespucci, Amerigo. "Third Voyage of Amerigo Vespucci." In *The Letters of Amerigo Vespucci and Other Documents Illustrative of his Career*. Intro. and notes by Clements R Markham, 34–52. London: Hakluyt Society, 1894.

———. (Albericus Vespucius). *Mundus Novus*. Trans. George Tyler Northup. Princeton: Princeton University Press, 1916.

Veyne, Paul. *Did the Greeks Believe in Their Myths?* Trans. Paula Wissing. Chicago: University of Chicago Press, 1988.

Viswanathan, Gauri. *Masks of Conquest: Literary Study and British Rule in India*. New York: Columbia University Press, 1989.

Vitoria, Francisco de. "On the American Indians." In *Francisco de Vitoria: Political Writings*, eds. Anthony Pagden and Jeremy Lawrence, 233–92. Cambridge: Cambridge University Press, 1991.

———. "On the Law of War." In *Francisco de Vitoria: Political Writings*, eds. Anthony Pagden and Jeremy Lawrence, 295–327. Cambridge: Cambridge University Press, 1991.

Voltaire, François Marie Arouet de. *Fragments on India*. Trans. Freda Bedi. Lahore: Contemporary India Publication, 1937.

———. "On History: Advice to a Journalist." In *The Varieties of History: From Voltaire to the Present*, ed. and trans. Fritz Stern, 36–38. London: Macmillan, 1970.

Wahrman, Dror. *The Making of the Modern Self*. New Haven, Conn.: Yale University Press, 2004.

Weber, Max. *From Max Weber*, eds., H. H. Gerth and C. Wright Mills. New York: Oxford University Press, 1958.

West, F. J. "On the Ruins of Feudalism—Capitalism?" In *Feudalism, Capitalism and Beyond*, eds. Eugene Kamenka and R. S. Neale, 50–61. Canberra: Australian National University Press, 1975.

White, Hayden. "The Forms of Wildness: Archaeology of an Idea." In *The Wild Man Within: An Image in Western Thought from the Renaissance to Romanticism*, eds. Edward Dudley and Maximillian E. Novak, 3–38. London: University of Pittsburgh Press.

———. *Metahistory: The Historical Imagination in Nineteenth-Century Europe*. Baltimore: Johns Hopkins University Press, 1973.

Williams, Raymond. *Keywords*. New York: Oxford University Press, 1983.

———. *Problems in Materialism and Culture*. London: Verso, 1980.

Wilson H. H. "Minutes of Evidence." *British Parliamentary Papers* 16 (1852–53): 273–92. Shannon: Irish University Press, 1970.

Wittkower, Rudolf. "Marvels of the East: A Study in the History of Monsters." *Journal of the Warburg and Courtauld Institute* 5 (1942): 159–97.

Wokler, Robert. "A Reply to Charvet: Rousseau and the Perfectibility of Man." *History of Political Thought* 1 (1980): 81–90.

———. "Deconstructing the Self on the Wild Side." In *Jean-Jacques Rousseau and the Sources of the Self*, ed. Timothy O'Hagan, 106–19. Aldershot: Avebury, 1997.

Wolf, Eric R. *Europe and the People without History*. Berkeley: University of California Press, 1982.

Wolin, Sheldon S. *Politics and Vision: Continuity and Innovation in Western Political Thought*. Boston: Little, Brown, 1960.

Womersley, D. J. "The Historical Writings of William Robertson." *Journal of the History of Ideas* 47 (1986): 497–506.

Yang, Mayfair Mei-Hui. "The Gift Economy and State Power in China." *Comparative Studies in Society and History* 31 (1989): 25–54.

Yapp, M. E. "Europe in the Turkish Mirror." *Past and Present* 137 (1992): 134–55.

Yates, W. "The Nalodaya or History of King Nala, a Sanskrit Poem by Kalidasa." *Calcutta Review* 13 (January–June 1845): 1–36.

Young, Robert M. *Colonial Desire: Hybridity in Theory, Culture and Race*. London: Routledge, 1995.

———. "Darwinism Is Social." In *The Darwinian Heritage*, ed. David Kohn, 609–38. Princeton: Princeton University Press, 1985.

Zastoupil, Lynn. *John Stuart Mill and India*. Stanford, Calif.: Stanford University Press, 1994.

*Iliad* (Homer), 126
imagination, Classical theories on, 191–95, 197–210
imagined community, eighteenth-century Europe as, 27–28
*Imago Mundi* (d'Ailley), 39
immigration policies, race and, 228–32
"Impact of the Concept of Culture on the Concept of Man, The" (Geertz), 62–63
imperialism, self-other concept and, 21–24
Inca empire, 54
India, 12–17, 124–27, 151–65; changing demographics in, 228; criminality and criminology in, 221–26; indigenous America compared with, 119–24; native traditions in, 147–51; racial theory in, 219–26; representation of antiquity in, 5, 119; self-other concept and caste system in, 234n7; Vedic culture and, 166–69
Indian Mutiny of 1857, 223–24
indifference, politics of, and New World, 36–45
indigenous Americans: Classical Age representations of, 207–10; colonial educational policy and, 159–60; Columbus's view of, 48–49; European view of, 38–45, 238n107, 238n112; genealogical representations of, 56–58, 100; gift-giving practices of, 85–86; Hegel's discussion of, 161–62; history of, European dismissal of, 133–37, 163–65; Hobbes's representation of, 75–78; Locke on, 82–86, 88–91, 94–100; native Indians compared with, 119–24; Renaissance view of, 21–24, 44–45; signatures of similitude and representations of, 45–58; social contract representations of, 14–15; Spanish colonialism and, 32–33, 41–42

individual identity, 136–37; absence of, in Renaissance, 184–85; history and, 129–31, 154–65, 251n139; Hobbes on, 66–78, 168; Locke on, 78–86; Rousseau on, 101–18, 136–37; social contract theory and, 14–15; subjectivity and, 61–65, 97–100
*Invention of Racism in Classical Antiquity, The* (Isaac), 173
*Invention of Tradition, The* (Hobsbawm and Ranger), 141–42
Isaac, Benjamin, 173
Islam: European preoccupation with threat of, 38–45; idea of Europe and role of, 26–36
Itard, Jean, 202

Jaucourt, Chevalier de, 198–99
Jerez, Francisco de, 37
*jihad,* evolution of, 32–33
Jones, William, 125–26, 147, 214
*Journal* of Christopher Columbus, 40, 48–49, 51–53, 94
just war exceptionalism, 76–77

Kabbani, Rana, 40
Kalidasa, 126, 166–67
knowledge: Arabic, in Middle Ages, 33–34; Classical view of reason and, 195–210; dehistoricization of, 59; Foucault on, 14, 45–48, 107, 128, 188, 195, 253n66; race theory and role of, 217–26; Renaissance representation of, 14, 130, 195; science and, 38–39
Kolb, David, 170
Koselleck, Reinhart, 139, 153–54
Kuhn, Thomas, 6–8

Laird, J., 65
language: colonial education policies and, 160–61; historical particularity in, 137; multiculturalism and, 229–32; nineteenth-century race theory and,

language (*cont.*)
214; race terminology and, 173; of representation, historical context for, 187–90

*La Nouvelle Héloise* (Rousseau), 135

La Peyrere, Isaac, 56

Laqueur, Thomas, 183, 191, 213

Las Casas, Bartolomé de, 41, 43–44, 54–55

Latin: decline of spoken, 27; Sanskrit affinity with, 12–13, 125–27

*Laws of Manu* (Kalidasa), 166–67

Leblanc, Marie-Angélique, 202–4

Léry, Jean de, 54–55

*Letter Concerning Toleration, A* (Locke), 78–79

*Leviathan* (Hobbes), 65–78

Linnaeus, Carl, 104–11, 116, 130–31, 133, 206–7, 213

Lloyd, Genieve, 243n92

Locke, John, 12, 59, 116; ahistorical time and work of, 97–100; on education, 201–2; on familial relations, 84–86, 168–69; historical legacy of, 129–30, 136–37; on imagination, 197–98; on individual identity, 62–65, 71–74, 76–86, 100; on knowledge, 14–15, 196; on tradition, 144–45

Lombroso, Cesare, 221–22

*London Ethnology* (journal), 214

Long, Edward, 207

Lovejoy, Arthur, 244n109

Lukács, Georg, 138–39

Macaulay, Thomas Babbington, 132, 160–61, 163–65

Macpherson, C. B., 81–82, 87, 92, 97

magic, capitalist transformation and eradication of, 209–10, 254n84

*Mahabharata*, 126

Maine, Henry Sumner, 137, 167–69

Malcolm, John, 147

Malik, Kenan, 173–74, 207

Maliki tradition of jurisprudence, 32–33

Malthus, T. R., 210–12

*Man and Citizen* (Hobbes), 70, 73

Mandeville, John, 48, 50, 55, 178

Mani, Lata, 149

market forces, Locke's contractarian theory and, 89–91

Martin, John, 64

Martyr, Peter, 37, 50

*Marvelous Possessions* (Greenblatt), 21, 40

Marx, Karl, 99, 116, 145

maternal imagination: Classical theories of body and, 194–95; monstrous bodies and, 190–91; in religion and culture, 181–83

Matthey, 197–98

Mauss, Marcel, 85–86

McClintock, Anne, 9

mechanical philosophy, 194, 253n61

Mehta, Uday Singh, 80–82, 91, 97–98, 197

mercantile economics, colonialism and, 92–97

Merchant Adventurers, 92–93

*Mere Nature Delineated* (Defoe), 201

metaphysics, historical specificity of self-other and, 20–24

Michelet, Jules, 132

Middle Ages: Arabic knowledge in, 33–34; body images in, 180–90; idea of Europe in, 25–36; maternal religious images in, 181–83; otherness concepts in, 39; race terminology, 173–74, 251n4; savage representations in, 103–5; supernatural images in, 178–80, 190–91; Voltaire's concept of, 135–37; wild man imagery in, 177–78

Mignolo, Walter, 163–65

Mill, James, 146, 149

"proto-racism," European representations and, 3
Ptolemy, 178–79
Pufendorf, Samuel von, 86

Quiroga, Vasco de, 50

race, racial theory, 173–75; anthropometry and, 2–3; Classical understanding of, 205–10, 216–26, 255n102; culture and, 228–32; epistemic context for, 4–5; history of, 3, 16–17, 173–226; India's role in, 219–26; Middle Ages and Renaissance body imagery and, 187–90, 251n4; nineteenth-century representations of, 212–26; self-other concept and, 29, 235n37
Raleigh, Walter, 56
Ranger, Terence, 141–42, 150, 157
Ranke, Leopold von, 132, 152, 162–63, 250n120, 251n139
*Rape of Europe* (Dürer painting), 24–25
Ray, John, 130–31
Raynal, Abbé, 119–24, 132, 134
reason: Classical debates concering, 193–210; Locke's emphasis on, 91–100; styles of, 7–8; tradition and, 144–46
*Reflections on the Revolution in France* (Burke), 144, 184, 249n92
religion: body concepts in, 176, 180–90; colonialism and, 30–31, 100; as conceptual category, 186–90; contract theory and, 69; history and, 129–37; knowledge and, 195–96; Locke on, 91–97; monster imagery and, 177–79; native traditions and, 146–51; race and racial theory and, 188–90; reason and, 198–99
Renaissance: body representation in, 16–17, 176–77, 184–92, 212; fascination of, with hermaphroditism, 184; genealogy and, 55–58; idea of Europe and, 27; knowledge formation in, 14,

130, 195–96, 208; monster representations in, 178–90; New World representations in, 21, 39, 42–45; race terminology in, 173–75, 206; signatures of similitude and, 45–58; supernatural images in, 178–80, 190–91
*Renaissance Self-Fashioning* (Greenblatt), 62–63, 185
representation: in Classical epistemology, 195–96; medieval and Renaissance history and language of, 187–90
reproduction, Classical Age theories on, 194
Requirement (*Regimento*), Spanish colonialism and, 32–33, 41–42
*Return of Martin Guerre, The* (Davis), 239n6
*Reveries of the Solitary Walker* (Rousseau), 101–2, 115
Revolution of 1688, 249n92
*Rg Vedas*, 166–67
Rievaulx, Aelred, 182
rights, self-other concept and, 22–24
Risley, H. H., 219–22, 256n136
Robertson, William, 119–24, 132, 134
*Robinson Crusoe* (Defoe), 51–52
Roger, Jacques, 244n109
Roman Empire: Europe and, 24–25; Said's orientalism and, 20–24
Romanticism: history and, 137–41; Rousseau and, 116, 245n122; suspicion of reason in, 217
Rousseau, G. S., 191
Rousseau, Jean-Jacques, 12, 14–15, 59, 97; on agency and adaptability, 111–13; biological determinism and, 207; botanical and naturalist studies of, 130–31; contractarian theory of, 101–18, 131–32, 246n32, 247n33; on education, 102, 115, 201–2; historical legacy of, 129–31, 136–37, 246n32, 247n52; on history and bourgeois man, 113–15; on

VANITA SETH is an associate professor of politics at
the University of California, Santa Cruz.

Library of Congress Cataloging-in-Publication Data

Seth, Vanita, 1968–
Europe's Indians : producing racial difference, 1500–1900 / Vanita Seth.
p. cm. — (Politics, history, and culture)
Includes bibliographical references and index.
ISBN 978-0-8223-4745-3 (cloth : alk. paper)
ISBN 978-0-8223-4764-4 (pbk. : alk. paper)
1. Indians—Public opinion. 2. Public opinion—Europe.
3. Indians—History. 4. Indians—First contact with Europeans.
I. Title. II. Series: Politics, history, and culture.
E59.P89.S48 2010   970.01'8—dc22
2010004454